LIBRARY OF HEBREW BIBLE/
OLD TESTAMENT STUDIES

485

Formerly Journal for the Study of the Old Testament Supplement Series

The Origins of Biblical Israel

Philip R. Davies

t & t clark

NEW YORK • LONDON

Copyright © 2007 by Philip R. Davies

T & T Clark International, 80 Maiden Lane, New York, NY 10038

T & T Clark International, The Tower Building, 11 York Road, London SE1 7NX

T & T Clark International is a Continuum imprint.

Library of Congress Cataloging-in-Publication Data
    Davies, Philip R.
    The Origins of biblical Israel / Philip R. Davies.
      p. cm. -- (The library of Hebrew Bible/Old Testament studies ; . 485)
    Includes bibliographical references and index.
    ISBN-13: 978-0-567-04381-8 (hardcover : alk. paper)
    ISBN-10: 0-567-04381-9 (hardcover : alk. paper) 1. Bible. O.T.--History of Biblical events. 2. Jews--History--To 70 A.D.--Historiography. 3. Palestine--History--To 70 A.D.-- Historiography 4. Bible. O.T.--Criticism, interpretation, etc. I. Title. II. Series.

BS1197.D35 2007
221.9'5--dc22

                              2007036008

Printed in Great Britain by Biddles Ltd, King's Lynn, Norfolk

CONTENTS

Part III
JUDAH AND ISRAEL IN
CRITICAL HISTORICAL MEMORY

FOREWORD

This book seems to me to have ended up as a mixture of monograph, textbook and essay collection. I set out to argue a thesis, but the nature of the evidence makes that difficult; there are so many issues involved, so many points to make and so many uncertainties. I have ended up approaching my central question from several different angles and with various methods (including literary reading, literary-critical analysis and fictionalized cultural memory) and my efforts to integrate them all are probably unsatisfactory. But I do believe that literary, historical and archaeological forms of knowledge and argument can be combined, though they should not be forced together.

What holds this book together, if anything, is a single question that involves describing "biblical Israel." Hence, reading the biblical story of Israel must be the first step. And reading it can show, without the need for a knowledge of biblical criticism, that there is no single "biblical Israel" at all, but several, often jumbled together but still sometimes contradictory. Seen as the subject of an extended narrative, "Israel" changes its identity several times even within the same story.

The translation from story to history is a fraught one and is often managed by means of a simple alternative: true or false?—as if we had the means, in most cases, to tell. I have tried to make this transition by means of a social-scientific perspective in which truth and untruth (which relate to the past that is narrated) are less significant than function and meaning (in which the present is more important). I suggest that the concept of *cultural memory* is better than the long-favoured term "tradition": although both distinguish between the process of "handing on" and the content of what is "handed on," "tradition" has developed little theoretical or experimental resources for analysis, other than the rare use of folklore studies. "Cultural memory" can draw on the phenomenon of individual memory and its contribution to identity formation and maintenance, as well as on the social mechanisms that promote collective memories. In the case of biblical studies, this concept has the additional advantage of allowing "biblical" and "scriptural" to be paraphrased—and thus the ideological baggage that these terms carry, of sacredness, separateness and authority. In any case, canonical status is to a large degree a consequence, rather than the essence, of a literary work, even though certain works clearly have been modified as part of the process of becoming canonized.

The stories about the past told in ancient Judah, which their canon contains, can be treated as "Judean cultural memory."[1] Any "biblical Israel" is ultimately a "Judean Israel," since the literary works that express that memory are undoubtedly Judean, whatever other layers they may contain. "Judean" is for the historian a more useful label than "biblical," and "memory" better than "canon." I have also used "cultural memory" in an unusual and no doubt controversial way: excavating a Judean cultural memory to expose another layer of (earlier) memory that is Benjaminite. Benjaminite is of course also a certain form of "Judean," but Benjamin's complex identity as both "Israelite" and "Judean" is important, given the central place of identity in the process of all memory-building. By recreating (conjecturally) such a memory, we can gain some perspective on Judean memory, showing that other memories of the same events (whether these events are real or created) not only are possible but must have existed. Identifying cultural memories with specific groups, and their development with a cultural process informed by ongoing social experience, is a safer, if still precarious, step in moving from literature to history. Memories are, after all, both products and agents of history. Events generate memory, but memories also modify, forget and even create "events." The memories also in their turn provoke action and can create communities that are themselves historical agents.

I finally ask, using more traditional literary-critical arguments, and with the aid of archaeological data, where these biblical Israels, these cultural memories, come from: what historical and social events gave rise to them. My hope is that the reader of this book will have anticipated these conclusions, or at least will not be surprised by them.

In view of the uncertainties (and also the polemics) of reconstructing the history of ancient Israel and Judah, I have avoided taking up a dogmatic position on many issues, preferring to follow the scholarly consensus where less is at stake and arguing against this only when I have reason to think it wrong and it is important to my case. Our understanding of the formation of "biblical Israel" must in any case be a gradual

---

1. "Judean" is used in this book of the entire history of the territory and its people. I am aware that some scholars use "Judahite" for the monarchic and premonarchic period. However, I use "Jewish" only of the religion or the *ethnos*, which does not necessarily connote birth or residence in Judah ("Israelite" is more complicated, since the name of part of the territory was changed in 722 to Samerina/Samaria).

process and no individual should pretend to be able to give a full answer. (It is paranoids who have an answer to everything.) How we try to frame answers, and what we may learn in the process, is also important. No doubt I shall continue to be understood by some mischievous critics as denying that there ever was an "ancient Israel." I hope that the contents of this book explain how completely wrong this charge is. But I will argue that there is no single, or simple, "biblical Israel."

My argument touches on a very wide range of issues, all of them hugely discussed in the scholarly literature. I cannot reference adequately all of this, not even all the work from which I have benefitted. Many readers will know when I am drawing on previous work unacknowledged; others should be aware that this is inevitable. The bibliography lists only works that are referred to, and I have referred to only a fraction of those I have read and used over the last forty years. I have become ever more appreciative of the fact that scholarship is a communal enterprise and that whatever I contribute is due to what I have learnt from listening to (and arguing with) others. It is of course unwise to mention names, but uncharitable not to. Among those to whom I especially owe gratitude for the thoughts expressed in this book, I might mention Graeme Auld, Ehud Ben Zvi, Joseph Blenkinsopp, Marc Zvi Brettler, the late Robert Carroll, Diana Edelman, Cynthia Edenburg, Israel Finkelstein, Lester Grabbe, Axel Knauf, Reinhard Kratz, Niels Peter Lemche, Mario Liverani, Oded Lipschits, Ami Mazar, Nadav Na'aman, John Rogerson, Thomas Römer, Thomas Thompson, John Van Seters and David Ussishkin: but I could mention very many more who deserve thanks, including the participants in Christopher Heard's weblog who provoked me to further thoughts. I know I have forgotten many others, and apologise for my defective memory. I am also indebted to many who have vigorously opposed my views, especially those who have done so without trying to distort them. Also due many thanks is Duncan Burns, whose careful editing saved me from numerous infelicities and inaccuracies and who kindly prepared the indexes as well.

As I finish writing this book, I am enjoying the Presidency of the British Society for Old Testament Study, of which I have been a member for thirty years. I can think of no better dedication of this book than to this generous, sociable and collegial group of friends and fellows.

Sheffield, April 2007

Chapter 1

THE PROBLEM OF "BIBLICAL ISRAEL"

Formulation

When I meet new doctoral students for the first time, I ask for their research topic in the form of a question. Then I ask "What kind of method will give you an answer?" (trying to solve historical questions with literary or theological methods, or vice versa, is a common problem). Formulating a dissertation or thesis as an answer to a question also helps prevent straying from the point: at any moment, one can ask oneself, "Am I still answering the question here?" The next interrogation is: "Why is this question important?" "Why do *you* want to answer this question?" Last of all, "Has anyone asked this question before? If not, why not?—and if so, why are their answers wrong?" Before embarking on the topic of this book, I will try to answer all these questions myself, first briefly and then some of them at more length.

The *question* with which I begin is this: "Why did Judeans call themselves 'Israel'?" This question entails tracing the origins and history of the "Israel(s)" described in the Hebrew Bible, and that task comprises what follows. I hope I succeed in providing a plausible answer to the question.

By what methods will the question best be answered? The question is historical, but there is practically no non-biblical evidence before the Greco-Roman period that Judeans *did* call themselves "Israel." We must rely heavily on an examination of the texts in the Bible, though archaeological data will help determine how far Judah may have been historically linked with Israel. The biblical data are less unambiguous than might be anticipated or assumed: sometimes Judah is presented as part of Israel (Pentateuch, Chronicles) and sometimes not (Samuel–Kings). Sometimes "Israel" is an ethnic designation, sometimes a political state, sometimes the worshipping community of the cult of Yahweh. While these definitions are often combined, they are not wholly compatible. The kingdom of Israel is not at all the same as the Pentateuchal Israel in extent or composition. Even today there exist two Israels, one of which

goes by the name "Samaritan." These are not Judeans, but they do claim
to be descended from the inhabitants of the kingdom of Israel, while
Judeans claim to be Israel by virtue of descent from one (or two-and-a-
half) tribes of what *they* call the ancient nation of "Israel." The modern
investment of a Judean/Jewish *state* with the name of "Israel" is an
innovation. In ignorance of this fluctuating biblical definition, scholars
and non-scholars often continue to speak of "biblical Israel" as if this
were a single unproblematic ancient society. The first task is a demonstration, by means of a narratological analysis, that there is no stable
"biblical Israel" and that this is easily apparent from a surface reading. In
other words, a *proper* "Biblical History of Israel" needs to start out by
exposing just how variegated and problematic that subject is.[1]

Why is the question important? The relationship between Israel, Judah
and Judaism is important not only for our understanding of the history of
the ancient kingdoms of Israel and Judah (and their successors), but also
as an explanation of why much of the literature of the Hebrew Bible/Old
Testament was composed and canonized: why, in fact, we have a Bible.
For if the Hebrew Bible is about anything, it is about "Israel": its history,
culture, cult, ethics. But there is a third area of importance, which is the
re-emergence in the twentieth century of "Israel" as not just the self-
designation of a religion or a culture, but as a *race* and as a political *state*.
The idea of Jews as a race had, among other consequences, a dreadful
outcome in their designation as genetically inferior, even sub-human by a
regime that attempted to exterminate it. The State of Israel is officially
secular but in practice a Jewish state whose *Realpolitik* is conditioned by
claims to its territory (and to neighbouring territory) that derive from a
biblical identity. But to be an Israeli is not necessarily to be a Jew, just as
in ancient times to be an Israelite was not necessarily to be a worshipper
of Yahweh. The modern manifestation of Israel as religious, cultural,
ethnic and political—and the contradictions inherent in these definitions—invites an analysis of the biblical roots of the matter.

Why do I ask this question? I was first confronted with it when writing
In Search of "Ancient Israel" fifteen years ago.[2] But then I was concerned
with contrasting the historically reconstructed Israel and Judah with the
biblical Israel(s), and to question the scholarly habit of synthesizing them
by conflation, merging them into an artificial construct, "ancient Israel." I

---

1. I refer, of course, to I. Provan, V. Phillips Long and Tremper Longman II, *A
Biblical History of Israel* (Louisville: Westminster John Knox, 2003), which man-
ages to be neither biblical nor critical.

2. P. R. Davies, *In Search of "Ancient Israel"* (Sheffield: Sheffield Academic
Press, 1992).

suggested a different synthesis: viewing the biblical Israels as a product of historical Israel and Judah, proposing a historical society *producing* a literary society of the past, not in response to some divine prompting or as a natural cultural development, but under the pressure of a particular set of social, religious and political circumstances. The large discrepancy between what we know of Israelite and Judean origins and the biblical story, and the need to explain the production of the biblical histories, brought me to the Judah of the Persian period, to a need felt by a social and political elite that had recently immigrated from Babylonia into what they saw as their ancestral land, at the time occupied by other Judeans with similar (or even better) claims. I suggested that the biblical histories were essentially an effort at constructing an identity that was continuous with the past, and in so doing creating a past that mirrored the present.

Many scholars still think of the Pentateuch and the Deuteronomistic History (i.e. Genesis–Kings, the "First History") as largely composed during the monarchic period. The fundamental issue, however, is not the *dating* of the biblical "Israel" but its relationship to history—both the real history of Judah and Israel, and also the history during which it was written. Thus, even the current preference for dating the Deuteronomistic History (or rather, its first draft) to the time of Josiah,[3] towards the very end of the Judean monarchy, removes it far from many of the events it narrates, and although the "exilic" sixth century still seems to constitute a watershed for some scholars—a perception surely influenced by the biblical ideology—historically speaking, the life of Judah and its inhabitants continued. We are now beginning to repair our previous neglect of the majority of Judeans at this juncture by referring not to the "exilic period" but the "Neo-Babylonian period." The crucial difference between a Josianic date for the first Judean history of Israel and a Persian date is not the presumed degree of historicity that each entails, but the different *motivation* for creating a history that has to be supplied. Date cannot be separated from context and purpose. "Late dating" is a misleading label; indeed, the Josianic era is still sometimes called "late"!

In Search of "Ancient Israel" suggested that biblical Israel was born in Judah, but it did not occur to me to ask why the name "Israel" was adopted for that nation, the name also carried by a kingdom that was then

---

3. The most developed exposition of the Josianic date is found in I. Finkelstein and N. A. Silberman, *The Bible Unearthed: Archaeology's New Vision of Ancient Israel and the Origin of Its Sacred Texts* (New York and London: Free Press, 2001); their second book, *David and Solomon: In Search of the Bible's Sacred Kings and the Roots of the Western Tradition* (New York and London: Free Press, 2006), has a different scope but employs a more nuanced methodology.

defunct. It did not occur to me then to ask why Judeans should adopt the identity "Israel": indeed, "adopt" would have sounded strange. I assumed they *inherited* this identity. But I now want to question that assumption; I do not think we know that this identity *was* inherited, rather than adopted—and the arguments that have persuaded me are biblical as much as archaeological.[4]

What is the history of this question? In the last fifteen years or so there have been two important developments in the scholarship on these issues. First, the notion of a clear distinction between the history of monarchic Israel and Judah and the biblical history written about them has become more firmly entrenched. The recent treatment by Mario Liverani represents the first systematic attempt to separate the history of ancient Israel and Judah as we can critically reconstruct it (what he calls "normal history") from the biblical story, which reflects its own historical context and its agenda in a later period ("invented history").[5] The recent books of Israel Finkelstein and Neil Asher Silberman are also establishing a new set of correlations between the historical episodes in the history of Israel and Judah and the biblical constructions.[6] In each case, the authors conclude that the biblical history tells us more about its own time than the past (a principle, in fact, already well established in biblical scholarship by the end of the nineteenth century).

Additionally, a number of studies have been published that assume, rather than argue, that the social context of a great deal of the biblical literature in its present form (in particular, Pentateuch, Former Prophets, Latter Prophets) is to be sought in the Persian period.[7] Both the dating

---

4. The nature of "Israel" as a product of the history of "Israel" rather than the prerequisite was directly addressed by R. Kratz, "Israel als Staat und Volk," *ZTK* 97 (2000): 1–7, but without considering the place of Judah within this "Israel."

5. M. Liverani, *Israel's History and the History of Israel* (London: Equinox. 2005).

6. Finkelstein and Silberman, *The Bible Unearthed* and *David and Solomon*.

7. To cite just a few examples: T. Mullen, Jr., *Ethnic Myths and Pentateuchal Foundations: A New Approach to the Formation of the Pentateuch* (Atlanta: Scholars Press, 1997); Mullen, *Narrative History and Ethnic Boundaries: The Deuteronomistic Historian and the Creation of Israelite National Identity* (Atlanta: Scholars Press, 1993); J. R. Linville, *Israel in the Book of Kings: The Past as a Project of Social Identity* (Sheffield: Sheffield Academic Press, 1998); J. W. Watts, *Persia and Torah: The Theory of Imperial Authorization of the Pentateuch* (Atlanta: Society of Biblical Literature, 2001); R. C. Heard, *Dynamics of Diselection: Ambiguity in Genesis 12–36 and Ethnic Boundaries in Post-Exilic Judah* (Atlanta: Scholars Press, 2001); R. F. Person, Jr., *The Deuteronomic School: History, Social Setting, and Literature* (Atlanta: Scholars Press, 2002); E. Ben Zvi, *Signs of Jonah: Reading and Rereading in Ancient Yehud* (London: Sheffield Academic Press, 2003).

of the biblical literature and explanation of its purpose and context are now more contested than they have been for some time. Despite the occasional and usually irrelevant polemics, the debate is valuable in its own right. The suggestion of a relatively low level of historical reliability in the texts, and a date removed from the time in which the events being described are set, have both been attacked as "revisionist." But in fact these ideas have been developing for several decades and the arguments used to advance them are those that biblical scholars have traditionally employed.

The remainder of this chapter consists of an expansion of these brief comments, in the form of a more traditional introduction to the problem of "biblical Israel(s)," namely a (brief) history of scholarly discussion, including an assessment of "wrong answers," and some comments on methodology. (The reader for whom such matters are a tiresome formality may move now to the next chapter.)

Biblical Israel(s)

The Pentateuch defines Israel's origins in a *family*, whose descendants become *tribes* that form a *nation*. But this "nation" is additionally defined as being uniquely bound to its own god (Exodus–Deuteronomy) and thus characterized by its *religion*. The genealogical and religious aspects are, of course, potentially in conflict: the descendants of Jacob often abandon their religious affiliation but remain "Israel," while non-Israelites can also worship the god of Israel. A further complication arrives with the political definition. Israel becomes one nation alongside Judah, both apparently in some way derived from the Pentateuchal Israel. But the division portrayed under Rehoboam does not *initiate* these two political units, for they are already separate when Saul is king of Israel and David simultaneously king of Judah. How, then, does Judah first become separated from Israel? No statement is given, but the distinction is already perceptible in the books of Joshua and Judges, while the books of Samuel and Kings hardly ever refer to an "Israel" embracing two nations: the issue is always political *union* under a Davidic king. Nevertheless, Israel and Judah are placed under the same covenantal obligations imposed by the same deity. Chronicles, on the other hand, holds that the "northern kingdom" (as we modern scholars have been accustomed to calling it) was differentiated from Judah by being religiously apostate from the Davidic line, and recognizes a religious and cultic Israel that embraces both kingdoms and a single line of genealogical descent. After the fall of Samaria, "Israel" survives, according to Kings, only in Judah—but in a cultural and ethnic, not in a *political* sense. There is no longer any kind of political Israel. After the end of the kingdom of Judah, while "Judah" remains as the name of the province, the identity of "Israel" persists in this religious sense only, though genealogy is used as a means of defining it! But no territorial claims to Samaria are implied, nor is the name "Israel" ever applied to the land of Judah, as distinct from its inhabitants.[8] "Israel" has a religious sense but also a genealogical one: an "Israelite" is defined by descent and religious affiliation. That identity continues, according to Ezra and Nehemiah, to be denied to the population of Samaria, which, like Judah, nevertheless continues to think of itself as "Israel" (as parts of the book of Jeremiah show: see below, Chapter 8).

This often confusing mixture of ethnic, political and religious criteria has infected modern scholarship. For instance, research into the origins of historical Israel still often looks for distinctively religious characteristics (as if this were the crucial criterion);[9] or the use of the term "northern kingdom," so avoiding the problem of how "Israel" is politically speaking only part of itself. Of course, the confusion originates in the biblical narratives themselves. But that is why scholarship should deal with it, not simply gloss over it.

The History of the Problem of "Israel"

What exactly is meant by "Israel" is an issue that has been incubating over many decades, and the contents of this book (as, indeed, of *In Search of "Ancient Israel"*) are not proposed as a radical departure. Rather, they are to be seen as the continuation of the principal lines

---

8.   The utopian vision of Ezekiel about the restoration of the territory of the twelve tribes is a different matter, for it seeks to restore a transformed Pentateuchal Israel. The ambitions of the Hasmoneans, who extended their territory to most of Palestine, is also a different matter: how far political opportunism and national ideology contributed to this expansion is difficult to say. But neither they nor anyone else ever called their extended kingdom "Israel," as distinct from the people, who are frequently referred to as "Israel" (e.g. in 1–2 Maccabees).

9.   For example, well after the death of W. F. Albright's "Mosaic monotheism," Norman Gottwald's *The Tribes of Yahweh: A Sociology of the Religion of Liberated Israel, 1250–1050 B.C.E* (Maryknoll, N.Y.: Orbis, 1979), still foregrounded religion as the essential component of ancient "Israelite" identity. Others have pointed to avoidance of pork among the earliest Iron age highland settlements. However, while customs such as male circumcision *may* be early ethnic markers, it did not distinguish most of the inhabitants of Canaan from each other and was hardly understood as exhibiting any distinctive religious beliefs or identity at this period. Likewise, the avoidance of pork, which became an ethnic marker later, may originally have been ecologically influenced.

of critical scholarship established already in the nineteenth century.[10] But until the beginning of the twentieth century, there was very little access to any historical Israel or Judah through extra-biblical sources or archaeological excavation or survey. The biblically based notion that the kingdoms of Judah and Israel were political manifestations of a single nation (and still sharing that common identity until the end of the kingdom of Israel) was taken for granted. Even so, the task of converting this biblical Israelite nation into something historical relied upon literary-historical critical methods.

The work of many scholars, culminating in Wellhausen's *Prolegomena* in 1878,[11] succeeded by these means in sketching an Israel whose religious history, at least, was different from what the biblical sources presented.[12] The Mosaic law, and in particular its elaborate cultic requirements, came to be situated towards the end, rather than the beginning, of that history, and with the Mosaic origin of the Pentateuch dismantled, doubt was also cast on the reliability of some of the origin traditions that these books contained. As the literary sources were fitted into later periods, their historical reliability regarding events that lay much earlier came into question.[13]

This reconstruction was tempered, under the influence of Romanticism and folklore studies, by an appeal to more ancient oral traditions that could be recovered by an analysis of literary form, a movement

10. I make this argument, in a more general context, in "What *Is* Minimalism, and Why Do So Many People Dislike It?," in *Historie og konstruktion. Festskrift til Niels Peter Lemche I anledning af 60 års fødselsdagen den 6. September 2005* (ed. M. Müller and T. L. Thompson; Copenhagen: Museum Tusculanums, 2005), 76–86.

11. J. Wellhausen, *Prolegomena to the History of Israel: With a Reprint of the Article Israel from the "Encyclopaedia Britannica"* (Preface by W. Robertson Smith; Edinburgh: A. & C. Black, 1985; repr. with Foreword by Douglas Knight; Atlanta: Scholars Press, 1994); trans. of *Prolegomena zur Geschichte Israels* (2d ed.; Berlin: G. Reimer, 1883).

12. The history of biblical criticism from the Enlightenment is contained in a number of earlier standard *Introductions* to the Hebrew Bible/Old Testament, especially those written by German scholars. For a readable and quite detailed treatment of this topic in English, see John Rogerson, *Old Testament Criticism in the Nineteenth Century: England and Germany* (London: SPCK, 1984).

13. It is fair to comment that such a view of early Judaism as a descent from prophetic ethical religion into legalism betrays a Protestant and even anti-Jewish ideology: but ideology does not of itself invalidate arguments or conclusions—and these conclusions have become widely accepted, for a number of reasons, though it is now clear that "Judaism" itself remained quite pluralistic at the end of the Second Temple period.

associated with the work of Hermann Gunkel.[14] However, the emergence
of archaeological investigation in Palestine was now already affording
the opportunity for independent and direct access to the material culture
of ancient Israel and Judah. But "biblical archaeology," as it was called,
was developed and maintained not as an independent approach, but in
the interests of confirming the biblical record.[15] The same can be said of
so-called Zionist archaeology, though this had a different basis.[16] As a
result of these motivations, the opportunity of providing a genuine critical stance by separating the archaeological from the biblical data was
virtually eliminated. Interest in biblical archaeology was predicated precisely on the assumption that the object of the search was the biblical
Israel, an entity whose history and culture was to be confirmed "scientifi-
cally." Such "confirmation" sustained the value of (and income for) this
archaeological work.[17]

It was left to biblical scholars to pursue a critical comparison of biblical and archaeological data that went beyond the search for "parallels."

14. Hermann Gunkel, *The Folktale in the Old Testament* (Sheffield: Almond,
1987); German original, *Das Märchen im Alten Testament* (Tübingen: Mohr, 1917);
The Legends of Genesis (New York: Schocken, 1964); ET of Introduction to *Die
Urgeschichte und die Patriarchen (das erste Buch Mosis) übersetzt, erklärt und mit
Einleitungen in die fünf Bücher Mosis und in die Sagen des ersten Buches Mosis
versehen* I (Göttingen: Vandenhoeck & Ruprecht, 1911).

15. Among the many accounts of "biblical archaeology," see Thomas W. Davis,
Shifting Sands: The Rise and Fall of Biblical Archaeology (Oxford: Oxford University Press, 2004), which is especially well informed and clear about the nature of this
peculiar movement. On the nationalistic and imperialistic agendas, see N. A. Silberman, *Digging for God and Country: Exploration, Archeology, and the Secret
Struggle for the Holy Land, 1799–1917* (New York: Knopf, 1982).

16. On "Zionist archaeology" see, e.g., Yaacov Shavit, "Archaeology, Political
Culture, and Culture in Israel," in *The Archaeology of Israel: Constructing the Past,
Interpreting the Present* (ed. N. A. Silberman and D. B. Small; Sheffield, Sheffield
Academic Press, 1997), 48–61; Nadia Abu El-Haj, *Facts on the Ground: Archaeo-
logical Practice and Territorial Self-Fashioning in Israeli Society* (Chicago: Univer-
sity of Chicago Press, 2001).

17. The obituary of "biblical archaeology" is in reality premature. It thrives, and
maintains its goal of excavating "biblical Israel," as exemplified in titles such as
Benjamin Mazar's *Biblical Israel: State and People* (Jerusalem: Magnes, 1992) and
P. J. King and L. E. Stager's, *Life in Biblical Israel* (Louisville: Westminster John
Knox, 2001). Both of these books turn out to be about the historical Israel, since they
rely mostly on archaeological and other cultural data *outside* the Bible. But if "biblical Israel" is supposed to mean "the Israel described in the Bible," an archaeologist
is hardly best qualified to deal with this issue. If it is intended to mean "ancient Israel
in the biblical period," then the term "biblical period" needs much more careful definition and qualification.

Albrecht Alt and Martin Noth, in particular, both with a firm grasp of the archaeological knowledge of their day,[18] attempted to synthesize rather than harmonize the two sources of information. Nevertheless, the historical result, as demonstrated in Noth's *History of Israel*,[19] was still a modified version of "biblical Israel." In Noth's view,[20] the Pentateuchal corpus, though represented in different documents that were subsequently edited into a single narrative (the Pentateuch), had an origin prior to any of the Pentateuchal source documents J and E. in the shape of an original outline that he called the *Grundschrift*. The historical basis for this account was a tribal league or amphictyony, formed within Palestine among the twelve (or notionally twelve) tribes. Even if the stories relating to earlier periods, such as those of the patriarchs, exodus, Sinai and the wilderness wanderings, were not treated by Noth as "history," they were reconstituted as the "traditions" of a society that directly corresponded to that portrayed in the Bible. While insisting that "Israel" came into existence only on the soil of Canaan, Noth nevertheless concluded that the biblical "traditions" represented the memories of that early society.[21] Such a view, despite the substitution of "history" by "traditions," nevertheless preserved fairly intact the equation between biblical and historical Israels. For it is questionable how any society *without* these traditions would correspond in any significant way to a biblical Israel. Hence, even if Noth's history can be favourably contrasted in terms of its critical approach with that of Bright, who purveyed the Albrightian view that the Bible was historically reliable and confirmed by archaeology,[22]

18. Noth's *The Old Testament World* (Philadelphia: Fortress, 1966) (original 1940, 4th edition 1964), is rather unjustly neglected in comparison with his literary-critical analyses.

19. M. Noth, *The History of Israel* (London: A. & C. Black, 1958).

20. See M. Noth, *A History of Pentateuchal Traditions* (Englewood Cliffs: Prentice–Hall, 1972); German original *Überlieferungsgeschichte des Pentateuch* (Stuttgart: Kohlhammer, 1948).

21. "Collective memory" is not the same as "cultural memory" in the sense exploited by Jan Assmann (*Religion and Cultural Memory: Ten Studies* [Stanford: Stanford University Press, 2006]) and others, which does not construe such "memory" simply as vague or inaccurate or exaggerated recollection of real events, but as forms of knowledge that enable cultural identity to be acquired and maintained. Nevertheless, it seems to me likely that Noth would have agreed substantially with such a definition: his well-known aetiological explanations (especially in his commentary on Joshua [*Das Buch Josua* (2d ed.; Tübingen: Mohr, 1953)]) and his notion of *Ortsgebundenheit*, of traditions being localized in places of significance, anticipates some aspects of the later theory.

22. The four editions of Bright's *A History of Israel* stretch from the first (Philadelphia: Westminster, 1959) to the (posthumous) fourth (Louisville: Westminster

the two *Histories*, seen from the beginning of the twenty-first century, now look more alike than different.

Nevertheless, Noth's view that it was political and social cooperation within Canaan (in the form of an amphictyony) that created Israel, rather than a more ancient ethnic origin, provided the foundation for what has now emerged as the consensus. Another important, but subsequently neglected line of analysis explored the possibility that the component tribes of Israel had found their way into Palestine in two independent groups. Half a century ago this had been a widely shared view:

> That the Joseph tribes and Judah entered into the possession of their territory in different periods is agreed by a very long line of modern scholars...[23]

But this conclusion, too, failed to follow up the possible implications. Rowley states a little later

> That all the tribes were of kindred stock, and that those who went into Egypt broke off from their kindred and about a century and a half later came and settled in their midst, is a view which is in substantial agreement with Biblical traditions, when freed from the fictitious unity that has been imposed on them.[24]

Two decades later, de Vaux's history of Israel[25] also devoted a lot of space to the analysis of separate tribal land occupation by Israel and Judah (441–620), though he places all the occupations in the second half of the thirteenth century (1250 BCE for the "southern groups" and 1200 for the "northern groups"). The idea of a common ancestor, an identical *external* point of origin, a shared experience of slavery in Egypt or a joint wilderness trek were thus questioned, but for reasons that were not made clear, belief in an inherited unity of some kind was maintained. Yet despite Rowley's assertion of a "common stock," there *is* no good argumentation behind it. The signposts were erected, but nobody followed them.

John Knox, 2000), during which time modifications of some views have occurred, though it remains close to the biblical presentation. Despite being critically obsolete, it clearly remains popular.

23. H. H. Rowley, *From Joseph to Joshua* (London: British Academy, 1950), 140.

24. Ibid., 162–63.

25. Roland de Vaux, *The Early History of Israel* (2 vols.; London: Darton, Longman & Todd, 1978); French original, *Histoire ancienne d'Israel* (Paris: Gabalda, 1971).

By this time, the biblical "conquest" had long been challenged, especially by Alt in his famous essay on the Israelite *Landnahme*.[26] In his commentary on Joshua, as in his *History*, Noth took his teacher's reconstruction further and argued that the stories were elaborated later, often as aetiological explanations (such as the ruin of Ai). This interpretation might have led to the question of how Israel and other population elements who had apparently *not* been substantially or even partly displaced, continued to coexist within the kingdom of Israel—whether indeed the subjects of the Israelite king were all really "Israelite" at all in the sense defined by the biblical narratives of origins. The opposition of "Israel" and "Canaan" and their respective cultures is a crucial element in the biblical definition of Israel presented by Deuteronomy (and reflected in many modern "Histories." But the power of the biblical image of Israel as a distinct culture seems to have obstructed such a line of reasoning. Despite Alt's influential thesis, the notion of an Israel intruding into an alien Canaanite culture and dominating it largely persisted, both in biblical scholarship and in archaeology. The older Israeli archaeological nomenclature of "Canaanite" (Bronze age) succeeded by "Israelite" (Iron age) was supplanted, but the question of how Canaan became "Israelite" is now one of the issues in the debate about chronology and Israelite and Judean state formation (see further in Chapter 9).

Scholarly awareness of "biblical Israel" as a *problem* rather than a datum can be traced back to two developments that occurred a few years after the publication of de Vaux's *Histoire* (1971). The first was the collapse of Noth's amphictyony theory.[27] Its demolition left a major problem—at least for his theory of the Pentateuchal tradition history: for where now did the original unity or identity of Israel lie? Where, when and how did these various tribal "traditions" merge into a single "memory"? Von Rad had, in fact, put this question rather well when he stated several years earlier, but in respect of the patriarchs, that[28]

---

26. A. Alt, *Die Landnahme der Israeliten in Palästina* (Leipzig: Reformationsprogramm der Universität, 1925). The English translation appeared as "The Settlement of the Israelites in Palestine," in *Essays on Old Testament History and Religion* (Garden City, N.Y.: Doubleday, 1966), 133–69.

27. C. H. J. de Geus, *The Tribes of Israel: An Investigation into Some of the Presuppositions of Martin Noth's Amphictyony Hypothesis* (Assen: Van Gorcum, 1976); N. P. Lemche, "The Greek 'Amphictyony': Could It Be a Prototype for the Israelite Society in the Period of the Judges?," *JSOT* 4 (1977): 48–59; for a recent review, see his *The Israelites in History and Tradition* (Louisville: Westminster John Knox, 1998), 97–107.

28. G. von Rad, "The History of the Patriarchs," *ET* 72 (1960–61): 213–16 (quote from 214).

Such a homogeneous historical tradition would presuppose a corresponding historical bearer of the tradition. But where can we find the bearer of such a comprehensive and unified tradition?

When extended to the Pentateuchal traditions as a whole, the problem was compounded. Von Rad removed the Sinai episode from Noth's reconstructed Pentateuchal tradition complex, and suggested that it had been integrated later.[29] Two books in the early 1970s finally established what had been debated already for many years, that the "patriarchal period" (to which biblical archaeologists were still committing themselves), was a fiction;[30] and finally, the suggestion of George Mendenhall that the original Israelite society was composed of Canaanites who had withdrawn to the highlands was substantially developed by Norman Gottwald, who proposed that a revolt of Canaanite peasants led to the creation of Israel. This theory challenged the entire history of patriarchs, exodus *and* conquest.[31] All these conclusions—which, sometimes in modified form, have become the basis of the current consensus—were made by biblical scholars, not by archaeologists; although some archaeologists had by now begun to question much of the proposed patriarchal dating, talk of a historical background for these stories persisted (and still does in some quarters, as readers of *Biblical Archaeology Review* will know).[32]

But even among biblical scholars, the general assumption prevailed that some experiences of a genuine historical society called Israel underlay the Hexateuchal (Genesis–Joshua) traditions. Although their narratives could not be translated exactly into corresponding historical events, they developed among the earliest "Israelites" on the basis of some kind of historical experience and constituted part of its cultural unity. The patriarchal stories reflected elements of genuine ethnic affiliation—if not with Mesopotamia, then perhaps with Syria ("Paddan-Aram"), where

29. G. von Rad, "The Form-Critical Problem of the Hexateuch," in *The Problem of the Hexateuch and Other Essays* (Edinburgh: Oliver & Boyd, 1966), 1–78; German original, *Das formgeschichtliche Problem des Hexateuchs* (Stuttgart: Kohlhammer, 1938).

30. T. L. Thompson, *The Historicity of the Patriarchal Narratives* (Berlin: de Gruyter, 1974); J. Van Seters, *Abraham in History and Tradition* (New Haven: Yale University Press, 1975).

31. G. E. Mendenhall, "The Hebrew Conquest of Palestine," *BA* 25 (1962): 66–87; Gottwald, *The Tribes of Yahweh*.

32. E.g. W. G. Dever, "The Patriarchal Traditions," in *Israelite and Judaean History* (ed. J. H. Hayes and J. Maxwell Miller; London: SCM Press; Philadelphia: Trinity Press International, 1977), 102–20.

Abraham's family was said to have settled and from where Isaac and Jacob took their (primary) wives; the exodus story likewise reflected some kind of liberating event from Egyptian domination that a core group within Israel had experienced. The conquest could likewise be interpreted as a globalizing of one or two local military victories over fortified cities or their armies.[33] It was not considered that the entire Hexateuchal narrative, on which the foundation of biblical Israel's identity was built, might actually be a fiction and its Israel something invented. That perception would have led to a quite different agenda.

For a brief period, an interesting dispute over the *theological* value of this narrative flared up between German and American scholarship: for Noth and von Rad (and especially the latter) Israel's "sacred traditions" were the proper content of biblical theology, rather than the historical facts themselves on which they were based. For the "Biblical Theology" movement, led by G. Ernest Wright, the value of the tradition was its witness to the events. History, not the "word," was the medium of divine revelation and intervention.[34] Thus the way was cleared for the later replacement of "history" by "story" as a category for "doing theology."[35] But stories are not just of use to theology: they are also important for the historian, because they shed light on the inner workings of society. Stories are told for a purpose, and that purpose is itself part of social history.

The final stage in the hatching of the problem was enacted by archaeology, as a result of regional surveys carried out by Israeli archaeologists in the West Bank during the 1970s and 1980s.[36] These confirmed the verdict that the earliest Israelite society emerged within Canaan from either indigenous or closely neighbouring populations, and that the story

---

33. Note also the suggestion mentioned earlier that some of the tribes entered from the south and some from the north, each with its own separate settlement traditions.

34. The principles of each of these positions are best expounded in von Rad's *Old Testament Theology* (2 vols.; Edinburgh: Oliver & Boyd, 1962–65; repr. London: SCM Press, 1975); German original, *Theologie des Alten Testaments* (2 vols.; Munich: Kaiser, 1957–60); and in G. E. Wright, *God Who Acts: Biblical Theology as Recital* (London: SCM Press, 1952). An exchange of views between these two scholars is also found in Wright's note "History and the Patriarchs," *ExpT* 71 (1959–60): 292 and von Rad's rejoinder (above, n. 28). This theological difference also underlies the *Histories* of Noth and Bright, though not as explicitly.

35. See James Barr, "Story and History in Biblical Theology," *JR* 56 (1976): 1–17.

36. The fullest account is in I. Finkelstein, *The Archaeology of the Israelite Settlement* (Jerusalem: Israel Exploration Society, 1988).

of a pre-existing nation descended from a single patriarchal line, enslaved in Egypt and arriving in Canaan as conquerors, could no longer be addressed as history. As Mendenhall and Gottwald had argued, the Israelites were, if not "Canaanites," then at least part of the local population.[37] The consensus is now that the Israel of history began as a society of highland farmers who for fairly typical reasons and according to fairly typical processes (pooling of economic resources, exchanging goods, intermarrying) came to share a sense of common ethnicity. As Miller puts it:[38]

> ...it was rather a matter of the pan-Israelite consciousness gradually emerging in Palestine among tribal groups which had their own individual origins and still were loosely associated with each other at the time of the establishment of the monarchy.

Some scholars wish to call this ethnicity "Israelite," and refer to these farmers as "proto-Israelites," but the label is fairly meaningless except in the sense, possibly, that this population would in future comprise part of the kingdom of that name. The use of the term "Israel" is sometimes justified by its appearance in the Merneptah stela,[39] but the connection may be more complicated.[40]

One aspect of the highland settlement is particularly interesting. The West Bank survey results indicated that that the highland regions occupied by the later kingdom of Israel were much more densely populated than those occupied by the kingdom of Judah. The scarce population of the Judean hills in Iron I is explained by Finkelstein as the result of a

---

37. Cf. Ezek 16:45: "You are the daughter of your mother, who hated her husband and her children; and you are one of your sisters, who hated their husbands and their children. Your mother was a Hittite and your father an Amorite." But did the writer guess this, or was it common knowledge in his day? Using biblical texts to disprove biblical texts is a methodologically delicate if not precarious operation.

38. J. Maxwell Miller, "The Israelite Occupation of the Canaan," in Hayes and Miller, eds., *Israelite and Judaean History*, 213–84 (280).

39. For a detailed discussion of recent research on the Merneptah stela and its possible allusion to the highland farming communities, see M. G. Hasel, "*Israel* in the Merneptah Stela," *BASOR* 296 (1994): 45–61. A fine, earlier, discussion is also found in G. Ahlström, *The History of Ancient Palestine from the Palaeolithic Period to Alexander's Conquest* (Sheffield: Sheffield Academic Press, 1993), 282–88.

40. A local name is not necessarily perpetuated by the same ethnic group ("Briton" is a perfect example). Second, it is not clear why Merneptah would attack highland farmers. However, it is possible that they were *not* attacked, and that the claim of Merneptah is false. It is also possible that Merneptah is *not* referring to the hill country, but to some other region where "Israel" was then located. Not a great deal can be safely deduced beyond the antiquity of the name.

"thin trickle" from further north, or "sedentarizing pastoral groups who had already been active in the region."[41] Dense settlement of Judah occurred only later. Finkelstein's explanation is that the Judean terrain was less easy to farm and that it was exploited only when the central highlands became overcrowded. Hence, he prefers to think of this settlement as spreading from the north rather than the south and rejects the theories of "penetration into Judah from the south," on the basis of a "dearth of sites in the Beersheba valley and in the southern Hebron hills" that would have indicated settlement from this direction.[42] This is a valid objection to the theory as previously formulated (and discussed earlier). That theory supposed an entry from the direction of Egypt, based on the assumption of some kind of historical core to the exodus story. But the direction from which the highland settlers came, currently disputed, does not need to have been from the south, and there is no reason to suggest that Judah, any more than Israel, was settled from this direction. Separate settlement in the two areas, either from within Canaan or from the Transjordanian plateau, is still a persuasive explanation, and better accounts for the sense of social and political independence that apparently characterized the inhabitants of Judah from the earliest moment that we can trace.[43]

I will avoid discussion here of the debate over Iron age chronology, the archaeological evidence for a "United Monarchy" and the emergence of the Judean kingdom. Finkelstein and others who advocate the "low chronology" suggest that the formation of a state in Judah cannot have occurred much earlier than the eighth century; Mazar and others who support the "high" (or "modified high") chronology place it earlier.[44] This issue is not likely to be resolved in the near future, nor is the even more contentious argument over the status of Jerusalem at the purported time of David. While some compromise between the two positions is possible, the core period of disagreement coincides precisely with that in which David and Solomon would require to be placed. This problem reminds us

41. Finkelstein, *Archaeology of the Israelite Settlement*, 326; A. Ofer, "The Monarchic Period in the Judaean Highland: A Spatial Overview," in *Studies in the Archaeology of the Iron Age in Israel and Jordan* (ed. A. Mazar; Sheffield: Sheffield Academic Press, 2001), 14–37.

42. Finkelstein, *Archaeology of the Israelite Settlement*, 327.

43. The excellent discussion of the settlement by Ahlström, *History of Ancient Palestine*, 334–70, does not deal directly with the possibility of Israelite and Judean settlement as distinct, but does name "Israelites" and "Judahites" separately.

44. See, e.g., Mazar, "Remarks on Biblical Traditions and Archaeological Evidence Concerning Early Israel," in *Symbiosis, Symbolism and the Power of the Past: Canaan* (ed. W. G. Dever and S. Gitin; Winona Lake: Eisenbrauns, 2002), 85–98.

that the precision, objectivity and reliability of archaeological data and their interpretation all have limits.

But in any case the issues can be sidestepped because they have no direct bearing on whether or how an "Israelite" identity was adopted by the population of Judah. More interesting and important is the disagreement within the biblical presentation between the books of Samuel–Kings and Chronicles (see Chapters 4 and 5). In the former, David is presented as having been separately installed as king of Judah and of Israel, and he does not rule over a single "Israel," but over two "houses" (as does Rehoboam). The Chronicler offers a different view, and never speaks of David as king of Judah, but only of Israel. This divergence reflects a fracture in the later Judean memories of Judah's origin (and identity) in relation to Israel's.

A good deal of modern biblical scholarship, while preferring Samuel–Kings to Chronicles as a historical source, follows Chronicles (and the Pentateuch) in speaking of "Israel" in an undifferentiated way, so as to include Judah. The traditional title *History of Israel*, however, was already recognized as problematic in 1977, when Hayes and Miller entitled their (edited) volume *Israelite and Judean History*, and their (co-written) 1986 volume *A History of Ancient Israel and Judah*.[45] This title was taken up (now with the benefit of the Israeli survey data) by J. A. Soggin.[46] This new name for an old genre acknowledges that a modern critical history should not begin earlier than these political formations, and therefore one cannot assume a single ethnic "Israel" as a historical precursor. A "History of Israel" has now to be written as a history of two distinct kingdoms, not of a single nation in two political configurations.

The question of an original ethnic unity is not directly raised in either of these works, but it lurks there. In discussing the period *before* the two kingdoms, Miller and Hayes frequently speak of "Israel and Judah," but they use "Israel" and "Israelite" in reference to the tribal configuration prior to the monarchic period that is reflected in the book of Judges.[47] Yet, as they acknowledge, the "Israelite" perspective in Judges is clearly embedded in the editorial layer, which, according to long-standing scholarly opinion, is where the tribe of Judah makes its only appearance. The extent of Saul's "kingdom" is also discussed: again, assuming that it did really exist, the consensus is that it includes Benjamin, Ephraim and

45. Hayes and Miller, eds., *Israelite and Judean History*; J. M. Miller and J. H. Hayes, *A History of Ancient Israel and Judah* (Philadelphia: Westminster, 1986).

46. J. Alberto Soggin, *An Introduction to the History of Israel and Judah* (2d ed.; London: SCM Press, 1993).

47. Miller and Hayes, *A History of Ancient Israel and Judah*, 90–91.

Manasseh and not much else. Why do we call it "Israel"? *Was* that the name by which it knew itself, or was known by others? As described by the books of Samuel, it did not include Judah, but was it continuous with the later kingdom of Israel? In what sense *was* it an "Israelite" kingdom? Because it was a political entity in the territory later occupied by the later kingdom?

Miller and Hayes accept that Saul's kingdom did exist, for this is where they begin their historical reconstruction with Saul. Soggin, however, begins with David, and alludes to

> ...a fact I have already pointed out many times: the division between North and South (i.e. Israel in the strict sense, also called "house of Joseph" and "Ephraim," and Judah) is an original division on an ethnic and political level, and probably also (as far as we can establish) on the religious level, in that it already existed before the dissolution of the empire of David and Solomon...though in the present state of the sources it is not possible to discover much of the detail. There is no doubt that the two groups were ethnically and religiously akin: but there was also separation.[48]

But where *is* the evidence of ethnic and religious kinship? The Bible genealogically relates its Israel with Ammon, Moab, Aram and Edom as descended from Abraham; and this perceived kinship was probably based on a historical consciousness. But ethnic identities are formed from geographical contiguity, cultural (including especially linguistic) similarity and intermarriage. These independent political states also had their own religions, although they all reflected a similar pattern. The biblical narratives place Israel and Judah in a closer relationship, under the ancestry of Jacob; but here again we must resist automatically converting the biblical Israel into the historical. Both kingdoms emerged within a century or so of each other, sharing a common border[49] and probably enjoying a considerable degree of local trade and intermarriage. Both kingdoms, of course, shared the same general Canaanite religious culture as other populations in the region, including the generic gods El, Baal

48. Soggin, *An Introduction to the History of Israel and Judah*, 4.

49. It is worth bearing in mind here (and throughout this book) that ancient borders do not imply restriction of population movement, nor are they necessarily represented by firm boundary lines rather than by the rights of patronage (tax-collection) claimed by rulers over villages. Thus, for example, one cannot really call "Dan" an Israelite city, except periodically. At times it "belonged" to Israel and at other times to Aram. On the whole question of "borders" in biblical literature, see J. W. Rogerson, "Frontiers and Borders in the Old Testament," in *In Search of True Wisdom: Essays in Old Testament Interpretation in Honour of Ronald E. Clements* (ed. E. Ball; Sheffield: Sheffield Academic Press, 1999), 116–26.

and the goddess Asherah (or one of her other names).[50] All these things contribute to a sense of ethnicity. But current research on ethnicity shows that it is more elusive: however much archaeologists want, and need, to identify it in terms that archaeology can recognize, it is not necessarily indicated by material culture.[51] One cannot even propose an ethnic consciousness among the subjects of the kings of Israel, living as they did in a *territorial* state, not one based simply on kinship. The biblical elision of "Israelites" as participants of a religious cult and as subjects of the king of Israel is not to be disregarded, let alone perpetuated, for it conceals a very real problem.

The biblical Israel is always presented as *culturally unique.* Its way of life is not developed over generations but *imposed* by a set of laws at Sinai; it is not so much a *chosen* nation as a *created* one (the ancestors are primarily the chosen). What the biblical Israel does is not custom, but divine imprint. Its most significant characteristic is its religion, its adherence to Yahweh; but there is no evidence that this cult was an original and distinctive trait of the early Iron age highland societies or even of the

50. On the religion(s) of Israel and Judah, see the detailed (and somewhat different) treatments by R. Albertz, *History of Israelite Religion in the Old Testament Period* (2 vols.; London: SCM Press; Louisville: Westminster John Knox, 1994); German original, *Religionsgeschichte Israels in alttestamentlicher Zeit* (Göttingen: Vandenhoeck & Ruprecht, 1992); Z. Zevit, *The Religions of Ancient Israel: A Synthesis of Parallactic Approaches* (London: Continuum, 2000).

51. On the vexing question of ethnicity, a great deal has recently been written. The standard treatment is F. Barth, *Ethnic Groups and Boundaries* (Boston: Little, Brown & Co, 1969. A more sophisticated account is S. Jones's *The Archaeology of Ethnicity; Constructing Identities in the Past and Present* (London: Routledge, 1997). See also Ronald Cohen, "Ethnicity: Problem and Focus in Anthropology," *Annual Review of Anthropology* 7 (1978), 379-403, and M. Brett, ed., *Ethnicity and the Bible* (Leiden: Brill, 1996), especially the articles by Brett, "Interpreting Ethnicity: Method, Hermeneutics, Ethics," 3–23 and D. Edelman, "Ethnicity and Early Israel," 25–55; K. L. Sparks, *Ethnicity and Identity: Prolegomena to the Study of Ethnic Sentiments and their Expression in the Hebrew Bible* (Winona Lake: Eisenbrauns, 1998); specifically on the Pentateuch see F. V. Greifenhagen, "Ethnicity In, With, or Under the Pentateuch," *JRS* 3 (2001): 1–17; see further, A. Killebrew, *Biblical Peoples and Ethnicity: An Archaeological Study of Egyptians, Canaanites, Philistines, and Early Israel 1300–1100 B.C.E.* (Atlanta: Society of Biblical Literature, 2005). However, this treatment is not theoretically up-to-date, and while accepting the diverse origin of those who settled in the central hill country of Cisjordan and Transjordan, Killebrew postulates that their ethnic formation and identity stemmed from the epic narrative of Israel's origins contained in the Bible, while the worship of Yahweh formed the core ideology (see especially her Chapter 4 on Israel's ethnogenesis). However, both a common origin epic and a common cult are surely products rather than causes of ethnic solidarity.

kingdoms. Whether they originally shared a cult of Yahweh (presumably among other gods), and if so, whether exclusively or alongside other groups, we do not know. If we wish to appeal to Judges as historical evidence, it is notable that not one of them has a Yahwistic name, nor does any king of Israel before Joram/Jehoram. We might then suggest that this is the point at which Yahweh is adopted as a dynastic god in Israel and in Judah (especially if the two kings are really one; see below).[52] But perhaps biblical onomastica are not totally reliable indicators.

To return briefly to the quotation from Soggin above: the phrase "before the dissolution of the empire of David and Solomon" appears to be a statement about history. But this "empire" is no longer an agreed historical datum. As represented in the biblical "history," David *is* described as bringing together Judah and Israel, with the implication that they had *not previously been united*. And perhaps significantly, that narrative continues by describing the two "houses," and later the two kingdoms, as hostile. This contradicts the Pentateuchal portrait, of course. But that contradiction prompts us to ask whether Judah and Israel were either only temporarily politically united under David, or, indeed, if this era cannot be historically demonstrated, were ever politically united at all.

The purpose of this very sketchy review has not been to make an argument about the relationship between Israel and Judah at the time of their formation. I want only to illustrate how biblical scholarship has by various steps come to a position where the difference between historical Israel and Judah on the one hand, and biblical "Israel" on the other, has become an unavoidable issue, where the origins of the biblical Israels, in their different formats, have to be investigated as historical processes within a particular society. The biblical descriptions cannot be treated merely as slightly unreliable accounts of a single historical entity. If we want to put the matter in an even simpler way: if we had no biblical texts, would we have any clue that Israel and Judah were anything more than neighbouring states? We would, of course, be aware that Jews refer to themselves corporately as "Israel," but would we know why?

And so we have, I think, come inevitably to ponder how the biblical "Israel" came into existence—or to ask the underlying question, how did Judah "become" part of Israel, and indeed, claim to be its only remnant?

---

52. I am referring here to kings of Israel and Judah from Omri, after which we can be reasonably certain of the historicity of several of the rulers' names. Jonathan is, of course, a Yahwistic name, but this character may be unhistorical, given his role in the romance of David's career at Saul's court; the names given for Saul's other sons are not Yahwistic. 1 Sam 14.49 also names ישׁוי as a son of Saul, possibly a corruption of a Yahwistic name ישׁיו. But if so, the form is probably a corrupt or "corrected" or variant form of Ishbaal (=Ishbosheth).

Wrong Answers

The question of Judah's "Israelite" identity, we have come to see, cannot be addressed automatically, or even probably, in the context of a common prehistory. Nor can we assume that Judah's "Israelite" identity developed naturally from the gradual fusion of the populations of the two kingdoms into a single society, whether through political or cultural or even a cultic similarity, such as the worship of the same god (as might be inferred from the Yahwistic names of most of the later Judean and Israelite monarchs). There have indeed been numerous scholarly proposals of so-called northern traditions, what Louis Ginsberg called the "Israelian heritage of Judaism,"[53] penetrating and affecting Judah. The Pentateuchal Elohist source was once supposed to have emanated from here, while Deuteronomy too has been given a "northern" origin, along with certain Psalms. The Exodus tradition has been associated with Bethel (see further in Chapter 10 below), and of course the stories about the kingdom of Israel, especially the Elijah and Elisha cycles. The collections that comprise the book of Hosea (and, we should add, Amos) presumably reached Judah from Israel too. How did all these come to be included in what is obviously a Judean canon, whether that inclusion took place during the monarchic period or later?

The most common answer to this question has been to suggest that during the reigns of either Hezekiah or Josiah (or both), an integration of some Israelites and their traditions into Judah occurred, the former through an influx of refugees, the latter through an expansion of territory to the north.[54] These processes are usually taken to imply some degree of felt kinship on both sides, though a degree of shared culture and simple geographical proximity might in fact provide a sufficient pretext. There are, as I will discuss later, problems with both suggestions.

53. H. L. Ginsberg, *The Israelian Heritage of Judaism* (New York: Jewish Theological Seminary of America, 1982).

54. On both kings, see most recently Finkelstein and Silberman, *The Bible Unearthed*, 229–59 and *David and Solomon*, 129–38; for a fuller treatment, see their "Temple and Dynasty: Hezekiah: the Remaking of Judah and the Rise of the Pan-Israelite Ideology," *JSOT* 30 (2006): 259–85. This argument is dependent on the suggestion of Baruch Halpern, "Sybil, or the Two Nations," in *The Study of the Ancient Near East in the Twentieth Century* (ed. J. S. Cooper and G. M. Schwarz; Winona Lake: Eisenbrauns, 1996), 291–338. On Josiah, see Finkelstein and Silberman, *The Bible Unearthed*, 275–95 and *David and Solomon*, 183–207. The prehistory of these deductions/speculations can be observed in nearly every biblical history written.

Another possibility is a period in which the kingdom of Israel might have imposed its name on Judah by annexation. The biblical narrative (2 Kgs 10–11) relates that the Omride princess Athaliah married Jehoram/Joram of Judah, and later became queen of Judah after her husband's death at the hand of Jehu. The fact that both Israel and Judah were purportedly ruled by a king of the same name (Jehoram) for what was precisely the same period (849–42 is a common calculation) has generated the suspicion that there was only a single king over both,[55] effectively creating a "United Monarchy." The Tel Dan stela may, on the other hand, if the popular reading "House of David" is indeed correct, imply that the territory of Judah was ruled by a chief who was a client of Israel (and later became remembered as the "founder" of the Judean royal line). It is possible that in these circumstances "Judah" was regarded as another "tribe" of Israel. But would Judeans (or their kings) have continued to insist on their unity with Israel after achieving a degree of independence from it? Or would not such vassalage or annexation make this outcome most unlikely? The suggestion is not as plausible as it may initially seem.

None of these scenarios can convincingly explain why the kingdom of Judah would have adopted the identity "Israel," a name that belonged to a neighbouring kingdom now vanished. It is virtually impossible to see, either, what kind of *gradual* process would result in Judeans accepting the self-definition "Israel." Unless there was previously a society that called itself "Israel" and from which both kingdoms derived (and the difficulties of establishing this have already been mentioned), there must be another explanation.

All the explanations so far mentioned assume that "Israel" was an identity shared with its northerly neighbour the kingdom of Judah. But a reading of the books of Samuel and Kings, as we shall see, suggests that this was not the case. The "Israelite" identity that Judeans came to embrace is not political. It has already been noted that the biblical Israels are essentially *religious* and *ethnic* rather than political. These two definitions converge on the figure of Jacob, the eponymous "Israel" and father of the tribes. The most explicit claims to membership of that family in Judean texts are not the Pentateuchal tribal genealogies but claims to descent from "Jacob" and allegiance to his deity ("god of Israel"). The name "Israel" is not necessarily adopted from a political

55. This is the conclusion adopted by Miller and Hayes, eds., *History of Ancient Israel and Judah*, 280–82. J. W. Rogerson, in Rogerson and Davies, *The Old Testament World* (2d ed.; London: T&T Clark International, 2005), 78, suggests rather that the Israelite Joram deposed Jehoshaphat.

state any more than from an ancient shared ethnic identity, but from a common cult and its ancestral founder. Such an origin might better explain the emergence of the biblical Israel in all its guises, as well as its afterlife, in which it became the self-designation of members of the cult of Yahweh.

I include the final item in this section also as a "wrong answer," which I think it is. But it is also a highly important answer to a problem that is well formulated and analyzed. The important work of Reinhard Kratz[56] is concerned to explain in detail how "the Israel of the literary traditions is not the Israel of history"[57] and specifically how the designation of a political entity was transformed into the name of a people defined by a relationship to a god. Here he points to what I think is the key to the question of Judah's "Israelite" identity: that it is not, in fact, a political claim but a religious one. While, as discussed earlier in this chapter, for Noth (but also for the majority of biblical scholars until recently) "Israel" as the name of the kingdom developed from "Israel" as the name of a people. In Noth's view, via the tribal amphictyony, this order should be reversed: the earliest mention of "Israel," in the Merneptah stela, does not designate a twelve-tribe nation but a group of people with a geographical location, while all subsequent extra-biblical references refer only to the kingdom of that name. Even the books of Samuel and Kings acknowledge two political entities, of which only one properly bears the name "Israel."[58] The starting point for any history of Israel is therefore a monarchy, not a people. Under the monarchies, Yhwh was the "god of Israel" and the "god of Judah," just as Chemosh was the "god of Moab."

Under the monarchies, Israel and Judah occasionally fought, and took up different positions over Assyria. But when in the eighth century BCE Samaria fell and Judah survived, the question of Judah's relationship to a now stateless Israel and their shared god arose acutely, and Yhwh's decision (as it was seen) to destroy Samaria raised the question of his intentions towards Judah, against which prophetic criticism was being

---

56. R. Kratz, *The Composition of the Narrative Books of the Old Testament* (London: T&T Clark International, 2005); trans. of *Die Komposition der erzählenden Bücher des Alten Testaments* (Göttingen: Vandehoeck & Ruprecht, 2000); see also his "Israel als Staat und Volk" (Kratz's related article, "Israel in the Book of Isaiah," is reviewed in Chapter 9.)

57. Kratz, *The Composition*, 309–22, provides a synthesis of the conclusions of the literary analyses.

58. In quoting Wellhausen, "The history of a people cannot be extended to a period in which that people was not in existence," Kratz comments that "this is just creative 'remembering'; nowadays one would say in 'cultural memory'" ("Israel als Staat," 4).

directed. In this climate developed "a notion of the unity of Yhwh and his people transcending the oppositions between Israel and Judah." This awareness is reflected in what Kratz sees as the seventh-century compositions contained in 1 Samuel 1–1 Kgs 2, the Yahwistic "Primal" and "Patriarchal Histories" (in Gen 2–35), and the Exodus narrative in Exod 2–Josh 12 (attributable to the Elohist). All of these utilized earlier sources but from them created a united "people of Israel" that previously had not been present. This "Israel" is also stamped with a religious character not previously present in either Israelite or Judean consciousness.

A further stage in the creation of the biblical Israel took place after 587 BCE when Judah also lost its independence. The Yahwistic History was adapted to reflect a wider circle of neighbouring nations and of diaspora communities; the core of Deuteronomy was incorporated into the Exodus narrative, affirming Judah as the centre of "Israel," from which the notion of a single monarchy was developed by the Deuteronomist responsible for the books of Kings. The notion of Yhwh as universal god was a further theological development.

To engage with Kratz's thesis in detail would require a discussion of his detailed literary analysis of the narrative books of the Hebrew Bible. I have offered much less detailed explanations of the material in Joshua–Kings and the book of Jeremiah, in which I point to a rather different account of the problem; the reader will have to decide which explanation, if either, seems more cogent.

I am, however, in any case dubious (see my comments later in this chapter) about the value of over-precise literary analysis, and Kratz is very precise indeed. I have also a few other general remarks. First, Kratz's explanation seems to be to attach a great deal of weight to abstract theological reflection. This account is by no means a religio-historical explanation. Wider social and cultural processes have no role to play in this, and political events provide no more than occasions for such ongoing reflection. If one is to reconstruct Judean theological reflection after 721 BCE, it is as plausible that Judah would distance itself from the defeated Israel both externally (in relation to Assyria) and internally (identification with a defeated neighbour and its god is bad for morale). This kind of speculation is, in the end, as unprovable as minute literary analysis.

Second, Kratz's explanation places a great deal of stress on the existence of a common cult in Judah and in Israel, namely the worship of Yhwh. But if he attributes so much of the biblical history to the creative work of theologians after 721 and again after 587, it is strange that he would not consider the notion of a shared god to be part of that created

history rather reflecting in theological terms a pre-existing cultural reality so profound that it prompted the definition of Israel as the "people of
Yhwh." He criticizes Noth for assuming an original "people of Israel" as
an explanation for the later kingdom, but he makes a similar assumption
himself: in place of a "people" comprising both Israel and Judah he
posits a common religious cult.

A more serious objection, which I have offered against other proposed
solutions, is why Judah should take the name Israel. Kratz has not
explained why Yhwh should be specially regarded as the god of Israel
rather than of Judah, or why Samarians should not have been encouraged
to worship Yhwh as the god of Judah who had abandoned Israel. But
despite these widespread disagreements between us, there are very wide
areas of agreement, and basically a recognition of the same fundamental
problem.

Methodology

In any exercise involving the Bible and history, three disciplines are
available to be harnessed: literary criticism (of various kinds) for the biblical materials, archaeology (excavation but increasingly survey) for the
material culture and social anthropology for analysis of cultural, social
and political history. The antinomy of "Bible" and "archaeology" is now
obsolete: each discipline has its own sphere of competence and antagonism is beginning to be replaced by positive engagement.[59] Methods of
integrating the two disciplines constructively are emerging, now that
many archaeologists see their job as understanding history and not
revealing the "reality" of "biblical Israel." If the biblical Israel is understood as a (developing) cultural product, an ideological artefact, and the
issues of historicity that used to dominate discussion are relegated to
their proper place, both disciplines can focus on the same question. The
recent works by Finkelstein and Silberman and by Liverani, though with
quite different approaches and outcomes, suggest how this integration
can be performed. Finkelstein and Silberman, in their *David and Solomon*, perform a kind of parallel stratigraphy in which archaeologically
reconstructed chronological periods are matched with literary layers in

---

59. The 2006 meeting of the *European Seminar on Historical Methodology*
brought the usual panel of biblical scholars together with a group of archaeologists,
with surprisingly valuable results. Each side (I believe) understood better its ignorance of the other and improved its understanding of their assumptions and
procedures. It is hard for me to see how we can write competent histories of ancient
Israel and Judah except by collaborating in this way.

the biblical stories of these kings to unfold the history of a biblical "tell."
Liverani's *Israel's History* constructs a "normal" history of Israel and
Judah from archaeological and ancient Near Eastern (including some
biblical) literary sources, then presents the biblical record as an "invented
history," whose ideology is traced to the tragedies and ideologies
employed by the returners from Babylon to consolidate their "Israelite"
status over the "remainees." Between the conclusions of these two exer-
cises lie two further differences: for Finkelstein and Silberman, the biblical narratives of David and Solomon are built up in layers over centuries
and culminate in the time of Josiah. For Liverani, while older materials
are not excluded, the shape of the biblical historiography is created by a
discrete historical-cultural process that took place in the Persian period.
Finkelstein and Silberman rely to a greater extent on the conventional
critical dating of biblical material, while Liverani is more sensitive to the
literary and ideological conventions of the ancient Near East. But it is
valuable to have different kinds of approaches to the same question.

In a book dealing with "biblical Israel," however, it seems important
to pay particular attention to what is, after all, a literary phenomenon.
The first step is not archaeological reconstruction, but a reading of the
biblical (hi)stories of Israel themselves. As has already been hinted in
several places in this chapter, these narratives do not offer a straightforward or coherent "Israel." But the awkward gaps and unanswered
questions that lie within and between these stories are the proper starting
point for an analysis. Problems need not be imposed on the biblical text:
it is quite capable of producing its own.

I will now comment briefly on literary, archaeological and sociologi-
cal methods relevant to the question.

Literary Reading
In Part I, I am adopting a literary reading of the biblical histories that
dispenses with sources, historicity, authors and audience in favour of the
"world of the text," "narrator" and "implied reader."[60] Such readings
often strain for integrity, making sense of the whole. But the assumption
that the text must be coherent is prejudiced and tends to impose on the
text something it may not possess. It displays the wrong kind of
"naïvety." We do not need to have read Derrida or Bakhtin to realize that
texts (especially large ones) can (must?) be contradictory and incoherent

60. For a useful introduction to the various "new" literary-critical methods (now
presumably quite familiar to all biblical scholars), see the Introduction in David J. A.
Clines and J. Cheryl Exum, *The New Literary Criticism and the Hebrew Bible*
(Sheffield: JSOT Press, 1993).

in some ways. A truly "naïve" reading often produces problems that can-not—and should not—be resolved on the literary level. As literary crit-ics, we are entitled simply to leave these as gaps or faults or even virtues and possibilities for the reader. We must especially be free to read the narrative literally without having "historicity" at the back of our minds; and for this, the techniques of "new" literary criticism are ideal. But if we want to *explain* or *solve* these inconsistencies, we must then employ a *literary-critical* method in which narrators become authors and the world of the text opens out to a real world of the context. We need to remember that authorship and readership of the scriptural scrolls do not correspond to our modern ways; texts were not always read through, and their author-ship was often created from many contributors in a linear process (this much we know from ancient manuscript evidence). That the end result should be entirely systematic and coherent is not a reasonable expecta-tion. A "literary" reading of the text is, in fact, no more natural or inno-cent than a literary-historical one. But it has value as an inevitable and important first step: it is wise to understand the shape and character of the whole before dissection begins, and to begin analysis with the end-product.

Of course the text should always be allowed to make sense when that is reasonable; but that "sense" is a narrative, and not a historical sense; for historical sense we must use literary-historical methods and historical data. We must also here be guided by our knowledge of other ancient Near Eastern literature, and a little common sense, which require among other things that we recognize "historicity" as a modern concept and acknowledge that it is not culturally relevant in ancient Near Eastern societies—largely because informed access to the past was not possible and had no useful function.

Archaeology

One of the problems with biblical archaeology is its ignorance of the social and political functions of text production in antiquity and a corre-sponding ignorance of the principles of literary-historical criticism. When archaeologists used to approach the biblical texts, they viewed them as an assemblage of historical data, rather like material artefacts.[61]

---

61. Finkelstein's and Silberman's *David and Solomon* must, like their *Bible Unearthed*, be excepted from much of this criticism. But it is still written from an archaeological viewpoint and follows archaeological categories of analysis. It is an intelligent application of literary stratigraphy that outstrips previous archaeo-logical approaches to biblical texts, but it does not move beyond the horizon of an

Their aim was generally to elicit historical data—but of one kind only. Concerned with the data contained *in* the text, they correlated the text with the periods it was supposed to be describing and not the period that produced the text, where the most direct correlation lies. "Stratigraphy" in this respect was simply ignored.[62] The fact that a majority of biblical archaeologists are religiously conservative does not help, because this reinforces their preference for literal interpretation as well as biblical historicity. It continues to be assumed in many circles that the contribution of archaeology to understanding the Bible lies only in retrieving "facts" reported in the Bible; and political as well as religious agendas have been served rather than scientific or historical ones. But in recent decades, much of this has begun to disappear, especially in Israel, and in excavations mounted by academic institutions. Biblical archaeology is no longer the rule: most archaeologists of ancient Israel reject its principles and dislike its practice.

It needs to be recognized, too, that archaeological and biblical data do not integrate as directly or precisely as is often claimed, especially when such integration focuses on points of "confirmation" or "convergence." In recent essays, Baruch Halpern and Hugh Williamson have each pointed out that the disciplines cover different kinds of data and different levels of historical activity, with rather little overlap.[63] The data used by each discipline generally testify to different kinds of human activity, different *levels* of historical event—indeed, archaeology is not well equipped to illuminate events, except where there are sharp changes in material culture (destruction layers, population changes). By contrast, the biblical text is full of detail, much of it relating to events that were not public but private. We need to be wary of this biblical detail: hardly any narratives are more detailed than the "court history" of David, or the books of Ruth and Esther. But all three are to some extent (if not totally) fictional, although they have precise temporal contexts.

archaeologically constructed history into the world of literary production and the sociology of ancient texts. It correlates textual data with the data of material culture.

62. The fact that biblical archaeology always tended to concentrate on the monarchic (and pre-monarchic) era and remains relatively uninformed about later periods—when the texts were produced—has not helped.

63. Baruch Halpern, "Text and Artifact: Two Monologues," in Silberman and Small, eds., *The Archaeology of Israel*, 311–40; H. G. M. Williamson, "Confirmation or Contradiction? Archaeology and Biblical History" (The St George's Cathedral Lecture 12, Perth, Australia, 2004). Halpern's comments do not seem to apply to his own prodigious integration of archaeology, text and imagination.

There remain other problems with archaeological data, which are not entirely the fault of archaeologists themselves. The external pressure that the media and financial backers place on archaeologists in Israel encourages the search for dramatic confirmation of biblical history, and then quick and sensational announcements, before the data have been properly revealed or understood. Similar pressures also obscure the huge extent to which archaeological data need to be interpreted. Archaeology is not wholly scientific; differences in interpretation abound, whether in major issues—over the pottery chronology of the tenth century BCE, over the size and status of Jerusalem before the eighth century, over the dating of the enlargement of Jerusalem after the fall of Samaria—or in questions of stratigraphy or the dating of pottery assemblages. Documented data often take years to appear after having been discovered.

The most serious problem in harnessing textual and archaeological disciplines is the mutual ignorance of many practitioners.[64] Too few biblical scholars, let alone the general public, are aware of the often sloppy practices of which archaeology has in the past been guilty, of the hidden agendas of several excavators (still today) and their patrons, the difficult and sometimes tendentious nature of some of the interpretation and the lack of properly documented publication. Archaeologists, however, are by and large entirely aware (and usually honest) about these limitations. Likewise, few archaeologists of ancient Israel and Judah have adequate training in how to analyse and use the literary data—a skill that requires extensive knowledge and expertise (sometimes dismissively dubbed "philology") but which tends to produce differences in interpretation much wider than generally found in archaeology. Given this largely inevitable state of affairs, the history of antagonism between the two disciplines has been understandable if unfortunate. But the situation is quickly improving.

History

It is not easy to say what *methods* history uses: these obviously depend on the subject matter. But the discipline is rife with methodological and philosophical debate. As far as our own topic is concerned, the most important issues are to do with scepticism, subjectivity and paucity of data.[65]

---

64. There are, of course, a number of biblical scholars who, like Noth and Alt, have archaeological experience, and several can write with equal authority about both archaeology and biblical criticism.

65. An excellent discussion of the philosophical issues underlying recent historiography of ancient Israel has been written by Megan Bishop Moore, *Philosophy and*

The historian can approach evidence with a broadly "sceptical" or a "credulous" attitude. These attitudes have no *moral* value—gossip columnists are typically credulous, investigative reporters typically sceptical, of their sources. Historians may prefer a fuller but less certain account to a more reliable one with large gaps. In theory, a sceptical attitude will develop positively when more evidence accumulates to quench doubt; the more credulous attitude should correspondingly develop negatively when the evidence quenches credulity. Thus, both postures ideally tend towards convergence though they never meet. Because of the religious investment that permeates any topic relating to the Bible, the credulous approach (for "credulous," read "faithful" or "believing") is sometimes encouraged while a sceptical approach ("nihilistic," "doubting") criticized. My own preference is not to accept any unsupported statement as true, whether in the Bible or not. This is not the same as disbelieving, though reports that defy common experience or sense are usually disbelieved (and rightly) by ordinary people (floating axe-heads and a lack of solar motion fall into this category). Historians who prefer to give biblical reports the benefit of the doubt may of course do so, but they need to satisfy themselves and others that this is a general principle and not a special case—for example, that a "biblical history of Israel" is no worse or better than a "Homeric history of Greece."

But whatever the approach, the fact is that in most cases we will remain ignorant. Not all sites can be excavated, the textual remains are sparse and large swathes of history remain beyond our capacity to recover. In the case of ancient Israelite and Judean history, even the relatively extensive textual details often cannot be verified, leaving a very large amount of narrative in a kind of limbo. This is a situation that many historians find unsatisfactory, and the temptation to abhor a vacuum is understandable. That does not, however, make the historicity of these narratives any more or less likely. Part of the answer may lie with moving attention away from unverifiable details towards larger historical events and processes that can be measured by a range of information. This brings the subject closer to the social sciences than to traditional humanistic history—which perhaps is not a bad thing (see below).

A second issue is that of subjectivity. Is there an objective history, a sequence of facts independent of attestation, point of view or interpretation? Such a view can still be encountered, but most historians now accept the distinction between the chaotic mass of facts that constitute the totality of the past and a meaningful selection and ordering of these

Practice in Writing a History of Ancient Israel (New York: T. & T. Clark, 2006), a book that had I encountered it earlier I would have discussed in this chapter.

facts into a story. If history has a meaning, then the meaning arises from the observer, just as the impressions of colour, smell and sound are created by human perception and do not reside in objects. For history to have an objective meaning, there has to be an objective interpreter: perhaps God. But the historian cannot deal with such a figure since it must lie outside history. This is not to say a historian must be an atheist. But once divine intervention is allowed (and it will always be an interpretation rather than a fact), it can be invoked at any time and place, and will destroy the tissue that history creates: of a theoretically seamless interaction of human acts and natural events.

A particular application of this principle is that all histories have their point of view and their biases, including those in the Bible. It would be interesting to read how Philistines or Canaanites or Assyrians viewed the events in first-millennium BCE Palestine, or indeed, how the population of Samaria viewed them. The fact is that the biblical histories are Judean and their canonization by Judeans does not alter this evaluation. Partly in order to compensate for that, I have tried to reconstruct a non-Judean history—which indeed in my opinion may once have existed (though its existence does not matter greatly).

Both of these issues lead naturally into a consideration of sociology, or at least two aspects of it.[66]

Sociology: New Historicism and Cultural Memory

New Historicism grew in the USA from British cultural materialism (and disguised some of its Marxist influences in the process). It focuses on the cultural context, rather than the aesthetics, of literary works.[67] Images and narratives are regarded as historically effective, as a medium for the working out of social ideologies and the social interaction of various groups and interests. New Historicists seek the issues, crises, and conflicts that literature reflects, conceals or mediates[68] and try to relate interpretive or exegetical problems in literary works to cultural-historical problems that obsess authors, readers and their society and which the

66. For a recent presentation of a range of social-scientific approaches to the Hebrew Bible, see Philip Esler, ed., *Ancient Israel: The Old Testament in Its Social Context* (Minneapolis, Fortress, 2006).

67. H. A. Veeser, ed., *The New Historicism* (London: Routledge, 1989); J. Brannigan, *New Historicism and Cultural Materialism* (Basingstoke: Macmillan, 1998). For its application to biblical studies, see G. Hens-Piazza, *The New Historicism* (Minneapolis: Fortress, 2002).

68. These operations are what the cultural materialist Fredric Jameson means by the title of his *The Political Unconscious: Narrative as a Socially Symbolic Act* (Ithaca, N.Y.: Cornell University Press, 1981).

literary work both consciously and unconscious communicates. Authors are thus treated as participants in social and political discourse. This perspective is particularly helpful to the biblical scholar, to whom not a single individual biblical author is known.

One particularly useful concept that should be regarded as "new historicist," even though its origins are independent of the term, is "cultural memory," also known as "collective memory." It was established by Maurice Halbwachs,[69] and has more recently been introduced into archaeology by the Egyptologist Jan Assmann.[70] It has also been treated at some length by Paul Ricoeur.[71] "Cultural memory" is perhaps better than "collective memory," since it can be created by a small group or even an individual. It is not necessarily something automatically "remembered" by the majority, but can be introduced and disseminated as a kind of "ideological canon" in the absence of any prior reminiscence. "Memory" is not an ideal term, for cultural memory may be constituted by a written text without any oral prehistory and indeed it may not preserve memory at all but create it. "Memory" does not imply history. But in another sense "memory" *is* an appropriate term, for our own memories, as we say, not only "play tricks on us" but can often be shown to be invented as well as repressed. Our faculty of memory does not serve the past, but our present interests. It is continuously reshaping the past for us.

Halbwachs argued that that human memory functions *within* collective memory, and that both are selective; different groups as well as different individuals have different collective memories, which influence their constructions of identity and their behaviour. Assmann puts it slightly differently: cultural memory is the external dimension of human memory that includes "memory culture" and "reference to the past." The former refers to the way in which a society preserves its cultural continuity through collective knowledge, prompting each generation to reconstruct or to manage its cultural identity. "Reference to the past" undergirds this collective identity by providing a historical awareness of that identity in

---

69. Maurice Halbwachs, *On Collective Memory* (ed. and trans. Lewis A. Coser; Chicago: University of Chicago Press, 1992).

70. J. Assmann, *Das kulturelle Gedächtnis. Schrift, Erinnerung und politische Identität in frühen Hochkulturen* (2d ed.; Munich: Beck, 1999), and *Religion and Cultural Memory: Ten Studies*.

71. Paul Ricoeur, *Memory, History, Forgetting* (Chicago: University of Chicago Press, 2004), adopts a more philosophical approach. The question of why some historical events occupy the pages of history more than other equally important ones leads to the observation that history "remembers" some events over others, which are then comparatively "forgotten." This difference affects how we construe historical experience and produce historical narrative.

time and space through a shared story of the past. But this "reference" does not imply a direct link with a past event. The past is a construct, a time and a space, and both are essential for identity formation. It does not matter whether that past is "true": what matters is that this past makes sense of the present, and vice versa. It is not what happens to us that makes us, but what we "remember."

The study of cultural memory, therefore, does not concern itself directly with real events except insofar as this enables the historian to analyze the inventive aspects of the memory. More important is the identity that the memory creates, for that identity itself becomes an agent of history. Here Assmann makes a distinction borrowed from Lévi-Strauss, that of "cold" and "hot" cultures. "Cold" cultures rely on rigid inherited categories of understanding, while "hot" ones are dynamic and their myths develop to reflect ongoing perception and experience. Assmann suggests that "cold" cultures consider repetition as important for their memory, and feature repeatedly returning events, in continuity rather than discontinuity, while in "hot" cultures, variety, innovation, evolution, and even disaster have a meaning and importance and are committed to memory. I will not explore this useful distinction further, but it should be immediately clear how it can be applied (whether justifiably or not) in a comparison of the books of Kings with the books of Chronicles. More generally, it allows us to distinguish biblical portraits of "Israel" that show a permanent and hardly changing nature from those in which it is constantly evolving. Taken as a whole the biblical Israel is rather more "hot" than some recent histories of it. Its "Israel" is more fluctuating and dynamic than some contemporary biblical historians allow.

The high degree of applicability of the indispensable social phenomenon of cultural memory to "biblical Israel" must be immediately obvious. The mechanisms by which this memory is sustained include rituals and ceremonies, but can also feature canonized texts. Indeed, it can be argued that canons provide a particular subset of cultural identity. It is important to recognize that cultural memory does not aim at *reliable* statements about the past but rather at a narrative of the past that makes sense of (and in) the present and for the future. (This is, of course, also how personal memory functions.) Hence, it is a constitutive function of ethnicity, the *ethnos* being in this case the group bonded by the shared "memory" of the past. In his book on Moses as a figure of cultural memory over millennia, Assmann has coined the term "mnemohistory" to denote the study of this phenomenon.[72]

---

72. J. Assmann, *Moses the Egyptian: The Memory of Egypt in Western Monotheism* (Cambridge, Mass.: Harvard University Press, 1997).

Assmann's study of Moses prompts the observation that while the cultural memory encoded in the Bible has given rise to developing interpretations and to "re-remembering," its "reference to the past" enjoys a unique privilege. While modern scholarly history can reconstruct a quite different kind of "memory" (a critical one), that "memory" does not function culturally in such an obvious way: but given that Western civilization employs various memories of its own, including the biblical, to sustain its identity, it would not be inaccurate to allow for the fact that cultural memory is still at work.[73] Partly as a reflex of that modern cultural memorizing, the ancient Judean cultural memory is latched onto as a record of the past. Cultural memories are characteristically unaware of their earlier drafts; memory obliterates its own previous history, or, when confronted with it, treats it as "fact," as if to obscure the process of change in memory itself. In so doing, the social function of Judean memory is subordinated to its historical function: in other words, how far the memory is true comes to be more important than what it meant.[74]

As I indicated in the Foreword, the purpose of the "Benjaminite cultural memory" that I construct in Chapter 7, while offered as a serious hypothesis about the prehistory of the Judean narrative, also enables the biblical story to be assessed as *an account of Judah's identity as "Israel"* that differs from other accounts that might have been provided (and with equal validity). In this case, the Benjaminite memory itself has a history, as first Israelite and then Judean.[75]

How, then, do we read texts of cultural memory? As I said earlier, to begin with we read them attentively and seriously, not with a view to their literary structure or historical content; and when we see the gaps and tricks and lapses that memory always betrays, we are not surprised, and do not wish to remove them. We then read again in a literary-*critical* manner, observing the ideological contours of texts, the interests and conflicts that they mediate. This distinguishes the reading technique from traditional literary-historical methods, in which documentary sources,

---

73. This is a point that can be drawn from Moore, *Philosophy and Practice in Writing a History of Ancient Israel*.

74. One of the best essays on this topic, which explores precisely the mechanism of generating memory in ancient Judah and nicely balances the elements of genuine memory and creativity in the response to national crisis, is Joseph Blenkinsopp, "Memory: Tradition and the Construction of the Past in Ancient Israel," *BTB* 27 (1997): 76–82; repr. in Joseph Blenkinsopp, *Treasures Old and New* (Grand Rapids: Eerdmans, 2004), 1–17.

75. For the application of cultural memory to Judaism (and other societies) in the classical era, see Doron Mendels, *Memory in Jewish, Pagan and Christian Societies* (London: T&T Clark, 2004).

life-settings, glosses and other scribal interventions produce a theory of literary growth. Not that these features are always irrelevant; but the structure for which we are looking is not primarily a *literary* one. Indeed, given that nearly all biblical literature is the product of rewriting, earlier forms may no longer be recoverable in detail, nor the scribal activity that has transformed the text during its history. It is the shape of the wood rather than the details of the trees that matters—though this is not to embrace a "final form" hermeneutic, for none of the canonized texts exhibit a single "final form" and the texts themselves cannot be viewed as sacrosanct by the historian. While individual scribes (or even possibly "schools," though this is a sociologically ill-defined concept) have no doubt played their roles in shaping the textual form of the transmitted manuscripts, such individuals and their motives remain almost entirely invisible. When considering authorship we have to deal in terms of the *societies* and *classes* that manifest their presence through the authors and rewriters. For the historian, the biblical narratives relating the past are socially generated artefacts whose contents were created, and functioned, as cultural memory.

Such a way of reading can also help to circumvent a few of the difficulties inherent in traditional literary-historical exegesis, which is notoriously prone to generate precise but widely differing interpretation. Mario Liverani expresses the problem as follows:[76]

> As is well known, biblical literary criticism (conditioned by the postulate of divine inspiration) normally views the original materials as organic and coherent, and attributes the "contradictions" to later interventions, to the point of postulating as many interventions or layers as there are contradictions to be regularised. It is better to restrict oneself to pointing out significant interventions that are endowed with a literary and ideological specificity. And hence offer the possibility of an historical setting.

Folker Greifenhagen makes much the same point in mapping out the ideological functions of Egypt in the Pentateuch and locating the historical setting for such functions, but using "biblical imagination" in place of "cultural memory":[77]

> The focus of investigation will be on the final form of the text. This methodological implication is first meant to distinguish the ideological approach employed here from traditional historical-critical approaches

---

76. Mario Liverani, *Myth and Politics in Ancient Near Eastern Historiography* (ed. and with an Introduction by Zainab Bahrani and Marc Van De Mieroop; London: Equinox, 2002), 190 n. 37.

77. Folker V. Greifenhagen, *Egypt on the Pentateuch's Ideological Ma: Constructing Biblical Israel's Identity* (London: Sheffield Academic Press, 2002), 16.

that tend to dissect the biblical text into its various developmentally linked strata. In contrast, the focus of this study is not on the origin, development and history of traditions *in* the biblical text but rather on the "biblical imagination."

A fuller exploration of reading strategies, with the added ingredient of intertextuality, is also explored in some detail by David Aaron in his excellent analysis of the Decalogue,[78] a rich and complex study that touches on numerous aspects of literary history.

It is not simply a literary-critical fad to insist on the larger "sense" of literary compositions: such a perspective is required by our realization of the historical process of generating large corpora of texts; and this realization stems from a growing concern with the text as shaped, in time and space, by a community for whom that text functions interactively in composing a social world and an identity—as it has continued to do for successive generations of readers. It is, paradoxically, the results of text-critical analysis that force us to realize the ongoing manipulation and consequent variegation of texts even as they approach the form(s) in which they will eventually be (arbitrarily) frozen. This realization obliges us to deal with the larger shape of texts, not as "final forms" (here the literary critic's veneration comes close to reflecting that of the fundamentalist), but as meaningful configurations whose details may be constantly amended but whose purpose remains the provision of a cultural memory that defines the subject in time, revealing a trajectory also for the future.

It seems to me important to use a range of interpretative methods and techniques, but also to ensure that they cooperate (dare I say "converge"?) rather than compete. The obsessions with discrete historical "facts," with literary history and with an idealized sacred text that have characterized a good deal of scholarship (and still seem to capture the public understanding to an unhealthy degree) seem to me inadequate to address what is first and foremost a cultural artefact. If taken together, these various approaches can, in fact, answer the fundamental question of all biblical scholarship: why we have a Bible. Or at least they can nudge us a little further forward.

---

78. David Aaron, *Etched in Stone: The Emergence of the Decalogue* (London: T&T Clark International, 2006), 1–40.

Part I

"ISRAEL" IN JUDEAN HISTORIOGRAPHY

Chapter 2

OVERVIEW

Following a recent trend, I shall consider biblical historiography[1] as represented for the most part in two blocs. The first comprises the whole of Genesis–Kings (Torah and Former Prophets) and the second Chronicles–Ezra–Nehemiah. Both series present a sequential narrative, and I shall refer to them from now on as the "First" and "Second" Historiographies.[2] Whether either should be conceived as the conception of a single author (or group of authors) or resulting from the juxtaposition of shorter historiographies, or as the outcome of successive redactions of shorter narratives of the past, is not relevant to a narrative analysis. Likewise, "biblical Israel" is treated as the creation of this narrative, not as some reconstructed historical entity or entities to which it might correspond.

1. By this term I mean a *large-scale narrative composition that claims to describe the course of human affairs in the past*. "Historiography" is the most explicit vehicle of cultural memory and though it can be distinguished from "myth," which includes the non-human past or narrates something that lies beyond the past, in another time-frame historiography can also be distinguished from other narratives set in the past that present self-contained episodes (Jonah, Ruth, Esther), and from lists such as genealogies and chronicles that provide chronologically ordered data but no explicit narrative. All these distinctions are, however, less than clear-cut. Many historiographies, for instance (including biblical), reach back to myth as the sphere of ultimate origins, even the cause of history itself. "Historiographer" is used in distinction to "historian" to avoid confusion with contemporary historians, whose manner of working and principles are different.

2. I prefer "First History" to "Primary History," the term apparently coined by D. N. Freedman in "Deuteronomistic History, The," in *The Interpreter's Dictionary of the Bible: Supplementary Volume* (ed. K. Crim; Nashville: Abingdon, 1976), 226–28; "Second History" seems to have been used first by D. J. A Clines, "The Old Testament Histories," in *What Does Eve Do To Help? And Other Readerly Questions to the Old Testament* (Sheffield: JSOT Press, 1990), 85–105. (Clines included Esther in the Secondary History.)

The fact that these historiographies have been transmitted in separate scrolls is not purely the result of the limits of ancient writing technology; the division of contents between them usually corresponds to perceived junctures in the narrative, and the obvious opening and closing formulas to many of the individual scrolls should not be disregarded. We are thus often guided by the form of the narrative itself to consider each scroll as exhibiting its own characteristics, where these are self-evident, without detriment to the single shared narrative they construct. Cultural memory, like individual memory, is, after all, episodic and the connection of its episodes into a continuous sequence requires conscious effort, nearly always producing gaps, variations and contradictions (readers can try constructing a single continuous memory of their own life to illustrate this point). The scrolls of Chronicles and Ezra–Nehemiah, moreover, appear in the standard Masoretic (but not Greek) format even in a non-chronological sequence. The fact that the closing verses of Chronicles and opening verses of Ezra are identical suggests that their contents *are* nevertheless intended to be understood as sequential;[3] their ordering in the Masoretic canon is not really relevant.

Readers unfamiliar with the stories (or parts of them) presented in each of these two histories should certainly refresh their memories first, and may also want to revisit them during or after the reading of the next few chapters, both to check that I am correctly representing their contents and also to discover whether the story reads differently the second time (my experience is that it reads slightly differently *every* time). What

---

3. The possible divisions of this material are almost endless: here is a sample of some recent treatments. The Tetrateuch–Pentateuch–Hexateuch debate is longstanding (see conveniently A. G. Auld, *Joshua, Moses and the Land: Tetrateuch–Pentateuch–Hexateuch in a Generation since 1938* [Edinburgh: T. & T. Clark, 1980]). Stephen Chapman has argued for an Enneateuch in *The Law and the Prophets: A Study in OT Canon Formation* (Tübingen: Mohr, 2000); E. A. Knauf has revived the Hexateuch option in "Towards an Archaeology of the Hexateuch," in *Abschied vom Jahwisten: Die Komposition des Hexateuch in der jüngsten Diskussion* (ed. J. C. Gertz, K. Schmid and M. Witte; Berlin: de Gruyter, 2002), 275–94; the theory of a single Pentateuchal author has been defended by R. N. Whybray, *The Making of the Pentateuch: A Methodological Study* (Sheffield: Sheffield Academic Press, 1987). On the concept of a "First History," see J. W. Wesselius, *The Origin of the History of Israel: Herodotus' Histories as the Blueprint for the First Books of the Bible* (London: Sheffield Academic Press, 2002). On the unity of Chronicles–Ezra–Nehemiah views range from those who see a single author (usually the Chronicler), those who see Chronicles and Ezra–Nehemiah as from different authors; those who see them as separate works by the same author; and further, those who see Ezra and Nehemiah also as from different authors. For a presentation of the options and a bibliography, see Ralph W. Klein, "Chronicles, Book of 1–2," *ABD* 1:92–1002 (esp. 993–94).

follows is not, of course, a disinterested reading, nor a (pseudo-)naïve one. It is a reading by a scholar with the mind of a historian but wearing the hat of a narratologist (of perhaps just "reader of a story") and prompted by the general question: "What is the 'Israel' here?" in each stage of the story, and the more specific question: "Does this 'Israel' include Judah?". I shall be especially attentive, therefore, to points where the identity of that "Israel" becomes problematic or obscure, where the narrative logic breaks down or where there seem to be internal differences or contradictions, but purely as *literary* phenomena; the historical implications will come later.

The "First History"

The First History is inhabited by several Israels, which for much of the time overlap. Hence it cannot always be said that there is at any one juncture a single or a coherent portrait. At many points where one Israel is primarily in view, the image of other Israels hovers, interrupts, or lingers. There is nearly always a *dominant* profile, and this is obviously what I shall focus attention on, but without ignoring the traces of others. The reason for this overlapping or interpenetration can be to a limited extent explained in literary terms, as a device that blurs the distinctions between different configurations, making "biblical Israel" something flexible or multi-layered. But such explanations do not, of course, account for the presence of different configurations in the first place.

There are basically four Israels that interplay—and in terms of their narrative dominance one can say that they form a sequence—in the First History. The first is as a branch of the larger family of Abraham, namely the family of his grandson Jacob/Israel. The second is as a nation, its descent from Jacob still marked by its twelve-tribe structure, but constituted not merely or even primarily by descent but by a distinct religion and culture, which, via themes of election and promise, is further connected to the Abrahamic family (one symptom of the shift is the transformation of Levi from secular tribe into priestly caste). The relationship between this nation and other nations is now actually or potentially hostile, and includes a degree of antagonism towards its Abrahamic neighbours (and distant relatives). A third Israel consists of a small but indeterminate group of tribes, in which Benjamin plays a central role and Ephraim also plays a part; these "tribes" (and perhaps some others) form a political unit with its own king (Saul). This "Israel" later imperceptibly expands into a fourth: a group of ten tribes that later form the kingdom called "Israel" under Jeroboam. From both of these last two, Judah is excluded; there is a span of time in which Judah and "Israel" are politically unified, and during which "Israel" mutates from its more modest scale into the larger one. The Judah that remains after the end of the period of unification consists not only of the "tribe" of Judah but also the "tribe" of Benjamin, plus some from the now priestly tribe of Levi.

We get a glimpse of a fifth profile, though this time not a corporate entity. In most of the Judges narratives we encounter a collection of individual tribes acting mostly independently. This profile is strongly framed by a united Israel ruled by a single judge, which finally acts together against one of its number (though this time without a judge!)—another instance of that "overlapping" mentioned earlier. The activity of individual tribes may well be described deliberately as the starting point of a process of crystallization from which the Israel of Saul is created—not as the political expression of an already existing social organization, an Israelite nation, but the outcome of cooperation and alliance between smaller units. The narrative gives some hints of how this process is remembered, for example the offer of kingship to Gideon (and Abimelech?), and the figure of Samuel in 1 Samuel may all represent leadership of a larger tribal grouping. But this may be reading too much into the narrative, and literary-historical analysis may throw more light on the function of these memories. As the narrative stands, it is unclear whether kingship is anticipated as a welcome solution or an outcome to be avoided; both ideologies seem to play a part in the narrative.

The various Israels just introduced can to a large extent be schematized into a sequence of four episodes, separated by three points of transition. The episodes can be characterized as *unity–dissolution–re-unification–re-division*. Each displays one *dominant* profile of "Israel," but the transition from one to the next is never abrupt and traces of other Israels usually linger alongside the dominant one. Thus, the first episode of an original unity, represented by the Pentateuch, begins to disintegrate in the book of Joshua, where the smaller Israel in which Benjamin plays a dominant role makes a preliminary appearance in the stories of conquest. Within Judges the united Israel of twelve tribes becomes a rather flimsy framework only; the dominant profile is of individual tribal exploits. Yet here we find also traces of the "Benjaminite" Israel, as well as, at the beginning and end of the book, traces of a twelve-tribe Israel under the leadership not of a judge but of the tribe of Judah.

In 1 Samuel, the dissolution is complete: the twelve-tribe unity more or less disappears; the Israel of Samuel and Saul, centred on the tribes of Benjamin and Ephraim, takes centre stage. The arrival of David introduces Judah as a neighbouring kingdom, which David joins to Israel to form a joint realm. This constitutes the episode of "reunification," though in a modified configuration—a single king occupying two thrones, Judah and Israel. What was once a nation of twelve-tribes has become two "houses." During the reigns of David and his immediate successors, the house of Israel becomes magnified territorially, and its leadership is transferred from the family of Saul to the figure of Jeroboam. Under Rehoboam occurs the re-division: this Israel (composed of ten tribes, evoking the Pentateuchal Israel) secedes and so re-establishes the independent kingdom of Israel.

The process of redivision, however, leads to a fragmentation. The kingdom of Israel finally vanishes, and later the kingdom of Judah also. "Israel" now persists in various (contested) forms. According to Kings, the deportees from the kingdom of Israel disappear, to be replaced totally by foreigners, who, although they worship Yhwh, are not "Israel." The territories once comprising the kingdom of Israel are now (mostly) called "Samaria." "Israel" disappears completely.

We now turn to the Second History. In Chronicles, the unity of Pentateuchal Israel is sustained, though it is given a strong cultic emphasis, with the city and sanctuary of Jerusalem as its core. Since the narrative commences with the death of Saul, several other profiles of Israel found in the First History can be disregarded: Saul and then David are presented as ruling over that twelve-tribe nation. Although ten of these tribes secede from the Davidic dynasty, the consequences of this political break, and the existence of a kingdom of Israel separate from Judah, are almost entirely ignored. With the end of the kingdom of Israel, the division is over and the true Israel regains its political unity; Hezekiah is again the king of the complete Israel, and as such invites members of the former "northern" kingdom to his Passover. While Chronicles' story ends with the exile of *all* Judeans to Babylonia, the reader is left with the impression that a twelve-tribe Israel remains a possibility for the future.

But this possibility is excluded by Ezra–Nehemiah, where "Israel" is used only as a self-designation for the tribes of Judah, Benjamin and Levi who return from Babylonian exile. The non-deported population of Judah are no more regarded as "Israel" than the residents of Samaria. Although elsewhere in the Bible and early Jewish literature we find references to the "lost tribes" of the erstwhile kingdom of Israel—and perhaps Ezekiel expresses the unspoken hope of the Chronicler for a reunion of the twelve tribes (Ezek 37:15–28; 47–48)—the Second History finally equates "Israel" with a specific group of Judeans. Genealogy thus makes a return, but unlike Genesis and Chronicles, where it distinguishes Israel from the nations, it here divides one Judean from another. The use of "Israel" to designate exclusively Judeans ("Jews")—the state of affairs that finally prevailed—in fact makes no appearance at all in the First or Second History!

Chapter 3

ISRAEL IN THE FIRST HISTORY:
THE PENTATEUCH

The contents of the Pentateuch correspond more or less with the first of
the episodes mentioned in the previous chapter, expounding the original
unity of Israel's twelve tribes. The narrative recounts the formation of a
nation first through genealogical descent (Genesis), then through adoption by/of its own deity, through its "constitution" (laws) and finally
through acquisition of its own land. The flow of the narrative is impeded
by a large block (or blocks) of "law," in which the deity issues instructions at Sinai, and later it is also held up by a speech from Moses in
which this "law" (and some of the narrative) is repeated, though with
differences. One effect of these blocks in the narrative is to add a different dimension to the characterization of the people whose creation the
narrative unfolds: as the people chosen by the deity and identified/
marked out by their observance of this law. When Moses says in Deut
5:3, "Not with our ancestors did Yhwh make this treaty, but with us, who
are all of us here alive today," he underlines the permanent and defining
character of that law for Israel. But in comparing the laws in Leviticus
and Deuteronomy and the narrative in Numbers we can extract three
portrayals of that "Israel," which, if not always incompatible, are inconsistent with each other. At the high point of Israel's biblical definition,
the portrait fragments like a cubist painting.

The Prehistory of Israel

The book of Genesis is entirely occupied with the emergence of Israel
from among the human population of the earth. After the world is
created, and then the human species, the various "families of the earth"
are distributed across its surface (Gen 10; 11:1–9), each family becoming
a nation ("in their lands, with their own language, by their families, in
their nations"). In 11:10–26, the line of Peleg, one of the two sons of

Eber, is extended to Abraham's father Terah, who begets three sons, Abram, Nahor and Haran. Abraham migrates from Ur, settles in Haran, and is called from there to the land his descendants will occupy. (Although Haran dies in Ur, the connection between ancestors and names of cities is well-established already in the genealogies; at all events, this connection underlines Terah's family's roots in Aram.)

We may choose to see this migration as a microscopic view of what other nations also experienced—their allocation being subject to similar fortunes[1]—but whether or not this is the case, Abraham makes a *further* movement, away from his family's chosen territory, in response to a divine call and promise; but we note, too, that his destination is for the moment possessed by (allocated to?) others. So Abraham behaves as a *ger*, a foreign resident, in a land that is not yet his own: he buys some property (a cave for his wife's burial), but does not *settle*. He and Haran's son Lot share the land between them for herding; Lot takes the Jordan valley. The (cultural) memory of being settlers in a land promised but currently occupied by others is striking, but more curious is Abraham's easy compliance with this state of affairs and, indeed, his willingness to travel outside it, specifically on a visit to Egypt that is terminated only by divine command (Gen 12)—as if he would not have returned of his own accord.

In 17:5 Abraham is made a "father of nations" in another theophany. The sign of circumcision now bestowed (17:9–27) extends to all his offspring and not only those who become the people of Israel. The promises of land, too, must therefore be understood as promises not to Israel only, but to all Abraham's descendants; even after the near-sacrifice of Isaac, this promise remains with Abraham's *descendants*, not with his *heirs*. The heirs are distinguished rather by *blessing*: Isaac is blessed by Abraham in 25:11, while Ishmael is blessed by the deity (17:20); Jacob, rather than Esau, is blessed by his father. But the blessing, while it includes the land promise, does not comprise an exclusive claim to all the promised *land*. Nowhere in Genesis is the land promise restricted *within* Abraham's family. The Abrahamic territory will include what later becomes the land of Israel but the land of Israel does not comprise all the promised territory.

This interpretation is confirmed when the extent of the land is finally declared in 15:18–20: "from the river of Egypt to the great river." This tract extends well beyond the borders of Israel and Judah and includes

---

1. This is how T. L. Thompson has read the story (*The Origin Tradition of Ancient Israel* [Sheffield: JSOT Press, 1987], 80). Such may also have been the view of the author of Amos 9:7.

the territory occupied by all of Abraham's kin. Ammon and Moab are slandered with a charge of incestuous origin, Edom and Jacob quarrel and Ishmael is at first rejected by Abraham, yet none of these disappears from Abraham's family, and all of them, together with Israel and Judah, inhabit their part of the promised territory. The status of Aram is not clear, however: whether Abraham's relatives in "Paddan-Aram," the home of Rachel and Rebekah, are included in this territory may depend on whether the territory is deemed to lie east or west of the Euphrates. The kingdom of Aram lay mostly to the west of the river. But does the promise extend to Abraham's own generation? An informed ancient reader would perhaps be expected to recognize that the promised territory comprises a precise and well-established geo-political region under the Assyrians, Neo-Babylonians and Persians: Eber-Nari, Abar-Nahara, "Beyond the River."[2]

The "Israel" of Genesis, that is, Jacob and his family, is thus part of a wider kin group that inherits the land promised to Abraham. The full significance of this has escaped a surprisingly large number of commentators. Even if the later removal of some "Canaanite" or "Amorite" nations who are not of Abraham's family is already predicted, peaceful co-existence for the time being is implied in the blessing of Melchizedek the king of Salem (ch. 14), the purchase of the cave near Hebron from Ephron the Hittite (ch. 23) and the intermarriage (ch. 34). Even the story of Abraham's visit to Egypt in ch. 12 hardly suggests the distaste that Egypt evokes later in the First History; this Pharaoh is no villain (nor is the Pharaoh of the Joseph story). The same is true of Abimelech of Gerar in chs. 20 and 26. Israel is therefore not (or will not be) an isolated nation quite distinct from all other nations, but part of a larger family with which it shares land promised to the ancestor; and the ancestors behaviour displays no xenophobic traits.[3] Even when later parts of this story focus on Israel's portion, the land of Canaan, the rights of Aram, Ammon, Moab and Edom to their territory are not in question. In 24:7 Isaac alludes to the promise to Abraham's descendants and in 26:3 he is given a promise of land for his own descendants (Esau and Jacob), but the territory is not specified; nor is it in 35:12 where Jacob is also promised land. This is, as we shall see, consistent with the remainder of the Pentateuch: an unspecified portion is promised to Israel, but Abraham's promised land is wider and inherited by other members of his family.

---

2. This region possibly has an eponymous ancestor by the name of Eber (Gen 10).

3. The attribution to David of a kingdom whose extent corresponds to this Abrahamic territory might well imply a Judean claim to hegemony over it all. But while David and Solomon rule over these lands, they do not dispossess the inhabitants.

This interpretation of the land promise might seem to be contradicted by Gen 12, where Abraham heads for the "land of Canaan" in response to the divine summons. The itinerary suggests that "Canaan" comprises the territory west of the Jordan, and in v. 7 his descendants are promised "this land."[4] But contradiction is not necessarily entailed here. The boundaries of "Canaan" are, as all kinds of ancient sources testify, extremely vague, and Transjordan is not necessarily excluded: "Canaan" may well be intended to refer here to the territory west of the Euphrates (as it is defined in Gen 15:18).

But what is Israel in Genesis? Almost unanimously it is Jacob himself, and this includes the three occurrences of "sons of Israel." Of the other uses, 49:7 has the phrase "in Israel," but paralleled to "in Jacob"[5] and ch. 49 has two references to "tribes of Israel." Genesis 47:27 has "Israel" settling in Egypt and acquiring land, and the transition from "Israel = Jacob" to "Israel = descendants of Jacob" is neatly conveyed here by the use of a singular "dwelt" (וישב) and a plural "gained land" (ויאחזו). The one anomaly is 34:7, which speaks of an "outrage in Israel," suggesting a quite different understanding of the term, perhaps influenced by a similar usage in 2 Sam 13:12, in another incident of sexual violence.[6]

The sons of Jacob are enumerated several times. First, their births are recorded in chronological order in Gen 29–30. Leah, Jacob's first wife, bears Reuben, Simeon, Levi, then Judah; then, since Rachel is barren, her maid Bilhah bears Dan and Naphtali; Leah is now past childbearing age and her maid Zilpah bears Gad and Asher; but subsequently Leah bears Issachar and Zebulun (and a daughter, Dinah). Finally, Rachel bears Joseph and dies after bearing Benjamin. In 35:23–26 the summary lists the sons of Jacob by their mothers—Leah, Rachel, Bilhah then Zilpah—rather than order of birth. All are said to have been born in Paddan-Aram, outside the land they will eventually occupy—though v. 16 puts Benjamin's birth near Ephrath. Otherwise, the scheme is completely consistent (see also 46:8–27; also ch. 49 with slight variations in order). But while Reuben is always the first-born, some passages assign the leading role to Judah, the fourth son of Leah. The "Blessing of Jacob" in 49:8–12 gives

---

4. On the imprecision of the term "Canaan," however, see N. P. Lemche, *The Canaanites and their Land: The Tradition of the Canaanites* (Sheffield: JSOT Press, 1991).

5. Gen 49:24 the divine epithet "Rock of Israel" is also paralleled to "Abir of Jacob."

6. Westermann, for example, makes the literary-historical conclusion that the "late author" of the phrase has expanded an older narrative; see C. Westermann, *Genesis 12–36: A Commentary* (London: SPCK, 1985), 539.

this tribe pre-eminence over the others ("your father's son shall bow down before you," reminiscent of Joseph's dreams in ch. 37). In the Joseph story, while Reuben usually issues the instructions and takes responsibility (37:21–22, 29; 42:22, 37), Judah takes on this role in 37:26; 43:3; 44; 46:28, as well as being featured alone in ch. 38. He takes a special interest in the welfare of the youngest son Benjamin, which may anticipate the political union narrated later in the First History.[7]

The book of Exodus lists those who came to Egypt as follows: the six Leah tribes, then Benjamin (Rachel's other son, Joseph, being already in Egypt), then the sons of the secondary wives (6:14 gives a truncated list of tribes containing only Reuben, Simeon and Levi). In Num 1 the order of census (excluding Levi) follows the sequence of (if we use Genesis as the template) Leah 1–Leah 2–Rachel–Bilhah+Zilpah together. This is followed in the "Blessing of Moses" (Deut 33), but with Simeon missing and Joseph replaced by Ephraim and Manasseh. The arrangement of the tribal camps in Num 2 follows no matriarchal ordering, and the disposition of six tribes each for the blessing and curse in Deut 27 likewise seems to reflect no particular priority or classification scheme. In general, while the listing in Genesis is consistent, Joseph and Ephraim/Manasseh alternate in Numbers and Deuteronomy, while Joseph is not a tribe in Exodus. The reader may suspect that the system, even though it varies only slightly, may be somewhat artificial and that its matriarchal arrangement reflects some other kind of classification or grouping, geographical, social or political. But these are literary-critical questions. The one purely literary observation important for our own topic is that Benjamin is associated with Joseph (to become Ephraim and Manasseh) as a son of Rachel, but attracts the special attention of Judah in Gen 43–44.

At the end of Genesis, the Abrahamic family has been narrowed down to Jacob and his family: the "sons of Israel." The one daughter, Dinah, figures only in ch. 34, and disappears afterwards (but cf. 46:15). At the beginning of Exodus, this family is quickly transformed into a *nation*. Exodus 1:1–7 effects this transition quite smoothly as they grow from seventy to a very large number and from a family into twelve tribes—according to Exod 12:40–41, over a period of 430 years.[8] Israel is thus

---

7.   The variation constitutes a major plank in the argument for a combination of sources within the Joseph story, but while it prompts a question from the reader, it creates no *narrative* contradiction.

8.   The alert reader may have noticed that Gen 15:16, which alludes to a return of Abraham's ancestors "in the fourth generation" (starting from what point? The fourth generation from Abraham is either Joseph or his children) supports the scholarly conclusion that the 430 years is part of a set of wider chronological schemes

now a "people" (1:9). This national identity carries with it a change in its attitude towards neighbours—and vice versa. From now on, the family ties that dominate Genesis seem to have been replaced by a more hostile attitude towards these other "nations" (as they too have become, but without leaving their lands in the process).

Episode 1: Unity

The new, hostile relationship between Israel and other nations is initiated by the arrival of a Pharaoh who "did not know Joseph." Israel and Egypt thus become enemies.[9] Hostile *difference*—and not merely with Egypt— is thereafter the norm, and for the most part Israel is either being attacked or attacking those with whom it comes into contact. The nation, as the original family has now become, is led out of Egypt and a religious identity is bestowed on it: rather than living under the promise of land from the patriarchal god, it now makes a national covenant with Yahweh, who is identified as the god of the patriarchs but whose promise is now conditioned by stipulations—a law to be obeyed in return for divine protection and gift of the land previously promised. This land is now required to be purged of its existing inhabitants: "For I will cast out nations before you, and enlarge your borders" (Exod 34:24: cf. Lev 18:24; Deut 4:38 and passim). These are the erstwhile neighbours of Abraham and his family in Canaan—not, as already noted, members of the *family of Abraham*, but they would include the "Hittites" such as Ephron (Gen 23:10) and Hamor the Hivite (Gen 34). The extensive social and cultic laws given on Sinai and repeated by Moses on the plains of Moab overwrite genealogical identity with a more powerful and determinative criterion. Israel and Canaan are now distinguished not by *kinship* but by *culture*. Israel's identity itself comes to rest on religious more than ethnic criteria. The membership of Israel has not changed, but the rules of membership have. Israel is different from other nations in a new and less "natural" way. The promise to Abraham, filtered down to Jacob as well as to other descendants, has been converted into a covenant with the latter's descendants that stipulates what they must do and be in order to be "Israel."

constructed within the entire First History. The statement of the Pharaoh that "they number more than we do" (1:8) is presumably exaggeration; the reader is surely supposed to infer several generations.

9. For a discussion of how relations between Israel and Egypt are ideologically constructed in the Pentateuch as an identity-forming mechanism, see Greifenhagen, *Egypt on the Pentateuch's Ideological Map*.

Yet three different constructions of that cultural identity emerge during the story of Israel's desert wandering that occupies the bulk of Exodus–Deuteronomy.[10] Leviticus, through its various priestly regulations, depicts a nation in which cultic criteria predominate. The nation is defined according to the categories of holiness and ritual correctness, clustered round a most holy centre where the deity is (sometimes) present, but the "camp" is also surrounded and threatened by the power of uncleanness. An underlying principle of *order*, expressed in terms of holy/profane and clean/unclean, embraces everything from the taxonomy of human sexual relations and bodily emissions to animals and to sacrifices. The book opens with sacrifices and the priesthood, culminating in the ordination of Aaron, then deals with matters that affect other Israelites (food, childbirth, disease), the slaughter of animals, sexual relations, cultic offerings, festivals and the sabbatical and jubilee years. But all these are viewed and prescribed wholly from a cultic point of view. The correct management of purity and impurity is the responsibility of both priests and nonpriests, and governance of Israel seems to be in the hands of the high priest, the representative of Aaron. Civil governance is not addressed, little reference is made to everyday social life and we find no concern for relations with other peoples or lands.

Deuteronomy offers a striking contrast to this: its Israel is regulated by a contract with its deity to adhere to laws in return for possession of the land. The relationship between deity and nation is that of patron and client, and the contract (covenant) that defines this applies to each individual as well as the nation corporately. There is no priestly (or royal) representative making the covenant on behalf of the people. Moses acts only as an *intermediary*, not representative here, and his profile is that of a prophet, a go-between. While idolatry is repeatedly forbidden, and certain religious practices specifically mentioned, there are no priestly regulations of the kind that occupy Leviticus; rather, the laws aim primarily at the social order of Israel. Religious behaviour (festivals, heeding prophets, cities of refuge) is considered within the dominant context of social relations: property, warfare, murder, the treatment of women and children, marriage and slavery. Familial relations, such as marriage and divorce, are also covered. Whereas Leviticus expresses no interest in what lies "beyond the camp," Deuteronomy insists on a strict separation from the dangerous culture of the surrounding Canaanites (Ammonites and Moabites, who are not "Canaanites," are not absolutely excluded

10. For a fuller description, see my "Biblical Foundations of Judaism," in *The Encyclopaedia of Judaism* (ed. J. Neusner, A. Avery-Peck and W. S. Green; 3 vols.; Leiden: Brill, 2000), 1:113–20.

from membership of Israel but "even to the tenth generation," 23:3).
Israel is ruled by what we would recognize as a constitutional monarch,
something entirely alien to the ancient Near East (ch. 17), but elders,
judges and levites (who are not differentiated from priests) are entrusted
with the daily administration of society. Leviticus and Deuteronomy
overlap only very slightly in their content and they differ widely in their
conception of how Israel is organized and indeed what it *is*.

The Israel of Numbers is mentioned last, since it is expressed mostly
in narrative and not, unlike the others, wholly in speech: it is also the
most curious of the three. The Numbers narrative moves the nation from
Sinai to the edge of Canaan and is characterized by an air of prepared-
ness, of organization, for warfare. The book opens with a census of those
"able to go to war" (1:3), and Israel is on the march towards a destination
to be conquered, living off the terrain and on the alert for attack. The
disposition of the camp and the order of marching are detailed, the latter
led by the ark: when it moves, Moses says "Arise, Yahweh, let your
enemies be scattered and your foes flee before you," and when it stops,
"Return, Yahweh of the massed armies of Israel."

The entire nation is thus constituted as a militia; families and tribes of
Israel are reconfigured as military units, providing specified numbers of
young men to fight. Towards the close of the book (ch. 34) attention
moves to the imminent occupation of the land and its divisions and the
disposition of tribal allotments is given, followed by allotments for the
Levites. The geography of the camp is thus converted, in anticipation,
into the geography of the land, the new home, the permanent "camp."

The military character of Israel is also reflected in the attitude towards
discipline. "Rebellion" is a constant theme (see chs. 14; 17; 20), and the
issue of Moses' leadership and the challenges to it by Miriam (ch. 12)
and by Korah, Dathan and Abiram (ch. 16) form one of the book's motifs.
Disobedience is harshly punished.

Although antagonism between Israel and Egypt has been initiated
already in Exod 17, where war with the Amalekites (descendants of Esau,
Gen 36:12)[11] results in a divine command to blot out their memory, further incidents of confrontation occupy the Numbers narrative. When the
territory of Edom (i.e. Esau) is reached (Num 20:14–21), the Edomites
refuse to allow Israel access, but now it turns away. Moab is crossed
without incident (21:10), but Sihon, king of the Amorites, who has conquered part of Moab, refuses access, encounters Israel in battle and is

11. Deut 25:17–18 has an expanded version with an (presumably unprovoked)
Amalekite attack, "when you were faint and weary, and struck down all who lagged
behind you."

defeated; his people are annihilated and the land is taken. (Amorites are not included in the Abrahamic family; see Gen 15:16.) Og, king of Bashan (Bashan does not appear in Genesis) is also defeated and the population exterminated. Despite the loss of Moab to Sihon, the Moabites are now encountered again; their king, Balak, commissions Balaam to curse them. After the lengthy account of Balaam's oracles, the Israelites intermingle with the Moabites and in one case, with a Midianite. Later (ch. 31) there is a war with Midian (descended from Abraham, Gen 25:2); all Midianite males and non-virgins are subsequently killed. In Num 32 we are told of the settlement of the tribes of Gad, Reuben and half of Manasseh in the Transjordanian territory once ruled by Sihon and Og. The book closes, appropriately, with preparations for the conquest of Canaan.

It is worth noting that land is taken only from non-Abrahamic nations (Amorites); but the treatment of Abrahamic nations varies. Edom's land is not crossed and Moab's territory is not taken, but only the "land of the Amorites" ruled by Sihon. The Midianites, like the Amalekites, are defeated and killed, but their territory is not occupied. Indeed, here for the first time (ch. 34) the boundaries of the land awarded to Israel are defined—the part of that larger territory promised to the Abrahamic family in Genesis but presently unoccupied by any family members. In Deuteronomy, the land is mentioned quite often, but never delimited and named only once as the "land of Canaan" (32:49). It is, however, referred to several times as "the land I promised your ancestors, Abraham, Isaac and Jacob." It is not clear whether this formulation modifies the scheme in Genesis, where the promise of land to all of Abraham's descendants is reiterated to Isaac and Jacob, but without implying that it is being redefined or *narrowed down* to the line of Jacob. The wording here might imply that the promise made on each occasion was identical and exclusive to one line of descent. Such an implication would fit with Deuteronomy's perspective of indifference, suspicion or hostility to all other nations outside Israel; but on the other hand, Deuteronomy also appears to acknowledge the territorial rights of the Abrahamic nations in narrating Israel's transit to Canaan.

What do the different portraits of Israel in Leviticus, Numbers and Deuteronomy mean? Two of the portraits delineate the kind of developed society that requires a land and we can read these as ideal descriptions, the possibilities or rather requirements for the Israel just created once it has reached its geographical destination. Numbers depicts a society under migratory conditions. But in this case we may also reckon with a utopian vision, if the wilderness functions not simply (or even mainly?) as a space or a time, but as a utopia (as the book of Hosea imagines it). Perhaps here cultural memory displays a particular role in identity formation, capturing in the form of recollection a vision orientated to the future or to an ideally constructed present. But since the portraits differ, we must construe them as alternative cultural memories, or projects, that prescribe the differently conceived identities of different, even competing, Israels. But they have much in common: in particular, each promotes a sharp differentiation from neighbours and outsiders that ranges from exclusion from the divine realm (Leviticus), to rejection (Deuteronomy), to military aggression (Numbers). Differentiation of this kind is nowadays recognized as a major component of ethnicity, and these portraits, however we read them, make an important contribution to the process of nation-formation that the surrounding narrative describes in bringing Israel all the way from family to political state.[12]

In none of these three Israels is genealogy of primary importance. Throughout Numbers and in the "Blessings of Moses" at the end of Deuteronomy the tribal composition comes again to the fore, but this social structure does not constitute (so it seems to me) any great identity marker. In Deuteronomy the promise of the land to "your ancestors, Abraham, Isaac and Jacob" links the conditional covenant promise with the unconditional promise to the forefathers, but the juxtaposition really highlights the extent to which the patriarchal promises have been not so much fulfilled as superseded by being conditional on Israel fashioning itself according to the new cultural-religious identity. Very often the word "ancestors" ("fathers") omits the three names and actually refers to either to those generations who entered, or who left Egypt[13] or who trekked the

12. It may be worth observing that rabbinic Judaism conflated the Deuteronomic notion of "covenant" and the Levitical notion of "holiness," transferring the priestly functions and responsibility to every Jew. (This process can also be detected in the *haverim*, those groups who piously extended priestly purity laws to their own tables, and the groups described in the literature from Qumran.) The Israel of Numbers plays no role in rabbinic Judaism but might be observed both in the Hasmonean political project (which built on successful military resistance) and the modern state of Israel, in which military superiority is presented as a *sine qua non* of not just survival, but even identity.

13. More broadly, the "ancestors" are invoked in Exodus–Deuteronomy 61 times, and only eight times are explicitly identified with Abraham, Isaac and Jacob, always as a set phrase (Exod 3:15, 16; 4:5; Deut 1:8; 6:10; 9:5; 29:13; 30:20). But suggestions that the names are a secondary expansion, while cogent, are not pertinent to this literary reading. See John Van Seters, "The So-Called Deuteronomistic Redaction of the Pentateuch," in *Congress Volume, Leuven: 1989* (ed. J. A. Emerton; Leiden: Brill, 1991), 58–77. Lev 26:40, 45 also refers to "ancestors" in Egypt and perhaps Num 20:15 "…our ancestors went down to Egypt, and we lived in Egypt a long time."

wilderness. Deuteronomy fittingly brings the Pentateuch to an end (almost) with Moses' blessings on the twelve tribes, but these blessings make no reference to the tribes' descent but rather celebrate tribal characteristics. In Exodus–Deuteronomy as a whole, and recapitulated in Deuteronomy especially, Israel's history becomes less a memory of common descent from a single line but of escape, covenant, migration and finally (but not yet) occupation of the land. Thus, the Pentateuch offers two sets of ancestors and origins: the introduction of Abraham and his family in the region, and the rescue of a group from Egypt. Although these are narratively connected, each, taken separately, construed a different basis for Israelite identity and a different place in the world of other nations, especially those inhabiting and bordering on the land that "Israel" will occupy.

Chapter 4

ISRAEL IN THE FIRST HISTORY:
THE FORMER PROPHETS (JOSHUA TO KINGS)

Joshua

The transition from the Pentateuch to the Former Prophets is smoothed by the persistence of Deuteronomy's language and ideology into the book of Joshua—specifically its opposition of Israel and Canaan, its insistence on the divine initiative in giving the land and the covenanted conditionality of that land occupation. The first half of Joshua is occupied with the acquisition of the land, and the second part (from ch. 15) with its allotment among the tribes, fulfilling the Pentateuchal land promises to the Israelite line of Abraham's family.

The campaign of conquest begins with the destruction of Jericho and Ai, proceeds to a treaty with Gibeon and its dependent cities and to the defeat near Gibeon of a coalition of five "Amorite" kings from the territory to be allotted to Judah (Jerusalem, Hebron, Yarmuth, Lachish, Eglon[1]); these are pursued and killed near Makkedah (an unknown location, but apparently in the Shephelah). From there, the campaign continues to Libnah and Lachish, Gezer and Eglon, then moves to Hebron, Debir and "the whole Negeb...from Kadesh-barnea to Gaza" (Josh 10:41), before returning to Gilgal. This circuit is followed by a campaign to the north, where a coalition of kings from Hazor, Madon, Shimron and a multitude of other places is defeated at the waters of Merom.[2] The victory is followed by the sack of Hazor (ch. 11), and the

1. The king of Eglon is named Debir, which is also the name of a city, though apparently out of immediate range, in the Judean highlands.
2. The virtually unanimous view of all scholars is that this Hazor is the northern city and Merom a site nearby—apparently confirmed by the account in Judg 4–5 of the victory of Barak over another "Jabin of Hazor" in the Jezreel and the statement that "Hazor was the chief of all those kingdoms" (Josh 11:10). In Josh 19:36, Hazor is also assigned to the territory of Naphtali. However, Josh 15:25 lists among the towns of Judah "Kerioth-Hezron, that is Hazor," which raises the possibility that the

narrative is temporarily brought to a halt with three summaries: one (11:16–23) notes that "Joshua took all that land," a second lists the kings conquered by Moses east of the Jordan (12:1–6) and a third catalogues the kings conquered by Joshua (12:7–24).

The general profile of Israel here is of a unified nation acting in concert under a single leader, as in Exodus–Deuteronomy. However, it has long been noticed that while the conquests within the territory later assigned to Benjamin are narrated in detail, the two subsequent campaigns, into Judah and to the north, occupy much less room despite their wider geographical scope, while the remaining territories go completely unmentioned. The partial and uneven narrative coverage and the restricted compass of the operations described are complemented by repeated claims of conquest of the entire land (e.g. Josh 10:29–43: note the formulaic "and all Israel with him" here and in ch. 11). The geographical focus on an area largely assigned to the tribe of Benjamin[3]

---

campaign of Joshua against Hazor was an extension of the previous campaign in the territory of Judah. Indeed, in Judg 4 the wife of Jael is "Heber the Kenite." While Barak comes from Naphtali, Deborah seems to have been at home "between Bethel and Ramah," namely, in Benjamin! Merom ("waters of Merom," 11:5, 7) cannot be identified and occurs nowhere else in the Bible. The waters in the Judg 4 story are the wadi Kishon, which is mentioned only once elsewhere, apparently near Mt Carmel (1 Kgs 18:40). But there are strong grounds for concluding that some confusion between two Hazors has taken place in the complex evolution of the story of Jabin's defeat. Again, these points concern only the literary-historical critic, though some of the features may create some puzzlement even for the superficial reader.

3.   Two prominent heroes come from the "mount of Ephraim" and several other incidents connected with Benjamin are located there (see below). Joshua is usually taken to be Ephraimite because of 1 Chr 17:27, but this may only be an inference from a memory of his inheritance in the "mount of Ephraim" (Timnath-serah, Josh 19:50), where he was also buried. Samuel's birthplace, Ramah, is also in the "mount of Ephraim" (Ramathaim, 1 Sam 1:1) but according to Josh 18:25 the town lies in Benjamin. The Hebrew word *har* generally denotes a single mountain. According to George Adam Smith, however, the phrase denotes all of the northern hill country, which from an elevated distance can appear as a single *massif* (see G. A. Smith, *Historical Geography of the Holy Land* (25th ed.; London: Collins, 1983 [first published 1897]), 325. Smith points out that the "mountain of Ephraim" is paralleled in Jer 31:6 with "mountains (הרי) of Samaria" (31:5). He comments: "The name spread originally from the hill country north of Benjamin's territory, which fell to the tribe of Ephraim, and in which we must seek for the *city called Ephraim* (2 Chron xiii. 19, 2 Sam. x. iii. 23, John xi. 54)" (345 n. 2). I am not so sure that the "mount of Ephraim" is necessarily understood as territory belonging to the tribal territory of Ephraim. But at all events, it should be understood as being included when I refer in this book to the territory of "Benjamin."

represents another fashion in which—as noted in Chapter 2—points already to another Israel that will later emerge, faintly in Judges and strongly in 1 Samuel, centred on, or even confined to, this area. This is the Israel that Samuel judges and that Saul rules. Perhaps another shadow can also be detected: the sequence of land allocation (see below) opens with the Transjordanian territories, conquered under Moses, but then begins the enumeration of Cisjordanian tribal land with Caleb and then Judah (Caleb is not a tribe, but a subdivision of Judah). This looks like the Israel led by Judah, already encountered during the Joseph story and to be met again in Judges, foreshadowing the political configuration elaborated in 2 Samuel and continuing for the remainder of both Judean Histories. Even if the enumeration is broadly geographical, from south to north (not strictly followed: Benjamin follows Ephraim and Manasseh), we have a Judean perspective; south to north is not an usual sequence.

The division of the land into tribal lots in Josh 13 also marks two developments in the character of Israel: it now becomes a territorially defined nation, though one in which the "promised land" belongs less to the nation as a whole and attaches to individual tribes, whose demarcated borders (or rather, border towns) suggest a degree of autonomy and integrity and also prepare for the portrait in Judges of independent tribal activity. The second half of Joshua thus forms the climax, even the end-point, of the history of the united twelve-tribe Israel and the beginning of a dissolution into individual tribes, from which different configurations of Israel will emerge.

Episode 2: Dissolution

Soon after the summary statement in 11:23 that "Joshua took the whole land…and Joshua gave it as an inheritance to Israel…and the land had rest from warfare," we read "Now Joshua was old and advanced in years; and Yhwh said to him, 'You are old and advanced in years, and very much of the land remains to be possessed'" (13:1). This unconquered territory comprises areas inhabited by the Philistines (west), the Geshurites (south) and Phoenician lands to the north. These people Yahweh promises to drive out himself "before the Israelites" (13:6), but Joshua is commanded meanwhile to divide the lands "to the nine tribes and the half-tribe of Manasseh" (i.e. those west of the Jordan, v. 7). The integrity of the narrative as a whole can be salvaged in part if we accept that the land grant to many of the tribes is *provisional*, dependent upon subsequent conquest. The sequel tends to confirm this understanding, since there follows an account of the land given *and taken*, first east and then west of the Jordan. Caleb and Judah are extensively treated (14:6–15) with Jerusalem specifically excepted as an unconquered city ("to this day," 15:63). The lands of the "house of Joseph" (Ephraim and West Manasseh) follow, but these tribes are said to have been unable to occupy all of their territory. All the tribes then assemble at Shiloh where the land that is still *totally* unoccupied is assigned to the remaining seven tribes. Joshua tells them "How long will you be derelict in taking the land that Yahweh, god of your ancestors, has given you?" (18:3) and orders this land—outside Judah and Ephraim–Manasseh—to be divided into seven portions, then to be assigned by lot. The sequence of apportionment seems logical: first land already conquered, then land partly conquered, then land unconquered. Yet the territory assigned to Benjamin, whose conquest has already been so dramatically described, is now the first piece of *unconquered* land to be allocated![4] After the appointment of refuge and levitical cities, the Transjordanian tribes depart, and the book climaxes with a grand assembly of "all Israel" at Shechem for a covenant ceremony. Then Joshua dies (24:29).

Two major features in Joshua obstruct a coherent literary reading. First is the claim, later contradicted, that the entire land was conquered. It has been suggested by a number of commentators[5] that Josh 1–12 can be understood in the light of the obviously hyperbolic conquest accounts prevalent in the ancient Near East and that accordingly occupation and subjugation should be distinguished. It is hard to avoid this explanation, and the fact that the narrative of invasion ends with a list of *kings conquered* does indeed suggest that the claims of total conquest should not control the overall sense, which is of an incomplete, nominal possession. The *conquest* of local kings is not to be translated into land *possession*. It is also relevant to note that the tribal occupation of these lands is not described as having been carried out; it is just possible that such a process is implied in the consolidation of the kingdom of Israel and Judah. But no slaughter of the remaining nations of Canaan is credited to any of the Israelite or Judean kings. The unfinished agenda is quietly forgotten (the issue of population mix is also discussed under *Judges* below).

---

4. The five tribes already in possession or partial possession are Gad, Reuben and half of Manasseh east of the Jordan; Judah, Ephraim and the other half of Manasseh on the west. Levi has no territory, and Ephraim and Manasseh count as one (Joseph), making it possible for there to be twelve tribes and also twelve tribal territories! The seven tribes remaining to have their land allotted in 18:11–19:48 are 1. Benjamin, 2. Simeon, 3. Zebulun, 4. Issachar, 5. Asher, 6. Naphtali, and 7. Dan.

5. See in particular K. Lawson Younger Jr., *Ancient Conquest Accounts: A Study in Ancient Near Eastern and Biblical History Writing* (Sheffield: JSOT Press, 1990), 244–46.

The case of the territory of Benjamin is not solved as readily. Following the logic of the previous paragraph, we might deduce that despite the encampment at Gilgal and the capture of Jericho and Ai and the pact with Gibeon, this land too remained *unoccupied*. If so, the book of Joshua altogether is about *conquests*, namely, sacking of a few cities and the defeat of kings (31 in all: 12:24), *and not about occupation at all*. For while the catalogue of kings conquered by Moses specifically states that "Moses gave their land for a possession" (12:6), Joshua's list merely enumerates his victims. Is the silence meaningful?

If we follow this interpretation, the allocation of lands merely sets an agenda for subsequent occupation. Judah (including Caleb), Ephraim and Manasseh *have* apparently already occupied their lands (fully or partially), but for Benjamin (and others) the task remains. The only way to read the book coherently is to accept that three actions need to be separated: military defeat, assignation of land and occupation of land. In this case, Israel as a whole, under Joshua, scores military victories; Joshua allots land, and the individual tribes carry out their own conquests independently. This means that statements like 11:23 need to be carefully interpreted:

> So Joshua took the whole land, in accordance with all that Yhwh had said
> to Moses; and Joshua gave it as an inheritance to Israel according to their
> tribal allotments. And the land had rest from war.

This statement seems to suggest conquest, seizure, allocation, peace: the complete process. But perhaps "the land had rest from war" is not supposed to imply that conquest is achieved but rather that the process of military activity is *temporarily* over. It might therefore represent an attempt to relate the activity of the tribes in Judges to the activity of Joshua. The phrase "Joshua took the whole land" might also mean that the author of the statements regards the capture of frontier towns as equivalent to the subjugation of the entire territory.[6] If we nevertheless prefer to take the statement as a definitive assertion of the military conquest of the whole land, however, we must then accept that the book of Joshua does not present an unambiguous account and that some statements in it represent another view of the process. Absolute coherence cannot always be expected in a text whose authorship is represented by a succession of rewritings, any one of which might have interposed a variant opinion. A modern literary non-historical-critical reading strategy (unless it is trying to be deconstructive) should probably follow what seems the view of the larger part of the narrative and bracket out the

6. So Rogerson, "Frontiers and Borders in the Old Testament," 125.

contradiction. An additional consolation in this case is that military reports, throughout history, usually aim to misrepresent the true situation. "Truth is the first casualty of war," runs the proverb (though memory is not about this kind of truth).

There are further contradictions within this account of conquest and settlement in the book of Judges; some will be dealt with presently. But we must press the question of Benjamin. Benjamin plays a key role throughout both Histories, since at different times they assign its territory to Israel and to Judah. It forms the central part of Saul's kingdom and later is described as deserting the other tribes, who will form Israel, and joining the kingdom of Judah. The most detailed narratives of conquest are confined to what will be allotted to Benjamin, though when that actually takes place, Benjamin is separated from both Judah and Ephraim (whose territory it lies between; cf. Josh 18:11) and placed among those tribes whose land was allocated last but who did not occupy it. The same scheme both relegates Benjamin and elevates Judah, a characteristic of parts of Judges and of the entire narrative of Saul's succession by David, where political pre-eminence passes from the one tribe to the other.

Judges

The narrative of the book of Judges takes further the process of division of a now territorial Israel into its tribal units. From the beginning it reinforces the reading of Joshua as an account of military *victories* but not of *settlement*. Yet it simultaneously contradicts Joshua in giving the impression that *none* of the tribes had in fact begun the process of settlement during Joshua's lifetime. Like Josh 13–15, it privileges Judah and perhaps also relegates Benjamin. Judah is the first tribe to "go up" and its successes (including those of its component elements, such as Judah's "brother," Simeon) are recorded; the only failure is not to capture the coastal plain. Of the other tribes, only the failures are recorded (with one exception; see below): the implication may be that these other tribes did not conquer *any* territory.

Two cities, Jerusalem and Bethel, should attract special attention here. They both also concern Benjamin. Whereas in 1:8 Judah is said to attack Jerusalem and take it, in 1:21 Benjamin reportedly fails to capture Jerusalem—and that is the only reference to Benjamin in this review. The implication may be that Benjamin succeeded elsewhere, so that both the tribes that later comprised the kingdom of Judah achieved a complete conquest (once Jerusalem *had* been finally captured). But as the text now reads, the claims of Judah to Jerusalem exceed those of Benjamin (the later capture of the city by David is clearly a quite different and contradictory memory). Yet the allotment of Jerusalem to Benjamin is not erased. This contradiction is already in Joshua, where the city is assigned to Judah in Josh 15:63, but not captured. Yet according to Josh 18:21–28, "Jebus, that is Jerusalem" belongs to Benjamin. The same contradiction in both books clearly marks something significant about the claims to tribal possession of the city, which are not confined to Joshua and Judges. I will note in Chapter 5 the connections between Saul's family and Jerusalem in Chronicles and the curious formula "Judah and Jerusalem," predominantly in the Second History and in Jeremiah (see Chapter 8). We find a similar contradiction over Bethel in Judg 1:22–26:

> When the house of Joseph attacked Bethel, Yhwh was with them. When the Josephites spied out Bethel (it used to be called Luz), the spies spotted a man leaving the city. They said to him, "If you show us a secret entrance into the city, we will reward you." He showed them a secret entrance into the city, and they put the city to the sword. But they let the man and his extended family leave safely.

"House of Joseph" is a curious usage, since Ephraim and Manasseh are individually mentioned in the following list of tribal (non)-conquests; but the main curiosity is the singling out of Bethel, alongside Jerusalem, as individual targets. According to Josh 16:1 also, Bethel belongs to Joseph; and the books of Kings state that the city housed one of the two royal sanctuaries of the kingdom of Israel. Yet according to Josh 18:21–28, Bethel (as just noted, like Jerusalem) is assigned to Benjamin. These two major sanctuary cities (which are not far distant from each other) seem to be objects of contested tribal "ownership"—both involving claims on behalf of Benjamin. This phenomenon also beckons us towards literary-critical analysis.

Judges is not entirely about individual tribal activity. There is a tension between the tribal and pan-Israelite perspectives throughout: although each tribe conquers its own territory alone, in the period that follows, the judges are said to "judge Israel" as a whole, and it is also Israel, not the individual tribes, that sins, causing oppression (but only of a certain tribe or tribes) and then deliverance by a tribal hero who then becomes the next judge of Israel. The stories of individual tribes (occasionally helping out their neighbours)[7] are thus interspersed by a story of a corporate

---

7. The famous, and much debated exception is the Song of Deborah (Judg 5). Since it has widely been regarded as "early" and thus potentially of historical value, its enumeration of tribes (Ephraim, Benjamin, Machir [Manasseh], Zebulun, Issachar, Reuben, G[ile]ad and Dan) has been taken as evidence of an early confederation of tribes. But the prose account mentions only Zebulun and Naphtali as participating. It is, perhaps, enticing to accept the consensus on dating and thus make the omission of Judah evidence of Judah's original independence of Israel, but more honestly one

entity with a single governance. The combined picture looks as if both the united Israel led by Joshua and the individual tribes to whom he allocated land persist as narrative actors, but in some degree of tension. Certainly, each tribe is responsible for its acquisition and its defence, even if Israel as a whole is "judged." The contradictions, like those in Joshua, can be overridden up to a point, but no competent reader can fail to register them, especially since in juxtaposing "Israel" and individual tribes, they tend to reinforce each other.

The double death of Joshua in Judg 1:1 and 2:8 (which can be added to Josh 24:29) is obviously a very acute difficulty, and another is the confusion between the so-called major and minor judges as scholars call them). The national institution of judgeship at one level integrates the roles of individual saviours into a pattern of overall governance (and chronological sequence), but at a cost: the integration is clumsy and the differences between the so-called major ("saving") and minor judges (briefly listed in 10:1–5 and 12:8–15[8]) are not entirely removed by having the "major" judges go on to "judge" Israel themselves. Precisely what the "judging" of the "minor" judges entails is nowhere described here, but the pattern of military success that leads to political-judicial authority (in the case of the "major" judges) seems to follow the process by which kings themselves are first chosen (see below).

Yet another problem with the narrative is more directly relevant to the question of Israelite identity: the *permanent* failure to achieve occupation and the resulting population mix; 3:1–6 explains that certain nations were left in Canaan to give the Israelites experience in war (v. 2) or to test their faithfulness to the commandments of their god (v. 4), concluding that Israel intermarried with these people and adopted their religious customs. This obviously undermines the distinction between a Canaanite and an Israelite population, on both genealogical and religious definitions. It also resolves the issue of incomplete settlement of the land: a population emerges that is not "Israelite" and not "Canaanite," in the terms employed by Deuteronomy and Joshua, but *undifferentiated*. There is a faint allusion to this lack of differentiation in Josh 7, where Achan and his family are given exactly the treatment that is prescribed for the Canaanites, implying that Achan was now regarded as being no longer

---

should admit that this piece of poetry is of uncertain date and meaning and should not be burdened with too many inferences. (It is well known that Homer's Greek does not reflect the poet's contemporary language, if he is to be dated in the eighth century or later).

8.   Shamgar in 3:31 is an exceptional case: his notice reads like the other "minor" judges but he is said to have "rescued (וֹיּשַׁע)" Israel.

an Israelite and that likewise, those Israelites who integrated with the Canaanite population were presumably no longer to be treated as Israelites. But Judges is very confused on this matter, since it presents "Israel" as a clearly defined entity that intermarries with the local population and adopts its religion—though it is the religious apostasy that is most often mentioned. The enemies that the judges fight are not the "nations of Canaan": these are now apparently to be understood not as "internal" enemies to be fought, as Deuteronomy would have it, but indistinguishable members of the same society. The enemies lie *beyond the borders of the land*. A society in which Israelites and "Canaanites" live side-by-side can nevertheless be characterized as an "Israel" that "cries out to Yhwh" and is delivered by him—perhaps even with the aid of a "Canaanite" leader named Shamgar ben Anath. How *can* "Israel" identify itself from these "Canaanites" and yet still act corporately towards Yhwh? How, indeed, can "Israelites" any longer be distinguished—even by Yhwh himself—from other inhabitants? It is not possible: and we see a further and even more fundamental aspect of the dissolution of the Pentateuchal Israel: not just into partially autonomous tribes but into the surrounding population and its culture. This process is a step in the evolution of "Israel." From now on the only way to maintain a distinct "Israel" is to redefine it in *political* terms, to introduce a *king*, making every royal subject *de facto* an "Israelite"; to create Israel as a *territorial state*. And this, as we shall see, is what will happen, though this state, as far as possible, will also inherit the religious definition imparted in Exodus–Deuteronomy, in which the king will play the major role as representative. Indeed, it will be the king's behaviour that determines adherence to the covenant and thus the fate of his subjects. The ethnic definition will remain in an attenuated form only in the acknowledgment of tribal membership. But the worship of Yhwh will remain as an *ideal* definition, even as it most of the time fails to be represented in actual practice.

Indeed, the progress towards this redefining of Israel under kingship is already being anticipated in the stories of Gideon and Abimelech. After his exploits, Gideon is offered a hereditary kingship of Israel (8:22–23). The offer is rejected on the same grounds as implied in 1 Sam 8, that Yhwh is the true king of Israel. His son Abimelech later becomes king, but according to the narrative itself, apparently only of Shechem (9:6); although the statement in 9:22 has him ruling over Israel, this contradicts the entire remainder of the story and so the reader is prompted to override it.

The stories in the book of Judges provide further evidence of fluctuating definitions of Israel. These stories are fitted into a scheme of twelve judges that does not quite manage to assign a judge to each tribe,[9] but retains a pan-Israelite context to their exploits. The first two heroes are especially significant. Othniel is a brother of Caleb, the companion of Joshua (the chronology implicit in Judg 2:10 furnishes another little problem!) and appears in 1:13, as well as in Josh 15, which looks like another version of the same story. The territory with which Caleb is associated there includes Debir, a site either near Hebron (cf. Josh 10) or perhaps Tell Beit Mirsim or Khirbet er-Rabud—at all events, within Judah, though the city is mentioned nowhere else except in 1 Chr 6:58, as a city of refuge. But the oppressor whom he confronts is from the other end of the tribal territories, a king of Aram. Unlike all the other cases of military deliverance, the oppression here is not localized: "Yahweh gave King Cushan-rishathaim of Aram into his hand; and his hand prevailed over Cushan-rishathaim" (3:10). The first judge, then, apparently borrowed from elsewhere, is Judean, and the only one whose actions defeat a threat to all Israel. He is anomalous, but possibly intended, by the scale of his achievement, to be exemplary.

But succeeding the Judean judge is Ehud from Benjamin, and his opponent is the king of Moab, whose threat is apparently to that tribe alone: there is a specific reference to the "city of palms" (Jericho), a Benjaminite town. The references to "Israel" in the opening and closing frame (3:12–15, 30) can be taken together with similar comments throughout the book, and probably with the addition of Ammon and Amalek to the Moabite aggression (contrast vv. 28–30, where Moab alone is mentioned), as trying to suggest a broader context. But Ehud's localized activity sets the pattern for the remaining stories. He blows a horn "in the mount of Ephraim" (we have discussed this term earlier), and "the Israelites go down with him" (3:27). The "hill country of Ephraim," as noted previously, is associated with Benjaminite territory elsewhere (Joshua, Samuel). We should not immediately discount the use of "Israelite" (בני־ישראל) inside the narrative as an intrusive element belonging with the pan-Israelite framework. Rather, we are now

9. One might expect one from each tribe, but the data are: Othniel from Judah, Ehud from Benjamin, Barak from Naphtali, Gideon from Manasseh, Tola from Issachar (but living in Ephraim), Jair and Jephthah from Gilead, Ibzan from Judah, Elon from Zebulun and Samson from Dan. Shamgar cannot be assigned (he looks like an afterthought [see 4:1]; his killing of six hundred Philistines with an ox-goad [see 15:15–17] might suggest he is a doublet of Samson, as P. Guillaume (*Waiting for Joshua: The Judges* [London: T&T Clark International, 2004], 29) proposes. Deborah (who shares the story with Barak and so may lie outside the scheme) is apparently from Benjamin, and of Abdon we are told only that he was buried in Pirathon, which, according to 1 Chr 27:14, is in Ephraim.

encountering, perhaps, another "Israel," in the process of formation and on its way to becoming a kingdom centred on Benjamin and Ephraim (or "Joseph," including Manasseh), and again led from Benjamin.

The motif of Benjaminite left-handedness resurfaces in the final episode of the book (chs. 19–21), but this is preceded by a story that directs criticism at the sanctuary of Dan and its priesthood. The Ephraimite Micah, who has made an "idol" (פֶּסֶל), installs his son as a priest and hires a Levite from Bethlehem. The priest is visited by Danite spies on the way to Laish, who encamp at Kiriath-jearim, from where they revisit the priest and persuade him to accompany them to minister at their new sanctuary. Kiriath-jearim is yet another site of disputed ownership. According to Josh 15:9, 60 it is in Judah, but according to 18:14, 28 it is in Benjamin.[10] The location is significant because it figures in the story of the "return" of the ark in 1 Sam 6–7 and its carriage to Jerusalem in 2 Sam 6. Is the ark shown as being moved from Saul's tribal territory (= Israel) to David's city or is it already resting within Judah itself? The return is set in the time of Samuel, who has no connection with Judean territory. But this is just another of a series of issues already encountered involving disputed territory between Benjamin and Judah. The main charge of the Judges story is that the Danites massacred peaceful inhabitants and installed an idolatrous cult in their new city. It is a critique of one of the two royal sanctuaries of the later kingdom of Israel—the other being Bethel. As such it could have originated as easily in Bethel as in Jerusalem; the verdict depends on the significance of the Judean identity of the founding Levite.

The following story (chs. 20–21) also has a polemical purpose of more central relevance to our interests. It describes a breach of hospitality that involves three tribes: the Levite comes from Ephraim, the woman from Judah and the offence occurs in Gibeah in Benjamin, which is also the home town and capital of the future king, Saul. The sequel to the outrage is an all-Israel gathering at Mizpah (also in Benjamin: a strange setting for such a meeting), which demands a redress that the Benjaminites refuse, leading to a war between Benjamin and the other tribes in which the left-handed Benjaminites are initially successful but finally succumb to a ruse (with echoes of earlier stories in the First History: Lot in Sodom in Gen 19, and the attack on Ai in Josh 8.) The Israelites refuse to intermarry with the Benjaminites and instead find a pretext for war with Jabesh-Gilead, taking from the survivors four hundred virgins, whom they give to the Benjaminites. In a further provision, women from Shiloh are captured at a festival; the ban on Israelites giving their daughters is

10.   The MT actually reads "Kiriath" at 18:20; the LXX has "Kiriath-jearim."

thus circumvented, since these women were not "given" but taken. The inclusion of Jabesh-gilead anticipates the later connection between that city and Saul (1 Sam 11; 31; 2 Sam 2:5; 21:12).

Taken as a whole, it is possible to distinguish two strands in Judges. One is associated with a twelve-tribe Israel, the other with a group of tribes acting for the most part with perhaps some local cooperation. The first of these extends a unity that is presupposed; the second builds towards a new unity—and a new Israel. The former strand is stamped with Judean superiority, in the introduction, in Othniel's initial global exploit, in the final war against Benjamin. In the second strand, the series of local heroes begins and ends with Benjaminites: Ehud and Saul (and we might include Samuel).[11] One Israel is fading in the book of Judges and another is emerging. The clarity of this double process is paradoxically achieved by the clumsiness of their juxtaposition, and the conclusion illustrates yet again how a good literary reading often points away from itself to a literary-critical challenge: to find the historical setting and the process in which these Israels develop and then come together in a single story. But such a discussion must be postponed until Chapter 9.

This paradox is also displayed in a simple dispute: whether the book of Judges as a whole favours the institution of kingship (and thus the conversion of the nation into a political entity) or deplores it as a process leading to disaster. Is the development of Israel into a monarchy, "like other nations" (as 1 Sam 8:5, 20 puts it), recommended to the reader as a good thing? Is the phrase we find twice in these final chapters of Judges, "doing what is right in one's own eyes" (17:6; 21:5), meant to approve of the coming political order or not? We cannot really solve this unless we determine the narrative scope of our reading. In view of the presentation of Samuel as a "judge," it seems reasonable to understand the monarchy in terms of a development from judgeship, though a contested one (Gideon and Abimelech). In the light of the increasing chaos in Judges, culminating in civil war, kingship seems a desirable and even a logical step. But Saul's kingship is regarded by the judge Samuel as a threat to what is a theocracy; while later in the First History, the evaluation of native kingship becomes increasingly negative, and even the positive portraits of David and Solomon are themselves blemished (the Secondary History takes a different view).

---

11. On the literary-critical configuration of the second strand, see, e.g., W. Richter, *Traditonsgeschichtliche Untersuchungen zum Richterbuch* (Bonn: Hanstein, 1966); see more recently Guillaume, *Waiting for Joshua*, with bibliography and discussion of the entire Judges narrative.

A literary-historical answer may well nuance its conclusions in the light of the archaeology of the book itself. The monarch who will bring an end to the judges' era and inaugurate the new political Israel is Saul; but he is clearly neither favoured in the final text of Judges, where both he and his tribe play the villains (and "Israel" is led by Judah), nor in some parts of 1 Samuel. Signs of rivalry between Benjamin and Judah are again evident here; and in the stories of David's displacement of Saul and the enmity of their two households it is to become central—and will remain a key theme in the remainder of the First History, as the Judah that here leads Israel in one strand and the Israel that is being formed in the other strand begin to mould themselves into the two kingdoms of the future.

1 Samuel

The focus on Benjamin (explicitly) and Saul (implicitly) at the end of Judges furnishes a straightforward narrative continuity with 1 Samuel, underscored by the retention of Shiloh as the focus of action (Judg 18:31; 21:12, 19) and the depiction of Samuel as a judge (and, like Saul, the founder of a short hereditary line of office-holders). Shiloh is in Ephraim, but after the capture of the ark, Samuel moves to Mizpah in Benjamin and summons "all Israel" in order to "judge" them (7:5–6). Perhaps the move is occasioned by the destruction of Shiloh but such a destruction is not recorded here.[12] Samuel makes a tour only of cities in Benjaminite territory (Gilgal and Mizpah, 7:16; plus Bethel, of disputed tribal alloca-tion), strongly suggesting that like the "major" judges of the book of Judges, his activity is, in fact, confined to the territory of (and perhaps closely adjacent to) a single tribe —but a tribe that has recently fallen into disfavour (Judg 21). The site of Ramah, his birthplace, in the "mountain of Ephraim" places him in territory discussed earlier in connection with Benjaminite activity.

In the election and reign of Saul as king the shadow of the twelve-tribe Israel lingers faintly, but the action centres on Benjamin, just as does Samuel's judging: the elders of Israel gather at Ramah (8:4); Samuel meets Saul in his home town of Gibeah (10:10); Saul is chosen at Mizpah; Bezek (11:8) where Saul musters for the fight against Ammon, is unidentified, but the kingdom is "renewed" at Gilgal (11:14); Saul's army against the Philistines is mustered at Michmash, in the hill country

---

12. Though I will suggest in Chapter 7 that it should be assigned to Benjaminite cultural memory, since all four references to the destruction of Shiloh occur in Jeremiah (7:12, 14; 26:6, 9). We should not overlook, either, that the news of the capture of the ark is brought to Eli at Shiloh by a Benjaminite (1 Sam 4:12).

of Bethel and Gibeah (13:2), and moves to Gilgal, then Geba (13:13,16). Beyond Benjaminite lands, we find references to Saul chasing his father's donkeys into Ephraim (9:4). We also find "Israelites" again hiding in the "mountain of Ephraim"—that place already linked with Joshua and Samuel and connected with Benjaminite victories—to join the battle against the Philistines (14:22–23). Saul's association with Jabesh-gilead has been mentioned earlier (see on Judg 21:8–14); he rescues them from an Ammonite invasion in ch. 11. But what of Judah, which lies closer to his territory?

Again we find complications. Samuel is sent to Bethlehem to anoint David as king—presumably over Israel, since he is to replace Saul. But later in the story David appears as king over Judah, based in Hebron (much further from Jerusalem than Saul's domain). Before this, however, the arrival of David at Saul's court potentially brings Judah more directly into Saul's dealings, and Telaim, from where the battle against the Amalekites (ch. 15) is conducted, may be the same as Telem, which in Josh 15:24 is located in Judah. But whether or not we should imagine Saul's activities as sometimes involving Judah,[13] we are not permitted to understand Judah as part of his kingdom because several statements declare that Judah and Israel are separate. In 11:8, Saul musters "300,000 from Israel and 30,000[14] from Judah"; in 18:16, "all Israel and Judah loved David"; in 22:5, David is told to go to the "land of Judah," presumably to remain safe from Saul; in 1 Sam 24:2, Saul takes "three thousand select men from all Israel" to search for David; and finally, after the death of Saul, David is first made king of Judah, not Israel (2 Sam 2:4). One cannot really imagine that Judah is *part* of Saul's "Israel"—if so, why is this one tribe already spoken of separately and why does it have its own king later?

Saul's Israel is not the twelve-tribe Israel of the Pentateuch or Joshua. Nor do we find twelve individual tribes, as in the core of Judges. We have an Israel composed of a few cooperating tribes, and a separate Judah. The existence of two political entities will become familiar to us from now on, and entrenched when Jeroboam secedes to form his kingdom of Israel, which is clearly larger than Saul's and based outside Benjamin. But the division is older, and, surprisingly, after Judah's dominant role in Judg 19–21—nowhere explained or remarked on; it is mentioned casually, as a matter of fact, as if so much taken for granted by the narrative's

---

13. 1 Sam 8:2 has Samuel's sons "judging" in Beersheba; perhaps an isolated hint that Samuel's jurisdiction should be understood as extending over the twelve-tribe Israel like the figures in Judges rather than merely the Israel that Saul will rule.

14. LXX (and Qumran mss.) have 70,000.

audience that the need for an explanation did not arise. But the reader further removed in time and place can see more clearly that the Israel of Genesis to Judges, the Israel of Saul, the "united" kingdom of David and the later kingdom of Israel, even if the narrative suggests that they are continuous, in fact represent four quite distinct configurations.

Episode 3: (Re-)Unification

2 Samuel

The (re-)unification of Israel and Judah through David is quite correctly referred to in biblical scholarship as the "United Monarchy" because it brings together two elements that, as we have seen, are already separated—the "houses" of Israel and Judah. The way in which the kingdom of Saul is inherited by David, thus achieving that union, is complicated: the two protagonists meet for the first time on two occasions; David is Saul's armour-bearer, his court musician and his general; he ties into Saul's family in two ways: by marrying Michal and also by befriending Jonathan. But he also operates as a brigand leader, a client of the Philistines with his own power-base in Judah. For his part, Saul turns from hero to villain as soon as David is on the scene. David's succession is over-determined, even to the point of contradiction (Saul meets him twice for the first time). For the literary critic no less than the historian, problems multiply: Is David to be understood as an insider or an outsider? Does he rule Israel as a legitimate heir of Saul, through a Judean takeover, as a Philistine vassal, or by Israelite invitation? What the story appears anxious to convey is that David's displacement of Saul was more than amply justified.[15] But his unification is not complete. David remains, in effect, the monarch of two separate kingdoms and does not amalgamate them. He retains two separate militias (2 Kgs 2:32). There remains enmity between the "houses" of Israel and Judah (see especially 2 Sam 2; 19:11; 2 Kgs 2:32) and even more so between the families of David and Saul (despite 2 Sam 19:16, discussed below). Indeed, in 2 Sam 2:8–11 Ishbaal is made king over Israel, while "the house of Judah follows

15. Biographies of David have recently become popular, and they tend to agree that a David did exist, but that the biblical portrait has a high degree of fiction. See W. Brueggemann, *David's Truth in Israel's Imagination and Memory* (Philadelphia: Fortress, 1985); S. McKenzie, *King David: A Biography* (Oxford: Oxford University Press, 2000); B. Halpern, *David's Secret Demons: Messiah, Murderer, Traitor, King* (Grand Rapids: Eerdmans, 2001). The treatment of David by S. Heym, *The King David Report* (New York: Puttnam, 1973) is still in many ways superior to any modern "critical" biography in recognizing the limitations of the historian.

David." The story in 2 Sam 19:11–18 also emphasizes the distinction between "Israel" and the "elders of Judah," "Judah" and the "people of Judah"—David's "bone and flesh" (but note here also the separate mention of Benjamin).

However, the picture is not straightforward. The definition of Israel as a kingdom distinct from Judah alternates with a usage of "Israel" that apparently designates David's entire kingdom. Some of these passages that mention "Israel" only might nevertheless refer to the kingdom of his master and predecessor Saul, but others introduce an "Israel" that apparently includes Judah. This latter usage is found especially from 2 Sam 6 onwards, though here too we also encounter "Judah and Israel" separately named (in addition to the passages mentioned previously, see 11:11; 19:43; 20:2). As for the land, in Joshua–Kings there are only four occurrences of the term: in 1 Sam 13:19 it must mean the kingdom of Saul and certainly excludes Philistine territory; in 2 Kgs 5 (two occurrences), the story of Naaman has an exclusively Israelite setting, as does 2 Kgs 6:23, where the reference is to Aramean attacks on the kingdom of Israel. This corresponds to the dominant usage of "Israel" in these books.[16] However, we also encounter the phrase "from Dan to Beersheba" seven times. In two of these (2 Sam 3:10; 1 Kgs 4:25) it is glossed as "Israel and Judah," betraying an awareness of two separate kingdoms. But in Judg 20:1; 1 Sam 3:20; 2 Sam 17:11; 24:2, 15 it is preceded by the phrase "all Israel." So we have to reckon with the presence of a different conception of "Israel" in a (significant) minority of passages. The reader may be tempted to conclude that the distinction between the two Israels is meant to be blurred, and this is probably correct in a sense, though this does amount to an explanation of why there should be two different constructions that *need* blurring. Only a limited degree of coherence can be achieved from a purely literary reading. Historical-literary explanations are required for a proper account of the matter.

1 Kings
The dominant portrait presents not only David but also Solomon and Rehoboam as simultaneously kings of both Judah and Israel, not of a single "Israel" (1 Kgs 1:35: "I have appointed him [Solomon] to be ruler of Israel and Judah"), but the twelve-tribe Israel continues to intrude. While David is separately crowned king of Judah and then of Israel,

---

16.　More interestingly, one reference in Ezek 27:17 also has the same meaning: "Judah and the land of Israel"; see also 11:17 and (probably) 25:3, 6. In the remaining eighteen occurrences the phrase seems to refer to the combined territory of Israel and Judah.

Solomon receives a single coronation in the new "united" capital of Jerusalem—as we might have expected (1 Kgs 1:32–40). Instead, his visit to Gibeon and his sacrifice there (2 Kgs 3) hint at some recognition of a separate Israelite cultic tradition in which he felt obliged to participate. However, when Rehoboam succeeds Solomon, he goes to Shechem, "for all Israel had come to Shechem to make him king," and receives complaints about the "heavy yoke" that Solomon had imposed on them. Here, as many commentators suspect, the "Israel" in question is separate from Judah, and refers to the "house of Israel," the "ten tribes" that are promised to Jeroboam. This seems clear from 12:18, where Rehoboam's taskmaster is stoned to death by "all Israel" and Rehoboam flees to Jerusalem. If this is the correct reading, then Solomon's forced labour on "all Israel" probably (1 Kgs 5:13; 9:15) also excludes Judah.

First Kings 8[17] stands out as an extended account of a twelve-tribe kingdom of Israel. Perhaps we should connect this episode with the fact of Solomon's single coronation and read the narrative as implying that under Solomon alone such a unified kingdom of Israel once really existed. Or else, as elsewhere, we may prefer literary-critical explanations.

Episode 4: Re-Division

The "division" of the kingdom under Rehoboam brings to a head some of the contradictions just described. Rehoboam rules separately over Israel and Judah, as his predecessors (Solomon more ambiguously) had done. We should infer from his visit to Shechem to be crowned over Israel (1 Kgs 12) that Rehoboam had been crowned already in Jerusalem as king of Judah. The events that follow are therefore not a moment of division within Israel, but a restoration of the status quo—or even a *continuation* of the status quo, since if Rehoboam, like David, required separate coronations over Israel and Judah, it was also open to Israel to refuse him. The "division" that is narrated is of a joint kingdom, not a single one, and even less a single *nation*. In this episode, "Israel" is not seceding from "Israel" but from the dynasty of David. This is explicit as

---

17. 1 Kgs 4 also appears to describe a unified twelve-tribe kingdom. But while v. 7 mentions "twelve officials over all Israel" and provides the names, the list ends "and there was one official in the land," who is unnamed. Verse 20 reverts to the normal usage "Judah and Israel," and most English translations supply "Judah" also at the end of v. 19 (with LXX). But this brings the total of the officers to thirteen, not twelve. Hence we should presumably understand that Solomon had twelve officers over Israel only, and thus not one per tribe but, as v. 7 states, one for each month of the year.

Abijah addresses Jeroboam in 1 Kgs 11:32: Yhwh will "tear the kingdom from the hand of Solomon and will give you ten tribes. One tribe will remain his, *for the sake of my servant David and for the sake of Jerusalem, the city that I have chosen out of all the tribes of Israel.*" The "kingdom" being torn from Solomon is the kingdom of Israel, of course, which is not a future state of affairs but already in existence. Second Kings 12:19 puts the same case another way: "So Israel has been *in rebellion against the house of David* to this day." One of the two kingdoms ruled by the Davidic line has seceded.

In the same sense, the "Israelites" who were "living in the towns of Judah: Rehoboam reigned over them" (1 Kgs 12:17) are hardly Judeans.[18] They might conceivably refer to the tribe of Benjamin, but why the text would not simply say "Benjamin" is hard to explain (see below for more discussion of this matter). It means members of one kingdom living in another.

But the mention of "tribes" (especially "ten tribes") introduces complications. The term "all the tribes of Israel" in 11:32 appears to invoke an ethnic Israel that encompasses both kingdoms. One might translate differently: "Jerusalem, the city that I have chosen in preference to all the tribes of Israel," meaning that henceforth the election of this city overrides the election of the (ten) tribes of Israel; one will be abandoned for the sake of the other. This translation makes tolerable grammatical sense and fits very well the dominant ideology of 1–2 Kings: the promise to David of an eternal dynasty that supersedes any previous promises; Jerusalem is now the exclusive focus of divine election, so that the rejection of Jerusalem becomes in effect a rejection of Israel's election by Yhwh. But "tribes of Israel" can also be a taken as a reference to a nation constituted by both the kingdoms of Israel and Judah: twelve tribes.

But we cannot rush too quickly to a total of twelve tribes! For there is an arithmetical problem. *Ten* tribes will leave Solomon, and *one* tribe will remain his.[19] The error is repeated (12:20–21):

---

18. This verse is missing from the LXX, and so is part of only the MT "final form"; it is therefore suspected by literary critics of being a gloss. If so, the author may well have a different usage and mean "Judeans." But such solutions belong outside the reading strategy adopted here.

19. Again, "final form" readers still ought to be aware that they are reading only one "final form." The Greek text allows Solomon *two* tribes. But the rule of *lectio difficilior* surely applies here. For a convenient critical discussion of the issues raised by this passage, see G. H. Jones, *1 and 2 Kings*, vol. 1 (NCB; London: Marshall, Morgan & Scott, 1984), 243–45.

> When all Israel heard that Jeroboam had returned, they sent and called him to the assembly and made him king over all Israel.[20] There was no one who followed the house of David, *except the tribe of Judah alone*. When Rehoboam came to Jerusalem, he assembled all the house of Judah and the tribe of Benjamin, one hundred eighty thousand chosen troops to fight against the house of Israel, to restore the kingdom to Rehoboam son of Solomon.

The passage continues (vv. 22–23):

> But the word of God came to Shemaiah the man of God: Say to King Rehoboam of Judah, son of Solomon, *and to all the house of Judah and Benjamin*, and to the rest of the people [the "Israelites living in Judah? "Canaanites"?]...

Obviously Benjamin is in some way implicated in the arithmetic, and before tackling this problem, we should note the absence of any explanation for Benjamin's decision, which is as amazing as the earlier absence of any explanation for the separation of Judah from Israel in 1 Samuel. We are not only given no *reason* for what seems a perverse decision, but even *the decision itself* is not recorded. The reader of the narrative, recalling how at the end of Judges Judah had acted as the leader of the twelve tribes against Benjamin, and how such enmity had developed between the families of David and Saul, will surely find it odd that of all the tribes, Benjamin would feel any allegiance to the dynasty of David—or indeed that it would desert an "Israel" of which Saul had been the first king. Also curious is the way in which Benjamin is named: we have "house of Judah and tribe of Benjamin" in v. 21, and "house of Judah and Benjamin" in v. 23. What does the distinction between "house" and "tribe" signify? And what of "house of Benjamin" in 2 Sam 3:19? But the key question is whether Benjamin is or is not included in the ten tribes promised to Jeroboam (1 Kgs 11:31–32). Levi is another problem: according to Deuteronomy and Joshua it has no territory and will therefore split between the two kingdoms. It is not mentioned as belonging specifically with Judah (this association emerges only in the Second History). It is hardly possible that Benjamin is absorbed (like Simeon) into the "house of Judah" and loses its tribal status. So we have eleven tribes and no certainty over where Benjamin is to be counted. The dilemma is underlined when in 2 Kgs 17:18 we are told "Therefore Yhwh was very angry with Israel and removed them out of his sight; none was left but the tribe of Judah *alone*." This reiteration defeats what would

---

20. Note again that "all Israel" means no more than "all of the kingdom of Israel," not "Israel plus Judah."

otherwise be the best literary solution: that Benjamin was promised to Jeroboam but decided to stay with Judah, thus frustrating the divine plan. Instead we have two plain contradictions: Benjamin was not counted with Judah and Benjamin *was*: Jeroboam had ten tribes and Judah had one, yet there were twelve tribes altogether.

This is not the place to solve the riddle. I shall leave this topic with one final comment. Only one text in the books of Samuel and Kings mentions twelve as the number of tribes—1 Kgs 18:31, in connection with Elijah, where the context would suggest that the kingdom of Israel is to be understood. Otherwise the only enumeration is Jeroboam's ten in 1 Kgs 11.

Now to the question of Bethel (1 Kgs 12:25–33). Earlier we observed that Bethel was assigned in the book of Joshua to both Ephraim and Benjamin (16:2; 18:13). One could bear in mind that tribal boundaries in reality are not necessarily rigid at all. But the biblical narrative sometimes understands them in this way: at least it seems to believe in the integrity of tribal territory. For if Benjamin were attached to Judah when Jeroboam reigned, the Israelite sanctuary would of course have to be assigned to Ephraim. The uncertainty over Bethel's tribal allocation might, however, be connected with the uncertainty that 1 Kgs 11 invokes over Benjamin's attachment to Judah. The ambiguity extends into the later period as well: according to 1 Kgs 15:16–22 Baasha king of Israel (re)built Ramah and in response, Asa of Judah bribed Ben-hadad of Aram to attack Israel and cause Baasha to withdraw. Asa had the building stones removed from Ramah and with them built at Geba and Mizpah. Hence Geba and Mizpah (both in Benjamin) are presented as under the jurisdiction of Judah; but Ramah, the birthplace of Samuel, is apparently regarded as belonging first to Israel then to Judah, which translates, in tribal terms, to Ephraim and then to Benjamin (cf. Josh 18:25). The story of Josiah's attack on Bethel (2 Kgs 23) implies that this sanctuary too is now under his jurisdiction: he had the ashes of idolatrous temple vessels from Jerusalem carried to Bethel. His destruction of the shrines of the "towns of Samaria" (v. 19) belongs to a separate episode. Later, in Ezra (2:28) and Nehemiah (7:32; 11:31), Bethel seems to be part of the province of Judah. The narrative suggests what was concluded from Joshua about Bethel and might also be concluded about the birthplaces of both Joshua and Samuel—anything here regarded by the narrator as belonging to Judah must be assigned to Benjamin, while what belongs to Israel is assigned to Ephraim. Ramah and Bethel are two examples, and Kiriath-jearim possibly another. *Historically*, we might seek a resolution in the fact that borders are not fixed and some lands remains contested. Indeed the land of Benjamin immediately north of Jerusalem can be topographically divided in more than one way, having links to both north and south.[21] But this is not a *literary* explanation.

From this point onwards, "Israel" applies consistently to the kingdom of that name: the usage is entirely *political*. After the fall of Samaria in 722 BCE, the name "Israel" for Samaria/Samerina and its people disappears from the First History. But even after the fall of Samaria, "Israel" is still not applied to Judah or its inhabitants, either—with one partial and important exception: the term "god of Israel."[22] Hezekiah "trusted in Yhwh the god of Israel" (2 Kgs 18:5; see also 19:15, 20 and 22 ["holy one of Israel" in the mouth of Isaiah]). The term recurs in 2 Kgs 21 (once: Manasseh) and 22 (twice: Josiah). It is absent from the Pentateuch, though there are three references in Exodus to "god of Jacob" (3:6, 15; 4:5; always in the same formula, with Abraham and Isaac). Between the book of Joshua and the fall of Samaria (2 Kgs 17), it is used in contexts that denote several Israels: the kingdom of Saul (1 Sam 14:41; 20:12 etc.), the twelve-tribe Israel (throughout Joshua; Judg 21:3 etc.), the joint realm of David and Solomon (1 Kgs 1:30, 48; 8; 9:31; 11; etc.) and the later kingdom of Israel (1 Kgs 14:7, 13 etc.) It is thus a widely occurring phrase that accompanies every manifestation of Israel in the First History (outside the Pentateuch). It is implausible to conclude that the title is independent of the fluctuation definitions of "Israel" in which it appears. Hence, perhaps it does not apply to any of them, strictly speaking. From the time of Hezekiah onwards, for example, the "Israel" of the "god of Israel" can hardly be the now-vanished kingdom, and, since Judah is never called "Israel" during this era, the name probably does not apply to a people at all. To what "Israel" does it refer?

Here the story of the fall of Samaria in 2 Kgs 17 and its aftermath provides a useful clue. It records that the king of Assyria "carried the Israelites away to Assyria" (v. 6), and in an interesting but overlooked comment, it also blames Israel for having induced Judah to abandon the commandments of Yhwh and follow other customs and adds that Yhwh rejected "all the seed (זֶרַע) of Israel" (v. 20). "Seed of Israel" is

---

21. On the topography of Benjamin, see the still useful description of Smith, *The Historical Geography of the Holy Land*, 243–52, who points to the "natural boundary" but also its "ambiguity" (244), and notes three possible frontiers: south of Bethel, north of Bethel and more northerly still. Thus he explains the fluctuating frontier between the two territories.

22. 2 Kgs 21:7–9 does refer to "tribes of Israel" and "Israel" in an inclusive sense, but first as a statement from Yhwh to David and Solomon and then as a reference to the initial settlement of the land—in both cases this usage would be in accordance with the scheme of the First History. The same is true of 2 Kgs 23:22 and 24:13.

especially interesting: it occurs only here in the First History,[23] and is clearly an *inclusive* reference to both kingdoms, one rejected and the other later to be rejected, as the context shows. However, the term "Israel" by itself is used in the same verse in its usual sense, the kingdom of Israel. "Israel" in this phrase is clearly "Jacob." "God of Israel," which as we have seen can also be used inclusively, therefore probably means "god of Jacob," an *ancestral* deity. This conclusion is supported by the appearance of "god of Jacob" eighteen times in the Hebrew Bible: Exod 3:6, 15; 4:5 (mentioned earlier); 2 Sam 23:1; twelve times in the Psalms; Isa 2:3 and Mic 4:2 (both prophets associated with Judah). There is no doubt that both forms apply to Judah as well as Israel and should be regarded as synonymous. The usage implies that Judah and Israel were regarded as sharing the same cult. The view that Yhwh was worshipped by both is of course widely held, and is usually explained from a common cultural origin. But if such a common origin cannot be demonstrated, why would Judah come to worship the god of Jacob/Israel—or, if the cult of Yhwh was also indigenous to Judah, why give him this title? Whatever the answer, it is possible that *this common divine title forms the basis for the idea of an Israelite nation descended from the same ancestor, rather than the other way round.*

Judah's identity as "Israel" is therefore not at all *political*; the union of both kingdoms, if it were historical, would be a separate matter, an expression of another form of unity. Judah's "Israel" has nothing directly to do with the kingdom to its north, but with the god of its ancestor. Are there any further clues to this from a purely literary reading?

Perhaps 2 Kgs 17 is even more helpful. What does the story say of the other "seed of Jacob/Israel" in Samaria? The statement that "Israel was exiled from its own land to Assyria until this day" says two things. One is that "Israel" went elsewhere, and so either exists in other places or does not exist at all. The other is that the inhabitants of Samaria are no longer "Israel," despite living in the land once occupied by Israel. *All* of "Israel" went into exile, and the king of Assyria displaced them with foreigners (v. 24). These foreigners do not know the "god of the land" (as it is expressed to the Assyrian king), so he takes measures to have them instructed in the cult of Yhwh by one of the exiled priests (v. 27) who returned from deportation and lived in Bethel. Alongside this cult, however, the new inhabitants continued to make idols of their indigenous deities; "so they worshipped Yhwh but also served their own gods…to this day they continued to practise their previous customs" (v. 33). The

---

23. Some critics suggest that the verse is therefore a gloss. Other biblical occurrences are Isa 45:25; Jer 31:36–37; Ps 22:24; Neh 9:2; 1 Chr 16:13.

narrator continues, in blatant contradiction: "they do not worship Yhwh and do not follow the statutes...that Yhwh commanded *the children of Jacob, whom he named Israel*" (v. 34). The italicized words confirm the conclusion that "seed of Jacob" in v. 20 is a designation for members of a cult (it does not matter whether grammatically the object of the naming is Jacob or his descendants; these are effectively identical). The "children of Jacob" are defined genealogically by virtue of their adherence to an ancestral cult. The slide here from the genealogical to the religious definition replicates the move from the genealogical in Genesis to the cultic in the remainder of the Pentateuch. A descendant of Jacob is a worshipper of the god of Jacob. With the kingdom of Israel now defunct, this is what "Israel" will from now on always mean. The mention of Bethel as the home of the imported priest also confirms the connection between its sanctuary and the figure of Jacob. The cult of the god of Israel is *par excellence* the cult of Bethel.[24]

Yet the genealogical code now becomes important. The description of religious practices in Samaria given by the narrative is, as just observed, a confused one. The (new) inhabitants, who are not genealogically descended from Jacob, both *do* and *do not* worship Yahweh alongside their own gods. If they *do*, they are hardly different in respect of their religious custom from Judah (and indeed v. 20 seems to make the equation), or from their predecessors, upon whom the name "Israel" had been bestowed by the god of "Israel." So the code of ethnic descent becomes necessary here, after all: the former Israel *were* descendants of Israel/ Jacob. And Judah, too, apparently. The way is thus clear to deny the identity of "Israel" to Samarians but to allow it to Judeans. Both populations deemed to be descended from Jacob failed to respect their deity's commandments, and were exiled. The deportees from Samaria do not return, and so only Judah is left to bear that identity. The argument for excluding Samarians from Israel is thus, paradoxically, a *genealogical* one; and the argument for including Judah is thus also implicitly genealogical. That argument finds its ultimate goal in the incorporation of Judah within a twelve-tribe Israel.

But while the genealogical inclusion of Judah in Israel is implied in 2 Kgs 17, the First History does not, in fact, represent Judah as "Israel," even though it does represent Judah as worshipping the "god of Israel."

---

24. The meaning of "Jacob" in the Hebrew Bible is an interesting and important topic, for sometimes it refers to both Israel and Judah (e.g. Ezekiel), sometimes to Israel alone, in distinction to Judah (Amos, Hosea, Micah), and sometimes to Judah alone (Isaiah). In both Isaiah and Jeremiah it is used sometimes of Israel and sometimes of Israel plus Judah. See further the discussion in Chapter 8.

The reason may be partly that the story ends with the deportation of the Judean ruling caste and the end of the cult in Jerusalem. A brief note reports that Gedaliah was appointed over those who remained in Judah, but was killed and "all the people high and low" left for Egypt, while King Jehoiachin of Judah was released from prison in Babylon. The reader may infer that Israel consists only in those with the Davidic king. But while this will be the claim of part of the Second History, the First History does not go this far.

The First History can hardly be read as anything other than a tragedy. The Israel with which it started out has gone, and we are left with the Judean monarchy, the sole bearer of a divine promise and hope, and a ruined city that once symbolized divine election. For a less tragic presentation that takes us beyond catastrophe, we must turn to the Second History.

Finally, there is something important yet to be said about the religious definition of "Israel" implied by the term "god of Israel." Even where there is no "Israel" that unites the two kingdoms, the histories of both Judah and Israel are subject to the same religious criteria, the commandments of the same god. The religious unity of the two kingdoms is taken for granted. Indeed, the commandments themselves, and the language in which they are described, clearly reflect Deuteronomy, which, within the narrative of the First History, is a speech by Moses to all the tribes of Israel. It might then be argued that the First History takes for granted that Judah and Israel are indeed parts of the one single people, and that the Pentateuchal Israel is ever-present in the books of Kings also.

This conclusion should perhaps be accepted in one sense and not in another. As I have just argued, the most fundamental unity between Israel and Judah in the "Former Prophets" is constituted by a shared cult of a god known as "god of Israel" and as Yhwh, and by a view that the history of both is conditioned by the relationship that they both have with that one deity.

On the other hand, while at this level there is a continuity of identity between the Pentateuch and the Former Prophets, the latter do not, except sporadically, sustain the identity of that Pentateuchal nation. First individual tribal histories, then the kingdom of Saul, the double kingdom of David and the two kingdoms undermine that identity and point to alternative processes.

If we ask about the identity of "Israel" in the Pentateuch, we can point to variations, too, but there is a consistent image of twelve tribes. If we look for this Israel in the remainder of the First History, we cannot sustain this image, except in one (and important) sense—that "Israel" remains the subject of this History in whatever guise it appears. There can be no entirely coherent reading of "Israel" here; but the difficulties become crucial only when we try to break out of the narrative world and turn the biblical Israels into historical ones. Before we turn to that process there are other biblical Israels to be encountered.

Chapter 5

ISRAEL IN THE SECOND HISTORY: CHRONICLES

The story of Chronicles is continued directly in Ezra and this continuity is recognized and reinforced by the identical text at the end of Chronicles and beginning of Ezra.[1] Whether Chronicles and the combined Ezra–Nehemiah stem from the same author(s), whether Ezra and Nehemiah comprise a single composition, whether the overlap between the end of Chronicles and beginning of Ezra is intrinsic or to which book it originally belonged are all irrelevant to a literary reading. It should be said, however, that the ideological differences between Chronicles and Ezra–Nehemiah are at least as dramatic as those within the First History as regards the composition of "Israel."

Also irrelevant is the textual relationship between the two Histories, especially between 2 Samuel–2 Kings and 1–2 Chronicles, where much of the content is identical. The habit of reading Chronicles as a revision of Samuel–Kings is to be avoided because it encourages a harmonistic reading and obscures important differences.[2] In recent years, fortunately, the study of Chronicles has blossomed and as a result our understanding of its distinctive ideology has markedly improved.

1.   The canonical order, though sometimes invoked in literary readings, is also irrelevant. Even disregarding the fact that "order" is not physically represented before the first Jewish biblical codices, even the conventional ordering that places Chronicles last within the Writings is not universally attested even in printed Hebrew bibles.

2.   The consensus that Chronicles is dependent on Samuel–Kings has in any case been challenged by A. G. Auld in his *Kings Without Privilege: David and Moses in the Story of the Bible's Kings* (Edinburgh: T. & T. Clark, 1994), and is complicated by the fact that the MT text of Samuel–Kings does not represent the supposed original underlying both books, but has been revised subsequent to the common text. (On this, see also R. Rezetko, *Source and Revision in the Narratives of David's Transfer of the Ark* [London: T&T Clark International, 2007].) Intertextuality is, of course, a legitimate facet of a purely literary reading—as long as it is synchronic and not diachronic! (Likewise, the title "Second History" implies only canonical sequence and not hierarchical order.)

As in the previous chapter, we read with an eye on the conception of Israel and particularly Judah's place in it. In the light of our reading of the First History, we will also be alerted to the place of Benjamin and to Bethel.

Pre-monarchy

The continuous narrative of Chronicles commences only in ch. 9, but the genealogies that comprise chs. 1–9 deserve comment. The lack of a narrative from Adam to Saul tempts us to read Chronicles as an alternative *sequel* to the Pentateuch, or even to an Octateuch (Genesis–1 Samuel). Most scholars assume that Chronicles in any case alludes to the Pentateuchal narrative, and certainly there is a great deal of shared information. But here too, as with the parallels to 2 Samuel–Kings, there are also differences, not just in the length and form, but in content. There is no Exodus, which might be explained by the non-narrative form of chs. 1–9; but in addition, there is nothing from what source-critics assign to the Yahwistic narrative (e.g. Cain and the Cainite genealogy). It cannot be demonstrated that the writer assumes the reader to have all or part of the Pentateuchal narrative, as we now read it, in mind.

The use of genealogies, as a kind of minimal narrative form, fulfils two important rhetorical functions. It balances change with permanence. Generations succeed generations, but these genealogies exclude external events and thus almost eliminate what we would now term "history."[3] Instead, the perennial sequence of generational succession imparts an almost timeless quality. *Almost* timeless, because genealogies do require an archetypal ancestor; the notion of past and indeed of origins is therefore not obliterated. They also mark the succession of time, though this is a curious sort of time almost without incident. But the past also structures the present in a way that is characteristic of myth rather than our modern definition of history (it is a feature, all the same, of virtually all ancient historiography). The genealogies of Chronicles imply that "Israel" has always been the same: now as at the beginning, whatever history has inflicted in the meantime. Here is a strong contrast with the First History

---

3. But not totally: 1 Chr 1:10 seems to make an allusion to Mesopotamian empires in the phrase "warrior on the earth" (if that is the correct translation of the Hebrew). Admittedly, the phrase is borrowed from Gen 10, but it is the only such expansion to be borrowed. Note also that Nimrud is in the line of Ham, while Asshur is descended from Shem. There is also mention of the deportation of Reuben, Gad and the half-tribe of Manasseh in 5:26 and a few other brief allusions to the fates of tribes.

where, as we have seen, the definition of Israel fluctuates as well as develops.[4]

The very terse genealogies contain data found also in Gen 1, 5 and 10, culminating in Abraham (1 Chr 1:1–27). Abraham's *immediate* descendants are traced (no Lot, Ammon or Moab), but not exclusively to the "Israelite" line: Ishmael and Esau are both included, and Edom (Esau) is given a fairly extensive line of descent, including a king list (as in Gen 36). From ch. 2 onwards Israel only is described. Jacob's sons are briefly named (v. 1) and followed immediately by a genealogy of Judah (vv. 2–55), then of the house of David (ch. 3). The twelve tribal genealogies then begin, headed by Judah again, but in a different order from 2:1. Indeed, 5:1 states that while Reuben was the firstborn, he forfeited his birthright to the "sons of Joseph" because of a shameful act (Gen 25:32?), although Judah was the predominant son (Heb. גבר). Levi stands in the middle of the list and Benjamin occurs twice; first after Issachar and again, at more length, at the end. Hence the three tribes comprising the province of Judah stand at the beginning, middle and end of "Israel," perhaps symbolically embracing the whole. Levi's genealogy is prominent by its length, listing not only its settlements but also the musicians appointed by David, so linking Levi with Judah and the temple with the monarchy. The total of twelve tribes is achieved by dividing Joseph into Ephraim and Manasseh (which is conventional, but does not follow 2:1) but also omitting Zebulun and Dan. The two parts of Manasseh (Transjordanian and Cisjordanian) are mentioned respectively before and after Levi. Benjamin has two genealogical sections, 7:6–12 and ch. 8, and unless we count either Manasseh or Benjamin twice, we arrive at a total of only eleven tribes.

There is a marked emphasis on Jacob as ancestor. His name is much more commonly given, in fact, as "Israel" than "Jacob." In the opening genealogy (1:1–2:2), the schematic presentation mentions the secondary lines before the primary one leading to Israel, but once the line reaches Jacob, the genealogies are arranged in a different manner: the process of election has been reached. In fact, as Williamson has pointed out,[5] the

---

4. The contrast is one of the features that might classify Chronicles as a "cold" history in comparison with the First History's "hot" (see Chapter 1). For discussion of the genealogies, see W. Johnstone, *1 & 2 Chronicles* (2 vols.; Sheffield: Sheffield Academic Press, 1997), 1:24–129; R. L. Braun, "Reconstruction of the History of Israel," in *The Chronicler as Historian* (ed. M. P. Graham, K. G. Hoglund and S. L. McKenzie; Sheffield: Sheffield Academic Press, 1997), 92–105, esp. 98–101.

5. H. G. M. Williamson, *Israel in the Books of Chronicles* (Cambridge: Cambridge University Press, 1977), 62–64.

special emphasis on Jacob is also evident elsewhere. The wording of the promise to him in Gen 16:10 is also employed at 2 Chr 1:9 in Solomon's dream at Gibeon. Finally, the only occasion on which the root בהר is used of the people as a whole is at 1 Chr 16:13 (cf. v. 17), where it is descent from Jacob that determines their election ("seed of his servant Israel, children of Jacob, his chosen ones [זרע ישׂראל/בני יעקוב]). This feature was noted in the First History at 2 Kgs 17, but by contrast, Chronicles is ready to embrace both kingdoms within "Israel" while regarding the kingdom of Israel as also subject to the kingship of David, and thus to Jerusalem and its temple. The story of the dream at Gibeon contains details absent from the account in 1 Kgs 3: the "tent of meeting" is said to have been there, and its bronze altar. The Pentateuchal cultic centre is thus split between Jerusalem (ark) and Gibeon (cf. 1 Chr 16:31). This is one of the few clues in Chronicles to a division within Israel prior to the secession by Jeroboam; and once the temple in Jerusalem is built, the Gibeon altar is no longer mentioned.

The second part of the genealogy of Benjamin in ch. 8 also contains some noteworthy features. Despite its rather complicated structure,[6] it seems to begin with the immediate descendants of Benjamin (vv. 1–5); then breaks into a genealogy of Ehud (whose parentage is not given, vv. 6–7). Another new genealogy is that of Shaharaim who "had sons in the Moabite countryside"; his many sons were all heads of houses (ראשׁי אבות) and "lived in Jerusalem" (vv. 8–28). Finally we have the genealogy of Jeiel of Gibeon, the line of Saul (vv. 29–40); these also lived in Jerusalem alongside their kin (v. 32).

But the genealogy of Jeiel is again rehearsed in 9:35, where it extends to Saul and beyond, and locates the family in Gibeon. At this point the narrative proper begins with Saul's final battle and death. But his line continues. In both respects there is a contradiction with the First History, which locates Saul's home in Gibeah and recalls his attempt to extermi- nate the Gibeonites—an incident nowhere actually recorded but which results in a famine, in David's compensation to Gibeon and in their exe- cution of seven of Saul's sons (2 Sam 21)—and seems also to imply that Saul's descendants died out (Michal is barren; Mephibosheth is the sole survivor and leaves no family). The profile of Benjamin and Saul here is therefore much higher and also free of polemics.

But this Saulide genealogy follows the full description of all the com- ponents of Israel, which culminates in the statement in 9:1:

---

6. See the excellent analysis by Johnstone, *1 & 2 Chronicles*, 1:111–17. How- ever, I am not convinced of his conclusion that ch. 8 is a resumption of the earlier genealogy.

> All Israel was enrolled by genealogies;[7] and these were written in the
> scroll of the kings of Israel. But Judah was deported to Babylon because
> of their rebellion.

And this is immediately followed by (vv. 2–3):

> The first to settle on their property and in their cities were Israel, the
> priests, the Levites, and the temple servants. In Jerusalem settled some
> Judeans, some Benjaminites, some Ephraimites and Manassites.

The impression may be gained from v. 1b that vv. 4–34 define the lay,
priestly and Levitical population of Jerusalem *after* the resettlement
recorded in Ezra and Nehemiah.[8] Such an interpretation, however, would
require extending the time-frame of Chronicles, which ends with the edict
of Cyrus. Moreover, v. 3 speaks of people of Ephraim and Manasseh
being included among these inhabitants of Jerusalem; plausible for the
time of David, but not as likely for the Persian era. In v. 22, later in the
same passage, the gatekeepers are said to have been installed by David
and Samuel, and while the purpose of this might perhaps be to reinforce
the antiquity and legitimacy of the office and hint at a restoration of
arrangements made by David, it is preferable, as Johnstone has argued,[9]
to construe vv. 2–34 as a description of the settlement *at the time of
David* (cf. 6:31; 7:2).

This interpretation best accounts for the meaning of "Israel" in these
verses. Bearing in mind that v. 1 reads like the conclusion of one passage
and v. 2 like the beginning of another, v. 1 uses "Israel" to denote the
kingdom of Israel, as shown by the reference to a "book of the kings of
Israel" and by the mention of Judah separately. In v. 2, Israel presumably
means the non-priestly tribes, settled in their allotted possessions; of
these, some Judeans, Benjaminites, Ephraimites and Manassites live in
Jerusalem. This can be contrasted with Neh 11:3, where only Judeans
and Benjaminites are mentioned, and where we can see more clearly that
"Israel" denotes the lay tribes of the erstwhile kingdom of Judah only.
(Ephraim and Manasseh are represented in Nehemiah only in the "gate of
Ephraim" [Neh 8:16; 12:39] and as a personal name [Manasseh, Ezra
10:30].) Together with all scholarly commentators we can recognize that
the two lists have a common source:[10] about half of the names given in

---

7. The verb שׁי is exclusive to the Second History. Its use suggests that the Israel
of the post-monarchic period is constituted exactly as it had been earlier.

8. The NRSV clearly interprets this way by adding "again," not present in the
Hebrew.

9. Johnstone, *1 & 2 Chronicles*, 1:119–21.

10. Ibid., 1:120; S. Japhet, *I & II Chronicles* (London: SCM Press, 1993), 202–4,
has a full discussion of the relationship between the two.

1 Chr 9 recur in the genealogy of Nehemiah's contemporaries in 11:4–19:33. How does the reader of the Second History interpret this? Presumably as a claim that the situation in the mid-fifth century is to be seen as a reconstitution of the original state of affairs. First Chronicles 9 makes precisely this point in referring the names to the time of David. That the names themselves may belong to the later period only underlines that continuity. It means, however, that Chronicles imagines a fully united Israel under David, and not merely a yoking of two kingdoms: Jerusalem is fully the home of all Israel, *as much of Saul's family as David's*. (The selection of the tribes of Benjamin, Ephraim and Manasseh alongside Judah might even be taken as a reference to the actual domain of Saul were it not that Saul is actually presented as king of *all* Israel: see below.) Contrary to the portrait of the First History, David, Solomon and Rehoboam rule over an Israel that was politically as well as socially and cultically integrated.

Monarchy

The unification of Saul and David, and the centrality of Jerusalem, are underlined in the transition to a narrative that includes the Saulide genealogy in 9:35–44. This almost, but not quite, repeats the data in 8:29–40. But the point being made now is not of the integration of Israel and Judah, but the sin of Israel that begins with Saul and will bring about the end of both of the separated kingdoms. The first divine punishment for this "rebellion" (מעל) is Saul's death, with which the narrative then commences. The phrase "Judah was deported to Babylon because of their rebellion" (מעלם) in 9:1 is now set to receive its explanation, beginning with the rebellion of Saul (10:13–14).[11] Saul's replacement by David is thus much less extensively related than in the First History, and he is much more the first king of Israel—in the narrator's view, of *all* of Israel, Judah included. This treatment of Saul must surely be connected with the regular mention of Benjamin alongside Judah and the placing of Benjaminites in Jerusalem in the time of Saul and David, as a way of sharing a common royal history, capital and cult between them both. In all of these respects we have a strong contrast with the First History.

Again, unlike the First History, David is not a king of two separate kingdoms, and is crowned only once over the united Israel, in Hebron (11:1–3). The request to David to become king over Israel runs "we are

11. Hos 9:9; 10:9 makes the same point, but replaces "Gibeon" with "Gibeah." Whether the statements reflect an Israelite or a Judean perspective (both are present in the book) is an interesting question.

your bone and flesh; until just now, even while Saul was king, you commanded the army of Israel." David is Saul's successor over the same single Israel; the capture of Jerusalem—again by "all Israel"—follows immediately. During David's period in the wilderness (the phrase "because of Saul" in 12:1 is again a very restrained version of the extensive accounts of persecution in 1 Samuel) his warriors are "archers, and could shoot arrows and sling stones with either the right hand or the left; they were Benjaminites, Saul's kin" (12:2), and they included men from Anathoth and Gibeon. Men from Gad and Manasseh are also mentioned (vv. 8–15, 19–22). The impression is thus given that David drew support not only from non-Judean tribes but also from members of Saul's family (countering the First History's view that David had little or no support from these quarters). Chronicles' sunny view of both David and Solomon as kings without blemish is well known, but more important for our interest is the picture of harmony between an "Israel" and a "Judah" that are two parts of a single whole. Only one comment here draws attention to a separate Israel and Judah: when Joab is instructed to make a census of "Israel from Beersheba to Dan" (1 Chr 21:1–6)

> he did not include Levi and Benjamin in the accounting, because the royal command was abhorrent to Joab (v. 6)

Such a comment does not explain the difference in figures between this account and 2 Sam 24:9 (the numbers are also the same in the LXX). Yet this is the only place in which Chronicles makes a distinction between "Judah" and "Israel" until the time of Rehoboam, when these two tribes are reckoned with the kingdom of Judah: but at this moment, why should their association with Judah be anticipated, as it is? They are in fact being allocated *already* to Judah. But only implicitly; for in another sense, Chronicles avoids naming either tribe Israel or Judah! If we cannot understand why Chronicles simply does not provide a figure for "all Israel," we can certainly understand his sensibilities here, and they brings us neatly to the problem of the separation of the ten tribes.

Up to this point, the text has stressed the supremacy of Judah and Jerusalem, but avoided any implication of rivalry between Judah and Israel or David and Saul, or their families. Accordingly, there is also an important difference in the way that this secession is explained. First Kings 11:26–40 describes a prediction from Ahijah of the division of Solomon's realm, signified by the tearing of the prophet's garment. This is omitted in Chronicles. Instead, 2 Chr 9:29 alludes to the acts of Solomon "written in the history of the prophet Nathan, and in the prophecy of the prophet Ahijah, and in the visions of the seer Iddo concerning Jeroboam ben Nebat." As Williamson points out (see below), in

Chronicles' scheme of retribution, each king is punished for his own sins, and therefore the secession under Jeroboam is presented as the result of the sins of Rehoboam, not Solomon (an additional reason may be that Solomon is unblemished in the Chronicles portrait, though not in the entire Second History; see Neh 13:26). The First History had carefully represented the split as between "Israel" and the "house of David." The phrase "the people of Israel who were living in the cities of Judah" (1 Kgs 12:17) also occurs in 2 Chr 10:17, but there is now a different nuance. In 2 Kgs 12:23 the prophet Shemaiah is told to speak to Rehoboam and "all the house of Judah and Benjamin"; 2 Chr 11:3 has "all Israel in Judah and Benjamin." Chronicles also includes an additional section (11:13–17) recording the support of all priests and Levites for Rehoboam "from all their territories" in which Jeroboam had forbidden them to officiate; and so they came to Judah, and "all who had set their hearts to seek Yhwh god of Israel came after them from all the tribes of Israel to Jerusalem." According to Chronicles, then, Rehoboam thus remains king of *Israel*, an identity that attaches to Benjamin, Levi and all other tribal elements living in Judah. All of Judah is *Israel in Judah*. Thus, in 2 Chr 12:1 Rehoboam is said to abandon the law, "he and all Israel with him."

Until Williamson's analysis of the Chronicler's view of the "divided monarchy,"[12] the prevailing view had been that the narrator here regarded only those Israelites "in Judah and Benjamin" as members of the true Israel, despite his continued use of the term "Israel" for the "northern kingdom," so entailing two different connotations of the term "Israel." But just as Kings maintains, with a few exceptions, a consistent use of "Israel"—the kingdom of that name—so Chronicles also has a consistent understanding of "Israel," though it is obliged to acknowledge that *part* of that Israel also inhabits a kingdom by the same name. Since the secession under Rehoboam is presented here not as the permanent punishment for *Solomon's* sins, but as a temporary punishment for *Rehoboam's*, it was a valid apostasy only during that king's lifetime.[13] Thereafter, the kingdom of Israel becomes apostate. But it does not lie outside the "Israel" of Chronicles. Japhet argues that the division into "Judah and Benjamin" and the remaining tribes is purely geographical, that all twelve tribes constitute the nation still. The Chronicler, in her

---

12. Williamson, *Israel in the Books of Chronicles*. The following interpretation of "Israel" in Chronicles follows Williamson's interpretation.

13. Here Williamson (*Israel in the Books of Chronicles*, 98–101) follows A. C. Welch, *Post-Exilic Judaism* (Edinburgh: William Blackwood & Sons, 1935), 189–91.

view, portrays a steady expansion of Judah until it has absorbed the remaining territory—a geographical solution to the division. While for Japhet this is achieved in the reign of Josiah, whose reform covers "from Simeon as far as Naphtali" (2 Chr 34:6), Williamson points out that the same might be claimed for the reign of Hezekiah.[14] In any case, the Israel of Chronicles is never truly divided.

The instances in which Chronicles uses "Israel" of *both* kingdoms, separately, show that each is seen to have equal right to the name. The secession under Rehoboam was justified, but did not divide Israel's identity; and it should have ceased after the death of Rehoboam. Accordingly, the Chronicler describes Abijah's victory over Israel with approval. The king says "O *Israelites*, do not fight against Yhwh the god of your ancestors" (13:12)—and earlier refers to his realm as "the kingdom of Yhwh in the hand of the sons of David" (v. 8).

Williamson's phrase "double monarchy"[15] accurately characterizes how the Chronicler's "Israel" is governed. In 2 Chr 28, after the war between the two, the "northerners" recognize this state of affairs, acknowledge their own sin (28:13) and so anticipate the restoration that is shortly to happen. For the destruction of Samaria is not the end of the kingdom of Israel, but a restoration of the unity of its one single kingdom ruled from Jerusalem. Hezekiah reassumes his rule over those who remain in the north also (2 Chr 30). The geographical extent of Israel is again fully restored too, in that those remaining in the erstwhile kingdom of Israel are included. Whereas 2 Kings interleaves the histories of the two kingdoms, Chronicles narrates only events involving Judah. This means that no explanation is given of the fate of the kingdom of Israel or of its inhabitants. They simply become fully subjects of Hezekiah; the rebellion is over. Of the accusations in the First History that north of Judah's borders all are idolatrous foreigners there is not a hint. Accordingly, the Chronicler here uses the phrase "remnant of Israel" to denote those who, after the fall of Samaria and the Assyrian deportations, survived in the north (v. 6), as he does in 34:9; in 34:21 he uses it of those in "Israel and Judah" together, making it clear by using these terms that he includes both sets of populations. The Chronicler can use "Israel" from this moment onwards quite unambiguously to refer to the total population of both communities in both a religious and political sense,

---

14. Japhet, *I & II Chronicles*, 46: "after the defection of the northern tribes, there is a process of return to this original unity." See her fuller comments in *The Ideology of the Book of Chronicles and Its Place in Biblical Thought* (Frankfurt: Peter Lang, 1989), xxx–xxx. Cf. also Williamson, *Israel in the Books of Chronicles*, 101.

15. Williamson, *Israel in the Books of Chronicles*, 114.

ignoring the reality of the province of Samaria that 2 Kings describes so carefully.[16]

Since Hezekiah's reign represents a return to the situation under Solomon, the temple and the cult are renewed. "All Israel, from Beersheba to Dan" is invited to Hezekiah's Passover in Jerusalem. He addresses them as "people of Israel," and invokes the ancestry of "Abraham, Isaac and [note!] Israel." The response is mixed, but the principle is established, and despite the scornful reactions of many, some "repent" and accept the invitation. "Since the time of Solomon son of king David of Israel there had been nothing like this in Jerusalem" (30:26).

Not only are the "ten tribes" of Israel now formally reunited with Judah, but the land itself is healed. What is the extent of this land? 1 Chr 13:2, 5 has David refer to "lands [pl.] of Israel," meaning "all Israel from Shihor of Egypt to Lebo-Hamath" (the extent of his empire); this presumably remains the ideal extent thereafter (1 Chr 22:2; 2 Chr 2:16)—including the territory of the former kingdom of Israel (2 Chr 20:35 [Hezekiah]; 34:7 [Josiah]). The Chronicler's "land of Israel" is therefore larger than the First History's. Does this mean that the land promised in Gen 15:18 is not for the other Abrahamic nations of Ammon, Moab, Edom and Aram, but solely for Abraham's *chosen* descendants? Probably not: just as David ruled over these lands but did not incorporate them in "Israel," so the Chronicler probably reflects an ideal in which the entire territory is subject to Jerusalem. Perhaps this only makes explicit what Genesis hints at: a broader religious community extending beyond the borders of Israel itself.

The account of Josiah's religious purge (2 Chr 34) stresses the pan-Israelite scope that in Kings is no more than hinted at. The fact that this purge *precedes* rather than follows (as in Kings) the restoration of the temple in Jerusalem is appropriate to the Chronicler's understanding that the whole land of Israel is governed by the temple in Jerusalem and should be purified ahead of its sanctuary. This point is emphasized by noting that the gifts for the restoration come not only from Judah and Benjamin but from (mentioned first) "Manasseh and Ephraim and from all the remnant of Israel" (34:9). The Jerusalem temple thus becomes in fact and not just in theory, or even in the face of resistance (as under Hezekiah), the one sanctuary of Israel. Even so, the report of Josiah's desecration of the altar at Bethel that features so prominently in Kings is not found here: it is not part of the intention of *this* narrator to draw attention to disunity and we see again an unwillingness to antagonize non-Judean sympathies.

16. See the discussion in Williamson, *Israel in the Books of Chronicles*, 126–30.

The story of 1 Kgs 13 that is related to Josiah's desecration of Bethel is not recorded in Chronicles. Indeed, only two references to the place are found. The first is 1 Chr 7:28 (already mentioned) in which it is simply listed as one of the cities of Ephraim; the other (2 Chr 13:19) records that Bethel was taken by Abijah from Jeroboam. This capture of Bethel is absent from Kings, and it offers a concrete instance of the defeat of Jeroboam's illegitimate cult, in keeping with the theme of Abijah's speech. It also provides an explanation for a problem we noted in the First History: the assigning of Bethel to Benjamin as well as to Ephraim, and the inclusion of Bethel in the province of Judah later in the Second History. While the "golden calves" are specifically referred to in that speech (2 Chr 13:8), Bethel itself is not named in connection with them. The subsequent capture of Bethel also refers to it as a "city," with no mention of its sanctuary (though it is unlikely that any reader would be ignorant of the cult of Bethel). Since the treatment of Dan is similar (and it was noted earlier that even the tribe itself is absent from the genealogies), we might conclude that the Chronicler is either uninterested in, or wishes to pass over, the existence of rival sanctuaries in the northern part of his "Israel" and to focus exclusively on Jerusalem as the place where even pious "northerners" came to worship. But another implication is that Bethel quickly became, and remained, part of the kingdom of Judah. There is no record in Chronicles of its recapture by Israel. So Bethel joins Judah, in keeping with the focus of Chronicles on Jacob/Israel as Judah's ancestor too.

What does this treatment of Bethel signify? Why are the indications of rivalry between Jerusalem and Bethel that we find in the First History absent from the Second History? The contradiction with Kings is also a contradiction with the book of Amos, in which Bethel is also an Israelite sanctuary in the time of Jeroboam II. In keeping with his eirenic attitude towards the legitimacy of the "northern kingdom," does the Chronicler wish to ignore cultic rivalry? By bringing Bethel into Judah, is he "Judaizing" it?

Let us finally review some key contrasts between the First History and Chronicles relevant to their respective definitions of Israel. The connections between Saul and Benjamin are reinforced by detailed genealogies, and after Saul's death, the conflict between Saul's house and David (2 Sam 2–4) is omitted. The episode of 2 Sam 19:16–18, where the Saulide Shimei curses David, is also absent (though this may not be significant since the whole of 2 Sam 9–20 is unparalleled in Chronicles). Benjamin is regularly mentioned alongside Judah, unlike Kings: in the reign of Rehoboam (2 Chr 11:23), Asa (14:8; 15:2, 8–9), Jehoshaphat (17:17–18), Amaziah (25:5), Hezekiah (31:1) and Josiah (34:9, 32). Apart from the report of the secession under Rehoboam (1 Kgs 12:21–23), Judah and Benjamin are not associated in the First History.[17] The overall impression is of a desire to acknowledge Benjamin and its traditions within Judah.

The presentation of "Israel" in Chronicles also exhibits much less antagonism towards the kingdom than Kings (which may not be unconnected with the more sympathetic attitude towards Benjamin). Chronicles' silence over the internal affairs of this kingdom is not necessarily evidence of indifference or of hostility, as sometimes is concluded: it is even possible that this information was not available to him.[18] Its "Israel" always included the population of the kingdom of Israel, which remained in political and geographical separation from the legitimate part of "Israel" in Judah and Benjamin still ruled by the house of David and worshipped at the Jerusalem temple under the legitimate priesthood. Secession did not preclude some "northerners" from returning to the true Israel, nor does Chronicles absolve many Judean kings from apostasy. With the fall of Samaria, Israel was again united—or rather, the remnant of Israel, which included not only Judah and Benjamin, but those of the tribes remaining to the north. There was once again a united Davidic rule over all Israel, celebrated by Hezekiah and later by Josiah, both of whom effected a religious purge over the entire land and restored the temple, thus uniting "all Israel" under the single cult of Yhwh in Jerusalem. The status of Jerusalem as an *Israelite* (in Chronicles' terms) rather than merely a *Judean* city and sanctuary is also reinforced in two ways. First, as noticed earlier, it is made the home of part of Saul's family. Second, the term "Judah and Jerusalem" regularly appears, as if Jerusalem has a kind of autonomy. Such a usage appears only once in the First History (2 Kgs 23:1), and significantly, in the account of Josiah's reform, reflecting perhaps an ideology and a dating for this story that are not shared with the rest of the books of Kings. It occurs 20 times in Chronicles; and elsewhere four times in Ezra (4:6; 5:1; 7:14; 10:7) (but not Nehemiah), twice in Isaiah (1:1; 2:1, both superscriptions), three times in Jeremiah (19:7; 27:20; 29:2), twice in Joel (3:1, 6) and once in Malachi (3:4).

In general, Chronicles is markedly less *polemical* than Samuel–Kings, especially with respect to Benjamin and Bethel, regarding the supremacy of Jerusalem, the Davidic house and the rule of Judah over Israel. But

17. This silence about Benjamin as part of the kingdom of Judah is reflected in the prophetic literature, with the exception of Jeremiah (on which see Chapter 8)

18. Since we are not assuming the dependence of Chronicles on Samuel–Kings, we should not speak of "omission." It is even possible—if we venture into a critical explanation—that the stories about the kingdom of Israel were added to Kings after Chronicles was written, or later than the source responsible for the common text.

this is not to say that the Davidic dynasty and its capital and temple are not unequivocally presented as the legitimate centre of Israel.

Nothing has been said yet about the *ethnic* integrity of Israel, where the First History left some questions in leaving the extermination of the Canaanites unfulfilled. The category of *ger* (גר), resident alien, among the population of Israel is found only rarely there: it occurs only in Joshua (8:33, 35) and in 2 Sam 1:13, describing an individual who is the "son of a *ger*, an Amalekite." Chronicles, however, uses the word in the plural to designate a major category: in 1 Chr 22:2 David gathers "*gerim* (גרים) residing in the land of Israel" to dress stones for the temple; in 2 Chr 2:17 Solomon takes a census and finds 153,600 such residents; in 2 Chr 30:25, at the time of Hezekiah's Passover, *gerim* from the "land of Israel and from Judah" rejoice with "the whole assembly of Judah, the priests and the Levites, and the whole assembly that came out of Israel."[19] Although the status of these non-Israelites is not specified, it seems clear that they were positively accepted. Japhet notes that "there are no Gentiles in the land of Israel; all its dwellers are 'Israel,' either through their affiliation with the tribes or as the attached 'sojourners.'"[20] The implication is that the genealogies in Chronicles are clearly not meant to be understood too literally, but rather as a social map of "Israel" conforming, of course, to the way we know such genealogies usually work. But in the remainder of the Second History there is a dramatic reversal, as genealogy is used not as a means of expanding "Israel" but contracting it by exclusion.

Finally, where does Chronicles leave Israel at the end of its narrative? According to the First History, not all Judeans were deported and life continued in Judah under Gedaliah for a while. But it is possible that the text wishes us to regard the remainder as having fled to Egypt, leaving the land to foreigners. The Second History entirely overlooks this episode in the life of the province. Chronicles puts the position quite firmly: the "king of the Chaldeans"

> took into exile in Babylon those who had escaped from the sword, and they became his slaves to him and his sons until the founding of the kingdom of Persia, to fulfil the word of Yhwh by the mouth of Jeremiah, until the land had made up for its sabbaths. All the days that it lay desolate it kept sabbath, to fulfil seventy years. (2 Chr 36:20–21)

---

19. Note also the prayer of David in 1 Chr 29:15; "For we are גרים and תושבים before you, as were all our ancestors; our days on the earth are like a shadow, and there is no hope." But probably the metaphor here is one of individual human life and not presence in the land.

20. Japhet, *I & II Chronicles*, 46.

This scenario leaves an emphatically empty land. The conclusion might be drawn from this that we should understand all the inhabitants of Judah to have been regarded as "Israel" and all to have been either been killed or deported. But is it the case that Israel remains now only in Babylonia? Room seems to have been left elsewhere in Chronicles for at least some of the inhabitants of Samaria to be regarded as "Israel," and these remained in Samaria. What is the status of these? Chronicles' ideology of a land lying fallow surely requires that Samaria is also presented as being empty. The ideology of an Israel that includes some in Samaria also implies that after the end of the exile the restored Israel will also include Samaria. But we cannot be sure, since the narrative continues in Ezra and Nehemiah, where a rather different outlook towards Samaria is encountered, and where Judah itself is not "empty" either. Despite the numerous points of agreement between all its components, the Second History does not present us, any more than the First, with a consistent view of who belongs to Israel—and who does not.

Chapter 6

ISRAEL IN THE SECOND HISTORY:
EZRA AND NEHEMIAH

The story of Israel related in this part of the Second History is a more confusing one. The Masoretic tradition regards Ezra and Nehemiah as a single book but the Christian tradition, following the Greek, as two books. This does not in itself complicate a sequential narrative reading. But both books contain first- as well as third-person sections, and each apparently covers the same period yet presents a mostly independent narrative, which is thus not continuous but overlapping.

The problems of disentangling the sequence (chronology) of the main events and the figures and roles of Ezra and Nehemiah are well-charted in the scholarly literature, and are probably insurmountable, especially if there is no straightforward history underlying the account. The easiest way to approach them from the literary and historical point of view is to see them as different versions of a memory about the refounding of Israel in Judah by immigrants from Babylonia in the Persian period. But bringing the two characters together in time and space requires the reader to consider the contents of both as part of a single story.

The centrepiece of this combined narrative is enshrined in the great assembly in Neh 9–10, the one and only place where the characters Ezra and Nehemiah actually meet and where the new Israel is born (or the old one reborn), recapitulating the covenant(s) that inaugurated the earlier Israel. The great prayer uttered by Ezra in this ceremony tells the story of the earlier Israel, at some length, from Abram to the deportations, covering much of the story narrated by the First History. It focuses on Israelite religious apostasy, starting in the wilderness, then under the "saviours" (the judges) in 9:27 and recalls that disobedience was repeated until the final handing over to the "peoples of the lands" (v. 30). It mentions the afflictions that have come upon Israel "since the time of the kings of Assyria until today." Otherwise, however, there is no mention of the erstwhile kingdom of Israel or its successor in Samaria; v. 35 refers to "kingdom" in the singular. Perhaps this reads too much into the account, but nevertheless the territory of Samaria is entirely excluded from Israel in this part of the Second History. Indeed, in Ezra 4:10 the officials refer in their letter to the king to "the rest of the nations whom the great and noble Osnappar (= Ashurbanipal?) deported and settled in the cities of Samaria (referring to the name of the Assyrian province, not the city) and the rest of the satrapy…" We should thus probably infer that all of Israel is regarded as having been deported by the Assyrians. This is not what Chronicles suggests (see 2 Chr 30), but it corresponds to the First History's view.

These components of Israelite history are not necessarily revisited in the same order under Ezra and Nehemiah, but the recapitulation does create a huge typology of the kind that impressed later generations to regard Ezra as a second Moses. In short: the Israel of Ezra–Nehemiah is the old Israel restored, undergoing some of the same experiences, reviving the same memory. Indeed, immigration into a land inhabited by those from whom Israel must separate is a very precise recapitulation.

The centre of the Ezra–Nehemiah narrative is presented as the reconstitution of the old and rebellious Israel in new and obedient Judah, under a political regime that has authorized this restoration but is still characterized as "kings set over us because of our sins" (Neh 9:37). The narrative opens with a Persian decree authorizing the rebuilding of the temple—not a decree of *return*, as such, for the return of Judeans is mentioned only as an agency for the rebuilding. The returnees are to be accompanied by gifts (perhaps a deliberate reminiscence of the exodus; Exod 12:35–36), and the Persian king personally brings out the temple vessels—an important symbolic gesture, not only of authorization and continuity but of the transfer of the royal into the ecclesiastical, one of the key themes of Chronicles (in which "house of David" now becomes not dynasty but temple). The narrative is then interrupted by a list of the returning exiles: not Judeans, but "Israelites," returning to "Judah and Jerusalem." These lists include temple personnel, and the returnees give up their donations on arrival. The altar is rebuilt and the cult reinstated; the temple foundations are laid. The opponents of "Judah and Benjamin" offer to assist and are rebuffed (how they are "opposing" is not explained). The "people of the land" also resist, by intimidation and bribery. So do three named officials and their colleagues, by writing to the king.

The king's reply is that "Jerusalem has had mighty kings who ruled over the whole province of "Beyond the River" (Ezra 4:20). Here the "Abrahamic" territory, which according to Chronicles formed not only the lands ruled by David but the ideal kingdom of Israel—possibly the maximal "land of Israel" makes another appearance. It serves to explain the interest on the part of the officials who represent "Beyond the River," and it also serves to explain the concern and hostility that they are said to display. For them Jerusalem has claims over the whole territory (see below). As a result of their intervention, work in Jerusalem is ordered to be stopped, but is later resumed after an intervention from the satrap of Beyond the River and by Darius himself. Building is finally finished, Passover celebrated, and in ch. 7 Ezra arrives, authorized by Artaxerxes to allow any who wish to return to Judah to do so, and to convey money and gifts for the temple. According to the decree, Ezra is to receive financial assistance from governors throughout Beyond the River, and furthermore is to teach the law and appoint judges for all the people in the satrapy "who acknowledge the laws of your god and to teach those who do not know them" (7:25). It would be possible to read this and the following verse as a command to apply the Jewish law throughout "Beyond the River" but more plausibly it bestows upon Ezra and his law authority for what will become the *ethnos* of Judaism. Even this, how-ever, is somewhat in contradiction to the impression given in the remainder of Ezra–Nehemiah that the social boundaries of "Israel" are to be very strictly confined to those who returned from "exile." But there is one exception. The Passover in Ezra 6 is eaten by "the people of Israel who had returned from exile, and also by all who had joined them and separated themselves from the pollutions of the nations of the land to worship Yhwh, god of Israel" (v. 21). These are not described as "Judeans," and the point is that they "join" Israel: they are not already part of it. Beneath the strict genealogical code and the exclusivist lan-guage is something quite different here. From whom were these "joiners" taken? There is no category called *ger* in Ezra–Nehemiah, and no place for it, apart from this single verse. The literary solution is that such a policy obtained only before Ezra arrived, and was revoked.[1]

Ezra's main task within the book of Ezra is to deal with interbreeding. He learns that Israelites, priests and levites have intermarried with the "Canaanite nations" and others, mixing the "holy seed" (9:2). The phrase suggests that already the Israels of Deuteronomy (separation, covenant) and Leviticus (holiness) are being merged. Ezra offers a penitential prayer and has these marriages broken off. The book closes with a list of those who had renounced their wives. We must note that these "Israelites" are

---

1.   For those literary-historical critics who wish to separate the material in Ezra 1–6 from the material connected with Ezra, this difference provides a further piece of evidence.

all from among the community of "returnees," and the populations from whom wives have been taken are described in the language of Deuteronomy: they are the "nations of 'Canaan.'" Here again is a recapitulation of the first settlement of Israel in the promised land. On this occasion the "peoples of the lands" are also the indigenous population. According to the First History, they would have comprised largely Judeans who were not taken to Babylonia, but here the view of Chronicles is probably being endorsed: nothing of Israel was left in the land; all Israel had been deported. Unlike Chronicles (in all likelihood), the view probably includes all of Samaria as well, at the time of Samaria's destruction under Assyria. As remarked a little earlier, it is therefore hard to see how Ezra will apply the law to all in "Beyond the River" who belong to the cult of Yhwh.

The book of Nehemiah consists mainly of a first-person narrative (the "words of Nehemiah," 1:1). The hero, a slave of Artaxerxes, hears about the sad state of Jerusalem and after a penitential prayer, asks the king to allow him return to rebuild it. The implication is that in the middle of the fifth century (the 20th year of King Artaxerxes) Jerusalem remains unreconstructed and uninhabited ("no houses had been built," 7:4). The reader will find difficulty in reconciling this situation with Ezra 1–6, which describes the lengthy process of rebuilding the temple; the impression is rather that the reconstruction of Jerusalem (and the temple?) is Nehemiah's own initiative (as it is, apparently, in 2 Macc 1–2). Nehemiah is given official authorization and an armed escort. On arrival he starts rebuilding the walls, encountering opposition from Sanballat, Tobiah and Geshem, apparently officials of neighbouring territories. Later (ch. 4) Sanballat and his associates arrive with the "army of Samaria" and wish to prevent the work, though no attack or other venture is recorded. Here, therefore, as in Ezra, we find opposition from local officials; and, Samaria is explicitly named as hostile (cf. Ezra 4:17). Nehemiah also deals with the problem of usury, forbidding the charging of interest on loans to buy food during famine (ch. 5). Despite further opposition, the wall is finished and Nehemiah, wishing to hold a census, finds a written list of the returnees, whose names are given.

In ch. 8 Ezra appears and the first-person narration ceases until it resumes at some point in ch. 13. A celebration of the Day of Atonement follows, and a prayer of confession is recited (ch. 9), followed by the signing of a covenant (ch. 10). The signatories undertake to obey the law of Moses, separate from the "people of the lands," observe the Sabbath and sabbatical year, pay a temple tax and deliver first-fruit offerings and tithes. Jerusalem is now repopulated by conscripting one in ten (ch. 11); a list of the residents in Jerusalem and "in their towns" follows, plus a list of priests and levites. The city wall is dedicated and the temple cult (apparently) commences (again causing the reader to wonder what had been done in the temple up to this point; 12:27–47). Foreigners are then removed, Sabbath reforms made and (again) mixed marriages condemned. The last chapter reintroduces the first-person voice of Nehemiah who ends by commending himself to his god for his efforts at cleansing Israel from foreign pollution and establishing the priestly work.

The Israel of Ezra–Nehemiah is almost completely (see n. 1 above) consistent. Descent plays a major role throughout as an index of membership of the "people of Israel" (Ezra 6:16; see also 2:59), maintaining a strict social boundary between Israel and non-Israel. Both books also use another term for this corporation, "(children/returners of) the *golah*" (Ezra 1:11; 2:1; 4:1; 6:19–21; 8:35; 9:4; 10:6–8, 16; Neh 7:6). As already noted, the continuity of this Israel with previously remembered Israels is both linear (linking back to the remnant of a Judah that was also regarded as a remnant of a once larger Israel) and typological (entrance from outside the land, covenant, separation from inhabitants of the land). In these respects it recapitulates Deuteronomy, but with only three tribes. This new "Israel" does not correspond to any other Israels so far encountered in Judean memory. It is similar to Chronicles, but explicitly excludes Samaria.

The link between "Israel" and the kingdom of David is, as in Chronicles, entirely through the temple: every reference to David, apart from the list of names in Ezra 8:2 and "City of David" (Neh 3:15; 12:37; cf. "graves of David" in Neh 3:16), associates David with the temple worship; again, as in Chronicles, the temple is the symbol of national identity, by means of which a remembered political identity is converted into a religious one.

It is interesting to see how "Judah" and "Israel" are used in these books (Judah 41 times; Israel 53 times). While the two terms have some distinct connotations of their own, for the most part they overlap and are frequently synonymous. "Judah" is used in a *geographical and social* sense[2] (though in several cases which of the two is not clear).[3] Nehemiah 11:36

2. "Jerusalem in/and Judah" (Ezra 1:2–3; 2:1; 4:6; 5:1; 7:14; 10:7; Neh 7:6) and "province of Judah" (Ezra 5:8; Neh 2:5); or "land of Judah" (Neh 5:14). Similarly, "from Judah" (1:2); "in Judah" (13:15); "towns/cities of Judah" (11:3, 20). It is also a *tribal/social* entity: "Judah and Benjamin" (Ezra 1:5; 4:1; 10:9); "Judah" (Neh 4:10); "people of Judah" (contrasted with "people of the land": Ezra 4:4; "house of Judah" (Neh 4:16).

3. "Nobles of Judah" (Neh 6:17); "many in Judah" (6:18); "people of Judah" (11:25; 13:16); "officials of Judah" (12:32); "leaders of Judah" (12:31); "king in/of Judah" (6:7); "Sheshbazzar the prince of Judah" (Ezra 1:8); "nobles of Judah" (Neh

reads "some divisions of the Levites in Judah were joined to Benjamin," which must be either a social or territorial allocation, in which case, "Judah" and "Benjamin" *both* denote geographical or demographic distinctions as well as tribal affiliations (as in "heads of families of Judah and Benjamin," Ezra 1:5).

"Israel" refers to the unified kingdom of the past,[4] and, in the present, to a group defined by descent, especially favoured by Yhwh and obedient to his laws and his worship,[5] except when wrath comes on "Israel" for profaning the Sabbath (Neh 13:18). There is, in addition, a special technical sense (already met in Chronicles): the laity—non-levites and non-priests. This distinction more clearly reflects the liturgical hierarchy that the architecture of the Second Temple, in its various descriptions and realizations, also came to represent in its concentric courts.

In general, then, while "Judah" and "Israel" are co-extensive, the term "Judah" (sometimes with "Benjamin") is confined to the geographical and political, while "Israel" denotes the religious and the genealogical. But both sets of characteristics cohere in the same body. The religious and genealogical definitions of Israel that we have already met in both Histories combine here, except that they are applied to a very restricted group.

The most curious feature of Ezra–Nehemiah, as already mentioned, is the balance between proselytizing and isolationism, between an explicit contraction to Judah itself, and an implicit expansionism within "Beyond the River," representing the maximal extent of the land promised to Abraham's family and won by David and the land allotted to Judah and to Benjamin, the erstwhile "kingdom of Judah." How does the reader reconcile this tension? Perhaps it is not even noticed. But we should not forget that while the "Israel" of Ezra–Nehemiah has often been understood as the historical as well as ideological matrix of Judaism, we know very well that Judaism spread over much of Palestine and beyond, forming a very large diaspora. Had the narrow vision of Israel's community

13:17); "all Judah" (13:12); "language of Judah" (13:24); "Judah rejoiced" (12:44); "I saw in Judah" (13:15).

4.   "King of Israel" (Ezra 3:10; 5:11; Neh 13:26) and to the ideal family of tribes ("sin offering for all Israel...according to the number of the tribes of Israel [=twelve]," Ezra 6:17; cf. "twelve bulls for all Israel," Ezra 8:35).

5.   Ezra 2:59/Neh 7:61; Ezra 10:25; "they separated from Israel all those of foreign descent" (Neh 13:3). Cf. also: "his steadfast love endures forever toward Israel" (Ezra 3:11); the book of the law of Moses, which Yhwh had given to Israel (Neh 8:1); or "the statutes and ordinances in Israel" (Ezra 7:10, 11); "silver and gold...that the king...and all Israel...had offered" (Ezra 8:25); "make atonement for Israel (Neh 10:33).

and territorial extent given in these two books persisted, Judaism would have been a very different religion. What kind of cultural memory, then, is at work here, and constitutive of what kind of "Israel"? A literary reading does not oblige us to view these books as eye-witness accounts or even reliable portraits, but just as stories. But the historian, too, needs to beware of this all too common assumption. The stories may well reflect later Jewish groups who wished to view their origins in this exclusive manner.[6]

Despite its narrative unevenness, the Second History of Israel is less inconsistent than the First. There are unifying themes: the centrality of the Jerusalem cult and the liturgical orientation of nearly all Israelite activity, the importance of genealogy for legitimacy, the ideal extent of the "land of Israel" and the absence of any distinct Judean identity outside Israel. Yet, as with the First History, the definition of Israel does change along the way. It begins in Chronicles in an all-inclusive way, with the full twelve (eleven?) tribes and a unified Israelite kingdom of David and Solomon that politically enshrines that identity. The loss of the ten tribes is temporary, and the fall of Samaria restores unity, although Israel is now confined to the territory of Judah and Benjamin (the two are used together as a territorial and political designation in a way that they are not in the First History), and inhabited by these two tribes plus Levites.

In the deportation to Babylon, Chronicles' view is that all of Judah went into exile (1 Chr 9:1); in Ezra all Judah has become "all Israel" when it returns (6:21). Between the deportation and the return, the Second History creates an ideological as well as a chronological gulf. The history of the land during the exile is a gap in which, with the hindsight offered by Ezra–Nehemiah, there is no Israel in the land at all. Chronicles does not tell us how its "northern tribes" would have fitted in; we have only Ezra and Nehemiah, for whom there are only foreigners or "people of the land" whose idolatrous culture equates them with the "Canaanites" of Deuteronomy (apart from the curious mention in Ezra 6:21). The Second History ends with Nehemiah's claim to have cleansed Israel from "everything foreign."

One aspect of the Israel of Ezra and Nehemiah not yet noted is the nature of the covenant that codifies the relationship between the new Israel and its deity. The covenant with Abraham had, according to Genesis, been given without being asked for, and rests on a divine promise

---

6. The current scholarly view is that the rift between Jews and Samarians, which Nehemiah in particular seems to reflect, occurred later than the fifth century. Moreover, these stories simply do not account for the Samari(t)an Pentateuch.

(significantly, Neh 9:7–8 rewrites the promise through the lens of Deuteronomy, as pertaining to Israel and to its own land only). The covenant at Sinai/Horeb was also a divine initiative, but was then written down, and the people assented to it. The covenant in Neh 9–10 is a signed and sealed document with all the names of those who are party to it. It is also a human initiative. In this and other respects, both books reflect a sectarian mentality: a charter, a membership list with strict criteria, the ban on mixing with outsiders—this Israel (as scholars have noted) is neither a family, nor a nation, but a sect.[7]

7.   I have explored the possibility of Ezra and Nehemiah as sectarian foundation legends in "Scenes from the Early History of Judaism," in *The Triumph of Elohim* (ed. D. V. Edelman; Kampen: Kok Pharos, 1995), 145–82. For a consideration of the Samaritan aspect of the question, see I. Hjelm, *The Samaritans and Early Judaism: A Literary Analysis* (Sheffield: Sheffield Academic Press, 2000).

Part II

ISRAEL IN BENJAMINITE MEMORY

Chapter 7

BENJAMIN'S HISTORY OF ISRAEL

Why Remember Benjamin?

The biblical history/histories/stories that have been read in Part One are, like many histories, the possession, the "cultural memory," of a particular group—or groups—whose identity and self-understanding that memory creates and preserves. That group, or those groups, should almost certainly be identified within the Israel-in-Judah of the Persian and Greco-Roman periods. Both histories run up to, or into, the Persian era. The written and canonized form of these memories was more or less determined by the first century BCE[1] (or perhaps in the second), with additional memories among the diaspora; earlier written forms presumably existed, too, and in this part of the book we shall be dealing with such "sources."

It is important to acknowledge that these histories are Judean cultural memories, though in the case of the Pentateuch, these are shared with Samari(t)an memories. Other memories existed within Judah (within the books of Enoch, for example), and we should not equate Judean memory simply with the biblical texts, which are the canonized memories only, though as such they increasingly served as the history that Jews of later generations inherited, as the "Jewish" memories of ancient Israel. The memories of other Israels (of non-deported Judeans, of Samarians, of diaspora communities, of other Palestinian inhabitants that later adopted Judaism) have preserved little or nothing in literary form and cannot be retrieved, though for Samaritans there are written memories outside the Pentateuch. But without much additional resources we have nothing to correct, to balance, to contextualize, the Judean memory. In this part of the book, therefore, I will suggest that we can recover, with the aid of some literary-historical analysis and some imagination, the outline of one

1. The Qumran biblical manuscripts are, of course, the best evidence we have for the content and form of the scriptural books, as well as for some of the ways in which they were read.

set of memories different from those that have imposed themselves on the canonized texts of Judah. They can be discerned because the Judean memory itself has in part overlaid them without obliterating them. I am referring to the memories of Benjamin that survived perhaps at first outside, but then within Judah. These would have constituted memories of Benjamin itself, but also of the Israel of which Benjamin was once part as well as the Judah to which it later belonged, to a different "Israel." These have all left traces in the Judean memory itself—because Benjamin was part of Judah—and in this chapter I shall try and reconstruct some of these memories from clues that I have mostly indicated already in Part I.

Cultural memory, like all memory, is as much about forgetting as remembering. Judah's canonized memory has blocked out much of the sixth century, for example, mostly everything that occurred in its homeland between the fall of Jerusalem and the project to rebuild it, between the end of the kingdom of Judah and the return of the descendants of the deportees. A small part of this history is narrated in five verses of the First History: 2 Kgs 25:22–26. The Second History, as we have seen, leaves a total gap, for its view is that "Israel" had no history in Judah during that time. Such lapses of memory are not accidental or innocent: they are *deliberately* "forgotten," and it is therefore important to understand why, and to see where this memory may be preserved elsewhere. This is another reason why Benjamin's memories are important. Benjamin did not remember exile in its own history, but did remember what happened at home, as I shall explore in the following chapter.

The aim of this exercise in "memory recovery," then, is not only to relativize the Judean histories, to show that despite their scriptural status, their version of events is *a priori* no more or less "historical" or ideology-free than any other memory, but also to aid in the reconstruction of a modern critical history (our own "memory") of how the various biblical Israels came into being.

The reconstruction attempted here is analogous to that by which Freudian psychoanalysis retrieves the causes of traumas suffered by the patient as a result of repression. To which my reply is: A great deal of the past—almost anything recovered textually—is accessible only through memory—cultural memory, that is. Critical analysis of memory is an indispensable technique of the ancient historian for whom first-hand documentary sources are inadequate. Indeed, there is more to the analogy: where cultural memories "forget," they may be suspected of repressing a recollection that might otherwise be traumatic. Feminist, postcolonial and other ideological methods of reading texts have also shown us how we can recover submerged or suppressed voices and identities from dominant discourses or memories. Of course, Benjaminite and Judean memory will have been to some extent shared; modern Jewish memory does not distinguish them (as far as I know). But Judean memories at times *do* acknowledge Benjamin as a part of an "Israel" that did not include Judah: for example, as the heart of Saul's kingdom and as one of the tribes taken from Solomon and given to Jeroboam, though Judah remembers Benjamin as having decided not to go with Jeroboam. We can see, indeed, that Benjamin is clearly identified alongside Judah in the Second History; thirteen times we find the phrase "Judah and Benjamin"—contrasted with just one in the First History (1 Kgs 12:23). Is the First History "forgetting" something? At the risk of sounding too fashionable, we might call Benjamin "marginal," "liminal" or even hybrid, all terms used to designate areas where identity is dynamic, disturbed or disputed.[2] This is true both of its social identity with the various biblical "Israels" and also of its territory, which can, as mentioned earlier in the book, be regarded as continuous both with the Judean highlands and the Ephraimite highlands. No doubt the two facts are connected. The biblical way of treating tribes is, of course, genealogical, though in places territorial boundaries are prescribed. This supplies an over-simple definition that must in reality have been more complicated. I have no intention of discussing the problem of the biblical twelve-tribe system which, in common with most scholars who have studied it in detail, I would regard, in its canonized forms, as artificial. There are plenty of comparative data to show how such a tribal system may have developed.[3]

In this chapter and the next I am going to argue, then, not only that we can recover traces of Benjaminite memory from the Judean texts we call

2. I am, of course, adopting the notion from the concept invented by Homi Babha, *The Location of Culture* (London: Routledge, 1994).

3. Genesis portrays several other neighbouring "nations" as having twelve tribes: Edom (Gen 25:15–16) Ishmael (36:10–14) and the Horites (36:20–30). The classic studies of the tribal system are those of M. Noth, *Das System der zwölf Stämme Israels* (Stuttgart: Kohlhammer, 1930); and de Geus, *The Tribes of Israel*. See most recently Ulrike Schorn, *Ruben und das System der zwölf Stämme Israels* (Berlin: de Gruyter, 1997). But true cross-cultural comparison needs to go further afield. In 508/7 BCE, Cleisthenes proposed, as part of his "democratic" constitution for Athens, a re-organization of the citizens into ten tribes (*phulai*), though this was apparently aimed at preventing, rather than encouraging, territorial-based identities. Civic service was based on tribal identity. The tribes were named after mythical characters ("Eponymous Heroes"). The Roman tribal system consisted of smaller units (*gens, curia*) and corresponded to settlement areas, thus forming a better comparison with the biblical system. But throughout the course of history the number of tribes changed; it was finally set at thirty-five, functioning essentially as voting districts in the Republic.

"Histories" (and one that is not a "history" but a book of "prophecy"), but that a Benjaminite history was, in fact, at one time written down and then rewritten into the Judean First History. This "textual psychoanalysis" will rely very much on conventional literary-critical procedures. However, following my comments in Chapter 1 about method, I shall rely less on the usual minute source-critical and linguistic dissection—which does not always adequately take account of the complexities of literary (and textual) transmission and rarely produces any consensus on the details—and instead place emphasis on the broader ideological contours, in the manner of an aerial photograph.

Benjamin's History of Israel

To access Benjamin's "History of Israel" we must address the material in which it is now embedded. The invention, or discovery, of the "Deuteronomistic History" by Martin Noth[4] suggested a single exilic author/editor for a work running from Joshua–Kings and prefaced by Deuteronomy. This theory was modified by Cross[5] who proposed a first edition in the time of Josiah and a second after the fall of Judah; a "double redaction."[6] German-language scholarship has tended to follow Smend (formerly Noth's assistant), who proposed, rather than a single work, a sequence of "Deuteronomic" layers dating mostly to the exilic period.[7]

4. M. Noth, *Überlieferungsgeschichtliche Studien*. Vol. 1, *Die sammelnden und bearbeitenden Geschichtswerke im Alten Testament* (Halle: Niemeyer, 1943), 12; ET *The Deuteronomistic History* (Sheffield: JSOT Press, 1981); cf. also Alfred Jepsen, *Die Quellen des Königsbuches* (2d ed.; Halle: Niemeyer, 1956), 94–95.

5. Frank M. Cross, Jr., "The Structure of Deuteronomic History," in *Perspectives in Jewish Learning* (Chicago: College of Jewish Studies, 1968), 9–24; reprinted as "The Themes of the Book of Kings and the Structure of the Deuteronomistic History," in his *Canaanite Myth and Hebrew Epic: Essays in the History of the Religion of Israel* (Cambridge, Mass.: Harvard University Press, 1973), 274–89, and in G. N. Knoppers and J. G. McConville, eds., *Reconsidering Israel and Judah: Recent Studies in the Deuteronomistic History* (Winona Lake: Eisenbrauns, 2000), 79–94. Cross did not produce a systematic treatment, and dealt only with the books of Kings rather than the entire work. For a fuller discussion and defence of the Double Redaction theory, see R. D. Nelson, *The Double Redaction of the Deuteronomistic History* (Sheffield: JSOT Press, 1981).

6. For a convenient documentation of the original proposal and its American—and German—revisions, see Knoppers and McConville, eds., *Reconsidering Israel and Judah*. See also the excellent recent discussion by T. C. Römer, *The So-Called Deuteronomistic History* (London: T&T Clark International, 2005).

7. R. Smend, "Das Gesetz und die Völker," in *Probleme biblischer Theologie* (ed. H.W. Wolff; Munich: Kaiser, 1971), 494–509; W. Dietrich, *Prophetie und*

The basic theory of a Deuteronomistic composition, usually in one or other modified form, is still dominant, though in recent years it has been subjected to some vigorous debate.[8]

Noth's original "Deuteronomistic historian" has been both disintegrated and shifted by these revisions. As with Duhm's "Deutero-Isaiah," who had been located in Phoenicia, this author was also subsequently absorbed into the "exile" by later scholarship. For Noth had suggested a Palestinian/Judean place of composition, Mizpah, but only in a footnote, so that we do not know his reasoning.[9] Yet perhaps this suggestion deserves more consideration than it has received, for the reasoning is straightforward: if such a work were indeed composed substantially in a single effort (with or without the use of existing sources), after the latest events it describes, where else but the provincial capital were the resources to write such a work? The Cross theory, by supposing that the work was already created in the time of Josiah, requires only that it was updated in Babylonia, but the theory of a Josianic origin, while it remains popular, is based on an interpretation of Josiah's reign that is itself suspect as a Deuteronomistic romance.[10] It is also questionable whether even a rosy-tinted view of Josiah and his reign would provide a convincing context for the production of an unparalleled literary enterprise of this kind. In this regard, Noth's context looks at first sight much better, since it understands the work as the product of a trauma involving national identity—the kind of crisis that the production of written texts of cultural memory seem to fit best.

Geschichte (Göttingen: Vandenhoeck & Ruprecht, 1972); T. Veijola, *Die ewige Dynastie: David und die Entstehung seiner Dynastie nach der deuteronomistischen Darstellung* (Helsinki: Suomalainen Tiedeakatemia, 1975) and *Das Königtum in der Beurteilung der deuteronomistischen Historiographie* (Helsinki: Suomalainen Tiedeakatemia, 1977).

8. E.g., L. S. Schearing and S. L. McKenzie, eds., *Those Elusive Deuteronomists* (Sheffield: Sheffield Academic Press, 1999); see also several essays in S. L. McKenzie, T. Römer and H. H. Schmid, eds., *Rethinking the Foundations: Historiography in the Ancient World and in the Bible—Essays in Honor of John Van Seters* (Berlin: de Gruyter, 2000).

9. Noth, *Überliefeungschichtliche Studien*, 110 n. 1 (ET 145 n. 1); cf. also Jepsen, *Die Quellen des Königsbuches*, 94–95. But I can find no further exploration of the possibilities of this location.

10. N. Na'aman, *The Kingdom of Judah Under Josiah* (Tel Aviv: Institute of Archaeology, 1992) = "The Kingdom of Judah under Josiah," *Tel Aviv* 18 (1991): 3–71; P. R. Davies, "Josiah and the Law Book," in *Good Kings and Bad Kings* (ed. L. L. Grabbe; London: T&T Clark International, 2005), 65–77; for a defence of the "Josianic edition" see Römer, *The So-Called Deuteronomistic History*, 67–106.

But Mizpah does not fit Noth's Deuteronomistic History. Mizpah was a Benjaminite city and the biblical texts that refer to the period (2 Kings, but mainly Jeremiah) suggest that its aristocracy and its leading political activists were not "Zionists" (see Chapter 8). The Zionists had been exiled and their city and sanctuary destroyed; the appointed king/governor, Gedaliah, had been assassinated by a Davidide. Noth was right to suggest that a *Judean* history written from here would not be optimistic about Jerusalem, and in accordance with that reasoning he interprets its ending as pessimistic, not, as many other believe, holding out some promise for a restored Davidic monarchy. But it is questionable whether any history written from Mizpah would have promoted the house of David as the divinely elected dynasty or Jerusalem as the divinely chosen city. These themes would have undercut the prestige of Mizpah and its ruling elite, representing the city as a second-best, or even interim, locus, whereas it remained as the capital of Judah for up to 150 years.[11] It would hardly have presented Saul (or Benjamin itself) in such an unfavourable light, nor denigrated neighbouring Bethel. Had there been a history written in Mizpah, and subsequently preserved, it would have been produced under official patronage and thus represented the ideology of the Benjaminite ruling elite. But perhaps such a history *was* written and can be recovered from the present Judean "Deuteronomistic History."

I mentioned in my methodological discussion in Chapter 1 that I prefer ideological criteria as the best approach to an analysis of large-scale literary composition of this kind. According to such a criterion, the "Deuteronomistic History" can be stratified into three levels in each of which we find a different Israel: (a) a group comprising a few tribes (probably Benjamin, Ephraim, Manasseh) in Judges and especially 1 Samuel; (b) a kingdom with its capital in Samaria, a neighbour of the kingdom of Judah, both briefly united (2 Samuel–2 Kings); and (c) a nation comprising the inhabitants of both Israel and Judah, descended from the twelve sons of Jacob (Joshua, the framework of Judges, a few passages elsewhere). If placed in this sequence they represent an increasing integration of Judah into Israel; in the first level, Judah is absent, then as a separate kingdom neighbouring Israel and finally as part of a nation including both Israel and Judah.

An often overlooked but highly significant feature of the "Deuteronomistic History" is that it does not trace the emergence of the kingdom of Judah from Judah's own independent origins. Despite the fact that in

11. For a detailed discussion of this particular question, see D. Edelman, *The Origins of the "Second Temple": Persian Imperial Policy and the Rebuilding of Jerusalem* (London: Equinox, 2005).

1 Samuel onwards Judah appears as a separate "house," we are told almost nothing of the area or the people ruled by David as king of Judah before his assumption of the throne of Israel; it is only as king of *Israel*—a kingdom outside Judah itself—that the narrative has him anointed by Samuel. Of the prehistory of the kingdom of Judah we have only stories of land acquisition and defence that actually belong to its neighbours, and the later addition of Judah to these stories is quite transparent. Judah had, apparently, no such memories of its own (was its origin and settlement so unmemorable?); they were therefore taken from elsewhere. The only Judean material we have concerns David himself: the accounts of David's activities as leader of a small, private armed band, his dealings with the Philistines and installation as king of Judah in Hebron. Later stories about his reign over Israel and Judah are also, of course, Judean, but they tell us nothing about Judah itself before its unification with Israel. Judeans adopted (and subsequently amended) the memories of others for this, when or shortly before they came to "remember" themselves as part of "Israel" and inserted themselves as its dominant tribe. Stories about Judah in Genesis may, of course, be of independent Judean origin, such as the story of Judah and Tamar or about Isaac and Beersheba; but they may equally be embellishments of an ancestral scenario that postdates Judah's adoption of Israelite identity.

What would explain such a borrowing of another's history? The possibility I am suggesting here is that one canonized Judean memory—the "Deuteronomistic History"—is not an autonomous Judean creation but an account fashioned in ideological response to, and partly incorporating, another memory. The response has at least two stages: it advances a *political claim* on behalf of Judah to rule over Israel in a "United Monarchy," and it makes an *ethnic* claim that both Judah and Israel belong to the same people. The two stages can, I think, be isolated within the books of Joshua–Kings.

To what memory would the Judean "Deuteronomistic History" have been responding? The history that Noth believed to have been written at Mizpah, if it had been written, would have been conceived, composed and received in the territory of Benjamin at a time when it found itself in the astonishing position of Judah's capital city, when the city and sanctuary of Jerusalem, which had for a century dominated the region to the point where the Babylonian Chronicle calls it "the city of Judah," were in ruins, its rulers and priests deported. The reversal of fortunes that the fall of Jerusalem brought about not only affected relations between Judah and Benjamin but also between Samaria and Benjamin. We can assume that the government in Mizpah did not regard the restoration of the

Davidic dynasty as its goal, and was interested instead in justifying Jerusalem's demise, a purpose that we shall identify in the earliest form of the book of Jeremiah (ch. 8). A "Benjaminite History of Israel" would serve the complementary role of celebrating Benjamin's historic leadership of Israel in the first days of the kingdom, possibly also countering Judean propaganda about David, though the extent of Judean memories about David at this time are very hard to gauge. It is not at all unlikely that they combined his role as temple founder and composer of liturgies with a handful of stories about his warrior exploits.

The reading of the "Former Prophets" in Chapter 4 identified features that trace the contours of a history in which Benjamin plays the leading role. Its narrative begins in Joshua with the conquest of the territory around Benjamin under Joshua; it continues with a collection of tales of Israelite heroes, initiated by a left-handed Benjaminite, and ends with the judgeship of Samuel, exercised also in the Benjamin area (1 Sam 7:16: Bethel, Gilgal, Mizpah), which leads directly into the anointing of the first Israelite king, also from Benjamin.[12] We might also consider including an episode in which Benjamin defeated a coalition of other tribes, now converted into the climax of the story of Judg 19–21.[13]

These episodes are not extracted haphazardly from the narrative of Joshua–1 Samuel as a set of varied "sources" or "traditions"; they represent a coherent and extended cultural memory, forming a well-plotted sequence, in which the territory of Benjamin remains the orbit of activity (together with some of the Ephraimite hill country to the north), and featuring leaders from that same region: Joshua, Ehud, Samuel and Saul. The narrative is one of charismatic military exploits that lead to the formation of a state in the central Palestinian highlands. The enlargement of this core by other "judges," such as Barak, Gideon and Abimelech, does not upset this pattern; Gideon is a Manassite hero and Abimelech a king of Shechem, both perhaps within the orbit of the Israel that comes to be ruled (according to the narrative) by Saul. The Barak story, like Josh 11, expands the territory towards Hazor and may represent an enlargement of the scope to reflect the boundaries of the kingdom of Israel later in its history.

12.　I remarked earlier that while both Joshua and Samuel are assigned to the "hill country of Ephraim/Mt Ephraim, it does not necessarily follow that this territory is within Ephraim itself (see Chapter 4 n. 3).

13.　This has, in fact, been proposed by O. Eissfeldt, "Der Geschichtliche Hintergrund der Erzählung von Gibeas Schandtat (Richter 19–21)," in *Kleine Schriften*, vol. 2 (ed. R. Sellheim and F. Maass; Tübingen: Mohr, 1963), 54–80.

This is not the place to discuss at length the possible literary prehistory of the Mizpah history being proposed here. Following Richter's thesis of a "Book of Saviours,"[14] that formed the kernel of the later book of Judges, Knauf (followed but also modified by Guillaume) has suggested a composition produced at the Bethel "Seminary" in the immediate aftermath of the fall of Samaria that served to condemn native leadership and argue for integration into the Assyrian empire.[15] Such a literary prehistory should not be ruled out, and Knauf's case for a centre of literary production at nearby Bethel is not inconsistent with the thesis being proposed here.[16] But if the Mizpah history comprises not only purely Benjaminite memory but also some other memories from the kingdom of Israel, the predominance of the Benjamin region is striking, and the stories of Gideon and Abimelech in particular have apparently been moulded to serve the same purpose that Saul himself plays in the Judean memory of David: as examples of unsuccessful or premature attempts at kingship that highlight the successor. A "Book of Saviours" cannot now be isolated *thematically* (even if it can be source-critically) from other elements in Joshua–1 Samuel.

The other aspect of this narrative thread, and equally important, is the clear traces of Judean revision, which underline the absence of Judah from the core narrative, except possibly as falling (partly?) within the sphere of Saul's control (1 Sam 15:4, Telaim/Telem).[17] The conquest of Joshua now includes a tour around Judah; the conquest of the land in

14. Richter, *Traditionsgeschichtliche Untersuchungen zum Richterbuch*, and *Die Bearbeitung des "Retterbuches" in der deuteronomischen Epoche* (Bonn: Hanstein, 1964).

15. E. A. Knauf, "Does Deuteronomistic Historiography Exist?," in *Israel Constructs Its History* (ed. A. de Pury and T. Römer; Sheffield: Sheffield Academic Press, 2000), 388–98; Guillaume, *Waiting for Josiah*. Account should also be taken of the proposal of A. Rofé that an Ephraimite History might be found underlying part of the Deuteronomistic History. Rofé considers that this was written, like Knauf's version of the "Book of Saviours," soon after the fall of Samaria, and centred on the figure of Joshua. See A. Rofé, "Ephraimite versus Deuteronomistic History," in Knoppers and McConville, eds., *Reconsidering Israel and Judah*, 462–74.

16. I have suggested elsewhere that the book of Amos also began as a collection in Bethel, though it acquired its current shape and purpose in Jerusalem; see my "Amos, Man and Book," in *Israel's Prophets and Israel's Past: Essays on the Relationship of Prophetic Texts and Israelite History in Honor of John H. Hayes* (ed. B. E. Kelle and M. B. Moore; New York: T&T Clark International, 2006), 113–31.

17. The connections between Jerusalem and Benjamin in Joshua, Judges (and Chronicles) have already been observed. If there *is* any historical fact behind the story, perhaps archaeologists should be looking for a citadel of Saul rather than David in Jerusalem.

Judges is led by Judah; the first judge is from a Judean clan; Judah leads a war of the tribes against Benjamin, following a scandal at Gibeah (Saul's home town); and, finally, Saul is supplanted by David.[18] An additional feature of this Judean re-"memorizing" is the polemic against Saul and Benjamin in Judges and 1 Samuel. This, even more than other additions, suggests an antagonism that the Second History does not share and that requires an explanation. The most elaborate revision, the integration of Judean stories about David into the career of Saul, makes him Saul's legitimate successor and the greatest king of Israel, turning Saul into a disobedient and divinely rejected persecutor of their hero.[19] Because of this extensive rewriting, it is impossible to trace the original lines of the Israelite story beyond the death of Saul. Perhaps, as I have already hinted, it went no further; the rise of Saul story was perhaps its climax. If so, however, the point of the written account would logically have been the resurgence of Benjamin as a centre of kingship—and perhaps also as the focus of a new Israel that might arise.

The most plausible setting for such a history of Israel's origins lies in the period when the political and religious primacy of Benjamin was being reasserted, along with claims of religious and political solidarity with Samaria and even political leadership of Israel. My suggestion does not, of course, imply any particular degree of historicity: we are dealing with what is not only cultural memory but also political propaganda. The historical connection between Saul's kingdom, whether or whatever it was, and the kingdom later established in Samaria by the "house of Omri" is a different matter altogether, and in fact quite unclear.

If it is correct to identify a Benjaminite history embedded in the canonized Judean one, then the "Deuteronomistic History"—or at least this part of it—was probably written precisely for the purposes of such a revision. It is counter-propaganda, reasserting Judean and Jerusalemite political and religious centrality and criticizing Benjamin, Saul and the

18. Perhaps also, as part of this revision, the story of Saul's birth (see the etymology of Samuel in 1 Sam 20, remarked by several scholars) has been reassigned to Samuel. (In the same vein, Samuel becomes the vindicator of David rather than Saul, whom he is made to denounce.)

19. The story of 1 Sam 6, originally about the end of the line of Eli, is now recast as a story of the loss of the ark, which David recovered and transferred to Jerusalem. But this is not necessarily anti-Saul. He is not blamed for its loss (and according to the MT of 1 Sam 14.18—amended in the LXX for obvious reasons—he subsequently used the ark. There is no reason why he could not have done this if it lay at Kiriath-jearim. Possibly Judean memory simply chose not to remember Saul ever having had access to the ark—apart from this one verse.

kingdom of Israel.[20] As observed earlier, this raises questions about the existence of specifically Judean memories of its own origins, which presumably commenced with David.

The theory of a first "History of Israel" written at Mizpah is just that: a theory. It seems to me to account much better than other explanations for the shape and the content of the memories about Israel's origins in Palestine, the reason for a written text of these memories and a motive for the Judean "re-remembering" as the city regained political and religious leadership in the Persian period. If I am correct, substantial portions of the rewritten "memory" follow closely the lines of the earlier one, for which there was no parallel memory at all. But from the moment David enters, and Judean and Benjaminite memories collide, we should probably reckon with a very great amount of rewriting and invention. It still remains to be shown whether there is any historical counterpart to the stories that concern them both, or the stories about the unified kingdom.

But despite the arguments in favour of such a written work, is there any evidence that literary texts of this (or any other) kind were produced at Mizpah during its period as capital of Judah? Are there also further traces of Benjaminite cultural memory in the Hebrew Bible? I hope to show that the book of Jeremiah provides a positive answer to both questions.

20.   See further D. Edelman, "Did Saulide–Davidic Rivalry Resurface in Early Persian Yehud?," in *The Land That I Will Show You: Essays in the History and Archaeology of the Ancient Near East in Honor of J. Maxwell Miller* (ed. M.P. Graham and A. Dearman; Sheffield: Sheffield Academic Press, 2001), 70–92.

Chapter 8

THE BOOK OF JEREMIAH

Jeremiah is primarily not a narrative book but it enshrines cultural memories of a less distant past than most of the other texts. To a large extent these are quite simple to retrieve: they can, as with the Judean histories in Part I, be read off the page. But to read them as Benjaminite memories requires more than surface reading: it calls for literary analysis. For in its canonized forms, the Jeremiah book is of course a Judean one, and its memories Judean, even if by adoption. We have to ask now about the origins of this scroll and its shape and structures. On these questions there is an immense history of scholarship, which must somehow be allowed for without being immersed in. Opinions on the book's formation range from a virtual transcription of the prophet's sayings, along with some biographical sketches from his amanuensis Baruch, to a "rolling corpus" in which individual pieces of poetry or prose have generated in a fairly haphazard way further comments and expansions—with all kinds of opinions in between.[1] Fortunately, the problem of the two editions of the scroll (the Masoretic and the edition translated in the Septuagint) does not need to be discussed. I shall deal only with the

---

1. Obviously it is impossible to cover in a single chapter the vast scholarly output on Jeremiah. An excellent summary up to the early 1980s is given in L. G. Perdue. "Jeremiah in Modern Research," in *A Prophet to the Nations: Essays in Jeremiah Studies* (ed. L. G. Perdue and B. W. Kovacs; Winona Lake: Eisenbrauns, 1984), 1–32. Of the many commentaries available, the fullest, but also the least easy, is that of W. McKane, *Jeremiah* (2 vols.; Edinburgh: T. & T. Clark, 1986, 1996). For commentaries that argue at each end of the spectrum between maximal and minimal attribution to Jeremiah himself, and consequently historical reliability, see W. Holladay, *Jeremiah* (2 vols.; Hermeneia; Minneapolis: Fortress, 1986–89); J. R. Lundbom, *Jeremiah: A New Translation with Introduction and Commentary* (3 vols.; New York: Doubleday, 1999–2004) takes a similar position, as does R. P. Carroll, *Jeremiah: A Commentary* (OTL; Philadelphia: Westminster, 1986). The generally agreed division of Jeremiah materials goes back to B. Duhm, *Das Buch Jeremia* (KHAT; Tübingen: Mohr, 1901) and was later developed by S. Mowinckel, *Zur Komposition des Buches Jeremia* (Kristiania: J. Dybwad, 1913).

Masoretic edition here, but every analysis and conclusion made about that edition can be transferred or adapted to the other edition. The ideological profile of the two is, as far as I can tell, very similar.

It is important first of all to ask when where, why and by whom this scroll came into existence. Its formation presupposes an obsession with the central event of its hero's career, the end of the kingdom of Judah, along with its prelude and aftermath. But this concern is reflected in different kinds of text. The majority of commentators accept to some degree a classification into three major types. First, and on the general view, earliest, is some poetry mostly in the *qinah* metre typically used for lament, contained in chs. 1:1–23:15. Sommer's demonstration that Second Isaiah shows an awareness of this material but not the remainder of the book[2] is helpful in further isolating it, so long as we do not assume without question that this is the right direction of influence.[3]

The text that is generally regarded as having been added to this original poetic collection falls into two kinds: one is largely prose material that elaborates on the poetry; how the one generates the other has been debated without consensus, but the language of this prose (vocabulary and ideas) is similar to the literature influenced by Deuteronomy. Also Deuteronomistic is the third kind of material, the narrative that begins in ch. 36 and continues to ch. 43.

If there was a historical Jeremiah, he presumably lived as the book sets him, under the last three or four kings of Judah, and was critical of Judah and Jerusalem, predicting their destruction. His threats seem to have been unqualified, like the original words of Amos about Israel. There is very little by way of a positive gloss, and such as there is appears to be secondary to the majority analysis. For example, in chs. 23–24 there are good as well as bad figs among the people, but the good figs are the "exiles of Judah," a group with whom the poetic oracles

2. B. D. Sommer, "New Light on the Composition of Jeremiah," *CBQ* (1999): 646–66. He argues that Deutero-Isaiah knew A and D (30–33) (specifically chs 30–31), plus 27–29 and 33, but not B or C.

3. While the dating of Second Isaiah is conventionally to the sixth century, and written in Babylonia, the original identification of Second Isaiah by Duhm (*Das Buch Jesaia*; Göttingen: Vandenhoeck & Ruprecht, 1892) placed it in Palestine or Phoenicia. A setting within Judah—which I also endorse—was proposed by H. Barstad, "Lebte Deuterojesaja in Judäa?," *NTT* 83 (1982): 77–87, and *A Way in the Wilderness: The "Second Exodus" in the Message of Second Isaiah* (Manchester: Manchester University Press, 1989); P. R. Davies, "God of Cyrus, God of Israel: Some Religio-Historical Reflections on Isaiah 40–55," in *Words Remembered, Texts Renewed: Essays in Honour of John F. A. Sawyer* (ed. G. Harvey, W. Watson and J. Davies; Sheffield: Sheffield Academic Press, 1995), 207–25.

express no sympathy. We also find a promise of return from exile (e.g. 30:10) and restoration of the Davidic monarchy (e.g. 23:5), sentiments sparsely expressed, and contradicted elsewhere in the book by stringent denunciation; their presence here is reminiscent of the ending of Amos 9 (where they are also widely recognized as an expansion of an earlier corpus). The promised punishment on Babylon in 25:8–14 presumably belongs to this secondary layer too, since it hardly makes sense in the context provided for the original words of the prophet, nor does it seem to reflect his sentiments towards Babylon during the final days of the kingdom of Judah.

If chs. 1:1–25:15—or rather the original collection, represented more or less among these sayings—represents a corpus attributed to a prophet named Jeremiah, then here we have the beginnings of the process that formed the book. We do not need to assume that the portrait of the prophet in the book is accurate or based on reliable knowledge. But it should at least represent a plausible profile, and it is more likely that a collection of oracles originated from a single author than an editor assembling and expanding a diverse selection. This judgment is not certain, but merely probable. In any case, we should assume the normal ancient Near Eastern practice by which the words uttered by prophets were often written down and communicated to their recipient, who was usually the king, then deposited somewhere, in a palace or sanctuary.[4] Without some kind of originating hero or author the book's existence is hard to explain. Since we have a written text of these oracles, they would at first, according to the usual practice, have been retained in a temple or court archive. But where? Jerusalem comes first to mind, since it was the city in which Jeremiah is depicted as having spoken and the recipient of most of his remarks. But if so, the texts would not have survived unless they were transferred, presumably along with other administrative archives, to the new capital of Judah, Mizpah. Some transfer of texts probably did occur in order to facilitate continued administration of the province/kingdom. But it is unlikely, in any event, that they had by this stage been assembled into a collection, in scroll form, in either court or temple at Jerusalem. One can hardly see a reason for such a transcription having been undertaken, and certainly not completed, during the final days of the city. More probably the oracles were still recorded and archived separately.

At Mizpah, however—whether these were transferred from Jerusalem or first written down here—these texts would have become favourably

---

4. For a sketch of the model, see my "'Pen of Iron, Point of Diamond' (Jer 17:1): Prophecy as Writing," in *Writings and Speech in Israelite and Ancient Near Eastern Prophecy* (ed. M. Floyd and E. Ben Zvi; Atlanta: Scholars Press, 2000), 65–81.

regarded, retained, copied and expanded into a longer elaboration of the main themes. There are several reasons for this treatment. The most convincing is that some of these words are addressed to "Israel." In a number of cases it is clear that this "Israel" does not include "Judah." "House of Israel" occurs 14 times in MT 1:1–25:15 (40 times in the entire book). In five of these cases the phrase is set alongside "house of Judah" (3:18; 5:11; 11:10, 17; 13:11; [cf. 31:27, 31; 33:14]). We should add 9:26 (cf. also 48:13), where Judah is named separately, alongside Egypt, Edom, Ammon, Moab and others. Chapter 10 could well be viewed in the same way, though the language is reminiscent of Isa 40–55 and so *might* imply a similar audience and context, namely a redefined "Israel" and the "portion of Jacob" that includes Judean returnees, whether or not exclusively. In the six remaining cases of "house of Israel" we cannot be certain.[5] As in Amos 9:14, during the development of the scroll over time, "Israel" has come in a few places to be re-read as meaning "Judah," but, again as in Amos, the words are originally addressed to the kingdom of Israel. At the time in which the prophet Jeremiah is placed, that kingdom was defunct and in the memory preserved in the First History the name had been dropped as a term for the inhabitants of Samaria. But there is no reason why the inhabitants themselves would abandon the name, nor the people of Benjamin (including Jeremiah and the governors of Judah in Mizpah). Indeed, the Bethel cult must have kept the name alive (and even this is hinted at in 2 Kgs 17, where Bethel is the site from which the new settlers are said to have been taught the indigenous cult.

If we look at the term "Israel" alone in 1:1–22:14, excluding "house of Israel" and "god of Israel" (plus the divine title "hope of Israel" in 14:8 and 17:13) we find that in six and very probably eight of the seventeen cases it denotes what had once been the kingdom of that name: 3:6, 8, 11, 12; 16:15; 23:6, 13; probably also 2:3 and 7:12). Two cases (4:1 and 6:9) fit Judah better, and in the remaining cases it is impossible to be sure whether Israel, or Judah, or Israel plus Judah, is meant (and of course the meaning can have been interpreted differently at different periods).

"Jacob" also occurs four times in 1:1–25:14; in 2:4, 10:16 and 10:25 we cannot know the precise referent. In 5:20, however, the parallelism suggests Judah. "God of Israel" occurs eleven times, "hope of Israel" twice—in many or most cases probably applying to Judah, but often

---

5. The phrase in 2:4 ("house of Jacob, and all the families of the house of Israel") may include Judah; the contexts of 2:26 and 3:20 suggest that the kingdom of Israel may have been originally in mind, but has been reinterpreted as Judah, and the same is true of 18:5–6 (see also 31:33 and 33:17). In 23:8 either Israel or Israel plus Judah might be meant, but 5:15 seems more likely directed at Judah.

more than one meaning is possible. More significantly, in 13:12 and 21:4 "God of Israel" is identified as "Yahweh" and, more explicitly, "Yhwh Sebaoth, god of Israel" occurs altogether 35 times out of only 44 in the entire Hebrew Bible.[6] "God of Israel," as we have seen, is found throughout both Histories, in the context of the kingdom of Israel but also of Israel-plus-Judah, and it is often accompanied by the name Yhwh. The emphasis with which the book of Jeremiah seeks to equate "god of Israel" with "Yhwh Sebaoth" suggests that their identity needs affirming and is therefore of recent invention. Yahweh Sebaoth is usually associated with the Jerusalem cult, but if "god of Israel" is not a common synonym (as it is clearly not, given the rarity of the collocation outside Jeremiah) it belongs elsewhere, probably in the kingdom of Israel. If it is indeed synonymous with "god of Jacob," as I suggested in Chapter 4, it almost certainly points to the deity worshipped at Bethel, with "Israel" alluding primarily to the eponymous ancestor and his worshipping descendants. though the deity was probably also worshipped at the other Benjaminite cult centres and if Bethel was indeed a royal sanctuary, had been a title of the dynastic god. If this reasoning is correct, the book of Jeremiah is attempting an accommodation between the devotees of the Jerusalem cult and that of the sanctuaries of Benjamin, especially Bethel.

So, while we can take it for granted that the book as we have it is Judean, and that Jeremiah is understood to have been a Judean prophet whose words were directed at Judah, the presence of words addressed to Israel needs explaining, even if—and especially if—that "Israel" has been redefined or re-read as including Judah (the "Israel" of Chronicles), or even as referring to Judah exclusively (the "Israel" of Ezra–Nehemiah).

"Israel" and "Judah" cannot, however, be neatly separated within the book. The prophet who is represented as speaking to both Israel and Judah here (be he real or fictional is unimportant) is described as a Benjaminite, and he will therefore be expected to have participated in cultural memories that are both Israelite and Judean. He may be based in Jerusalem, but he is a native of Anathoth (1:1; cf. 32:8, 17), and at one point demonstrates his allegiance to his kin by calling on Benjaminites to flee Judah (6:1). The book reflects the geographical distinctiveness of the territory: 17:26 and 32:8, 44; 33:13 and 37:12 refer to the "land of Benjamin" (the "gate of Benjamin" is also named twice). "Land of Benjamin" occurs only four times elsewhere in the Bible (Judg 21:21; 1 Sam 9:4; 16; 2 Sam 21:4), and this concentration suggests a special Benjaminite awareness. But there is of course much more to this than mere

---

6. The occurrences outside Jeremiah are Isaiah (×3); 2 Samuel (×1); 1 Chronicles (×1); Psalms (×2); Zephaniah (×1); Malachi (×1).

consciousness, given the political context that the book projects (and to a large extent also reflects). Jeremiah is presented, during the closing years of the kingdom of Judah, as one of a number of people urging capitulation to Babylon. When Jerusalem falls, the Babylonians raze the temple, deport some or all of residents and transfer the capital to Mizpah, installing as ruler a Gedaliah who is mentioned in the book several times and is known to Jeremiah—indeed, gives him support. Gedaliah is assassinated by a member of the Judean royal family ("house of David"), but the consequences are not related, except that a number of Judeans asked Jeremiah what they should do; he advised them to stay, but they preferred to go to Egypt, taking Jeremiah with them. There he continued his activity, including denunciation of the host country. In broad terms at least, the public events recorded in the book *did* take place. Jerusalem was rendered incapable of functioning as a capital and its temple continued in use either not at all or in a very minor capacity. We can establish through archaeology that the area around Jerusalem was severely depopulated at this time, while settlement in the land of Benjamin, where little or no destruction took place, was most densely concentrated.[7] Jeremiah's reported move to Gedaliah in Mizpah (40:6) is exactly what such a character would have done and whether or not it is a historical datum, it testifies to a connection between the character, the book and Mizpah. Jeremiah's flight into Egypt, on the other hand, may or may not be a reliable datum. It is hard to understand how, if he had ended his life there, a book of his oracles would have come into existence unless there was already a substantial collection in Mizpah; such travels late in life are sometimes attributed to famous characters to link distant communities with figures from the homeland or bestow prestige on local sites and institutions (e.g. the apostles Paul in Spain and Peter in Rome, Joseph of Arimathea at Glastonbury). A colony of Benjaminites in Egypt might well at some later stage find have found this book ideologically quite congenial as well as an account of their colony's origin.

Many scholars nevertheless consider that the book was initiated as a single written text by Jeremiah in Jerusalem, and thus by the prophet himself, dictating to Baruch (the story in ch. 36 claims this was done twice), and that either written copies or memories of his spoken words were

---

7. For a full discussion of the evidence, see O. Lipschits, *The Fall and Rise of Jerusalem* (Winona Lake: Eisenbrauns, 2005); a useful survey of data and scholarly opinion is given in J. Middlemas, *The Troubles of Templeless Judah* (Oxford: Oxford University Press, 2005). Also of importance is O. Lipschits and J. Blenkinsopp, eds, *Judah and the Judeans in the Neo-Babylonian Period* (Winona Lake: Eisenbrauns, 2003); cf. also R. Albertz, *Die Exilzeit. 6 Jahrhundert v. Chr.* (Berlin: Kohlhammer, 2001).

taken to Babylonian by the deportees. The story of the origin of the scroll is hardly a reliable account:[8] for one thing, it presupposes that the contents had never been orally delivered before, expressing a curious notion of prophetic behaviour that separates the reception of the word and its delivery (and thus makes nonsense of the highly varied contents). Those deportees who are widely believed to have expanded the original collection were mostly supporters or servants of the royal house, groups that Jeremiah had opposed, some of whom are represented as trying to have him killed. It is implausible, if romantic, that such people would suddenly realize he was right and completely change their minds about him to the extent of carrying away his words to meditate, preserve and develop.[9] Those who, on the other hand, *would* have taken a sympathetic stance to Jeremiah remained in Judah and Benjamin. It is more likely that the scroll of Jeremiah began its life in these more sympathetic surroundings.

The least problematic, and indeed most obvious location for the origins of the book of Jeremiah is Mizpah, where Jeremiah reportedly ended up.[10] Here both a collection of oracles attributed to the prophet and an extended narrative about the events in which he took part are most likely to have occupied the local scribes, for specific reasons. The two kinds of material complement each other as in other prophetic books, but here more emphatically: the events vindicate the sayings, and the sayings explain the events. The narrative and the oracles belong together to form an argument that was, in this time and place, worth saying: that Jerusalem's fall was deserved.

Whether we can be more precise about the date of this collection other than to date it somewhere in the sixth century is another matter. The

8.   The literary and ideological construction of the story is widely acknowledged, as well as its Deuteronomistic language. Carroll (*Jeremiah: A Commentary*) regards it, like most of the biographical details of the prophet, as fictive. Many scholars nevertheless assume an underlying historical truth (for a restatement of this position, see J. A. Dearman, "Composition and Context in Jeremiah 36," *JBL* 109 [1990]: 403–21). Many of the points made by Dearman concerning the degree of historical reference in Jeremiah as a whole are well made.

9.   Such an explanation is offered by E. W. Nicholson, *Preaching to the Exiles: A Study of the Prose Tradition in the Book of Jeremiah* (Oxford: Blackwell, 1970).

10.   Thiel's major study of the Deuteronomistic redaction of the book also concluded that the book was more or less completed in Judah by 550 BCE; see W. Thiel, *Die deuteronomistische Redaktion von Jeremia 1–25* (Neukirchen: Neukirchener, 1973) and *Die deuteronomistische Redaktion von Jeremia 26–45* (Neukirchen: Neukirchener, 1981). Whether the Deuteronomic language and ideology can be connected with Mizpah or Bethel rather than Jerusalem is an interesting question: the book's "northern" origins have often been suspected. The ideology of the so-called *Deuteronomistic* literature, however, is clearly connected with Jerusalem.

important conclusion is that by the time Jerusalem resumed its role as capital of Judah, somewhere in the second half of the fifth century, this scroll existed, and was transferred, probably along with other documents, to Jerusalem (with the books of Amos and Hosea perhaps transferred from Bethel) and further edited, ultimately in two different versions.

If this reasoning is right, the scroll, though always in one sense "Judean," but more specifically Benjaminite, and its sympathies accordingly lay with the new regime. It celebrates the fall of Jerusalem with rather more *Schadenfreude* than grief, certainly by comparison with other biblical writings; it has, as we have noted, an ongoing interest in the "house of Israel," and it suggests a merging of the deities of Yhwh Sebaoth and El Yisrael, implying a union of Israelite and Judean cults. Indeed, these features complement those of the Benjaminite "history" discussed in the previous chapter, which celebrated Benjamin's political leadership and hint at an ambition to bring together both Israel and Judah (to both of which Benjamin belonged).

A number of scholars nevertheless hold that Jerusalem continued as a cult centre in a diminished way and even enjoyed allegiance from Samaria.[11] The strongest (only?) piece of evidence in support is the story in Jer 41:5 of 80 men from Shechem, Shiloh and Samaria "bringing grain offerings and incense to present at the temple of Yhwh." The usual view is that these men were on their way to Jerusalem, which was at the time in ruins. Joseph Blenkinsopp has argued, however, that they were on their way to Bethel (or it may have been Mizpah itself; the sites are only a few kilometres apart), and were killed in Mizpah by the Davidide Ishmael. Their murder makes less sense if they were, in fact, mourning for Jerusalem and intending to go there than if they were instead continuing their long-established ties with an Israelite sanctuary.[12] It actually makes little sense that Samarians would mourn the destruction of Jerusalem when the outcome had been of benefit to other sanctuaries that were closer, previously connected with the kingdom of Israel and now under a regime that was surely favourable to them. (We might also consider, given Judah's role in the events that had led to the destruction of their own kingdom, that Jerusalem was not regarded with especial affection.)

---

11. Most recently Middlemas, *The Troubles of Templeless Judah*, 125–44; M. D. Knowles, *Centrality Practiced: Jerusalem in the Religious Practices of Yehus and the Diaspora in the Persian Period* (Atlanta: Society of Biblical Literature, 2006), 30.

12. Ezra 4:2 is often cited as evidence for a continued cult of Yhwh in the province Samaria, where the "adversaries of Benjamin and Judah," as they are called, represent themselves as the descendants of those brought in by Esarhaddon [*sic*]. This merely endorses the view in 2 Kgs 17.

Since the story also does little credit to the line of David, it is much more likely to have been part of the earlier Jeremiah collection and perhaps intended to discredit that dynasty further. The reference to their shaven beards and torn clothing, however, makes no sense on this interpretation, and arises from a later Jerusalemite reinterpretation of the journey as a pilgrimage of grief to Jerusalem, underlining the superiority of that sanctuary to any other, even for Samarians.

If so, this adjustment would be part of a larger set of transformations in the book that reflect its relocation to a Jerusalem setting. The most striking transformation is in the prophet's own behaviour. Jeremiah is not represented in most of the words attributed to him as having felt much grief over the fall of Jerusalem and its temple and dynasty. The destruction of the old Israelite shrine of Shiloh is mentioned in three places in the book of Jeremiah—and nowhere else in the Bible (7:12–14; 26:6–9; 41:5). *Here* is a Benjaminite memory and it is used to put Jerusalem's destruction into its context. The Jerusalem additions to the book, however, have him desolated over what he has to say, largely by the device of including several anonymous laments that are made to appear as his inner speech to the deity and foreground his despair at being given his commission.

The original collection was also more interested in the future of Judah and Benjamin (and Israel) than of the deported Judean aristocracy, whom Jeremiah tells to stay where they are and forget about returning. By contrast, one long section, ch. 3, appears to be a promise of return of the Israelites deported from Samaria. It has of course been glossed from a Jerusalem perspective: v. 14 refers to Zion and v. 17 makes Jerusalem the "throne of Yhwh"; "all nations shall gather to it, to the presence of Yhwh in Jerusalem." But it also ends with "in those days the house of Judah shall join to the house of Israel, and together they shall come from the land of the north to the land that I gave your ancestors for a heritage" (v. 18). This might be a piece of Zionist redaction too, but the "joining" of Judah and Israel was already a possibility, even a policy, under the rule of Mizpah. This text (like others in the book) does not, however, speak of *reuniting* a single nation, but, like Kings, recognizes two "houses." Because of its "Deuteronomistic" prose, the book is more reminiscent of the books of Kings, but its attitude towards Israel is closer to Chronicles in its sympathy for what was now Samaria. Unlike Chronicles, however, its union of the two is not predicated on the centrality of Jerusalem, but on the liminal territory between Judah and Israel, the home of the ancestral cult of Israel and birthplace of the Israelite kingdom.

On this interpretation, the book of Jeremiah anticipates the union of Judah and Israel that will later be adopted as the orthodoxy of Jerusalem and become the "biblical" Israel that in various forms the Histories all exhibit. Let us take one detailed textual example of how this sort of development is reflected in the book. It is quite characteristic of the often complex structure and sometimes irretrievable history of many passages, but it illustrates the play between Israelite and Judean interests. Chapter 3 opens with an address to Israel, with the language of vv. 1–5 reminiscent of Hosea. It opens with a probable allusion to Deut 24:1–4 forbidding a man who has divorced his wife from remarrying her after she has mean-while been married to another. In both texts the law is clearly intended as a metaphor of Israel and its god. The closing in v. 5 "will he be angry forever, will he be indignant to the end?" suggests that the divorce has already taken place and there is no future. The prophet (again, we can speak of the implied author, not necessarily a historical person) com-ments (like Hosea but unlike Amos) as an insider on the religious life of Israel. Verse 5 is a predictable enough conclusion: "you have done all the evil you could"; but what follows is addressed to Judah: "you have seen what your sister did: but you are actually worse" (v. 10)! "Sister" may connote no more than "neighbour" or, from a Benjaminite point of view, something closer. But it invokes the parallel between the fates of the two neighbours in a way that brings them together; and indeed, their fates are now to be seen as the work of the god that they now share. The perspec-tive is "Israelite" ("your sister Judah"). But we then have the words "go and proclaim these words towards the north" and "I will bring you to Zion"; these imply a Judean perspective. The idea of return to Zion does not need to point to a perspective in Babylonia, but to those Judeans for whom exile and return (not necessarily recent) provided a determining experience, the perspective that drives the books of Ezra and Nehemiah (as well as Daniel and several of the Qumran scrolls). Here "return" means "come back home." But "return, faithless Israel" in v. 12 delivers the other meaning שׁוּב, not "come back" but "change your ways." Here is an original address to Israel (but also, not doubt also to Judah) now recycled to apply to Judeans whose memories of Jerusalem's period of demise recall Babylon, not their homeland. And the outcome also changes: at the outset it seems that no future is envisaged, while vv. 15–17 offer a rosy future in Zion (the same happens in Amos). This passage is instructive in several ways. It is a microcosm of the strategies by which the book has been made to serve several interests and deliver several messages, all of them involving in some way the question of Judean and Israelite relationships and identity.[13] But it also demonstrates

---

13. 23:13–15 also makes an unfavourable comparison of Judah with Samaria, but offers no promise to either.

a complexity that resists neat unravelling. We can see the kind of engagements that have produced this text, but we cannot produce an agreed account of how it reached its present form. Hence my own preference for drawing back from over-precise reconstructions of texts or authors in favour of broader ideological interests. Many other passages (especially ch. 31) provide equally good examples.

The themes, the literary history (in general, though not in detail) and the historical context projected by the book of Jeremiah all fit together to create a coherent picture of why the book came into being and was preserved. The two great ironies of the book are that a prophet initially projected as a Benjaminite chauvinist is later made into a Judean, Deuteronomistic prophet and the unified Israel that the book begins to intimate is overlaid by various "Zionist" projects in which either a united Israel is ruled from Jerusalem or, indeed, only exiled Judah survives to bear the Israelite identity. Jeremiah has been turned into a figure more amenable to a Judean "Israel." He is made to be reluctant over the harsh message he has to proclaim, and many of his sayings about Israel are now directed towards the new "Israel," now centred on Jerusalem. But just as Benjamin had brought a part of Israel into Judah, and the Neo-Babylonian period brought Israel and Judah somewhat closer together through the leadership of Benjamin, so the book of Jeremiah served to promote a cultural process that may well have been anticipated in this area for a century or more (both Judah and Samaria had been under Assyria before becoming Neo-Babylonian provinces) but could now flourish without the counterweight of Jerusalem: two societies were forming a single religious community, worshipping the same deity at some of the same sanctuaries. If there is a single birthplace of what we commonly think of as "biblical Israel," this is it. That this occurred precisely because Jerusalem no longer played any role perhaps constitutes the trauma that caused Judean cultural memory to forget this period entirely, to forget where its "Israelite" identity came from and to generate alternative stories with Judah and Jerusalem in the "correct" place.

Part III

JUDAH AND ISRAEL IN
CRITICAL HISTORICAL MEMORY

Chapter 9

JUDAH AND ISRAEL AS NEIGHBOURS

In this final part of the book, we put literary reading and ancient cultural memory to critical use. In a way, we lay our own kind of scholarly cultural memory over the memories of others and retell the story as we like to understand it, which is (ideally) from evidence and argument.[1] This is how critical historians try to "remember"; in a rational manner, by using data, critical analysis and reasoning. The results are not "objective," for all histories are narratives about a past that has itself no intrinsic narrative, only chronology. All connections in the past are interpreted. But this is how our modern historians do history, ostensibly more interested in the past for its own sake, and bothered by "what really happened" instead of addressing the historical phenomenon represented by cultural memories that have little interest (or knowledge of) an objective past, and in which factuality is no criterion, but the preference or necessity of ongoing cultural (re-)definition or action.

There are also the kinds of postmodern metahistory that deal less with facts and more with the way we construct history itself, which are equally important. For among other things they prompt us to realize that, at least in civilizations nurtured on the Bible, the scriptural histories of ancient Israel function as our history too, as part of our cultural origins. What the Bible itself "remembers" is part of an ongoing identity-affirming process, and to challenge it is still to challenge modern cultural identity. That is partly why biblical history differs so much from other ancient histories in the intensity with which it is debated.[2] Such debates are not merely about the events of two thousand and more years ago, but about what we are

1. It is hard to deny, however, that Jews, Christians and non-believers may have different cultural memories that affect the way they tell ancient Israelite and Judean history.

2. I have expanded these observations in "Whose History? Whose Israel? Whose Bible? Biblical Histories, Ancient and Modern," in *Can a History of Israel Be Written?* (ed. L. L. Grabbe; Sheffield: Sheffield Academic Press, 1997), 104–22.

and believe here and now. Are modern critical histories of ancient Israel also a form of cultural memory? It's an intriguing question, and I am inclined to reply that they are not, but that they are consciously engaging, whether they like it or not, with modern cultural memories and indeed, they also themselves tend to be influenced by them. Debates about the reliability or otherwise of the biblical story are debates about the validity of a memory and identity, and even where the historian sets out to resist this cultural influence, it shows itself inescapable, whether in overreaction or compromise. But that does not mean that the principles of critical history are themselves defective, and in the end I prefer to believe that we can and should approach ancient Israelite history as we would ancient Chinese or Mayan history—the only difference being in the nature of the source-material, and not in the way we approach the task of accumulating data—interpreting it and fashioning a rational narrative. The difference between a critical and uncritical history in the end is that a critical one can be challenged by using it own rules. It is in principle self-correcting. Cultural memory does not work that way.

In reviewing the ancient cultural memories of Israel and Judah, I indicated now and then places where a literary reading was unable to move beyond the contradictions and paradoxes that it observed, and noted that if such questions were to be addressed, literary-historical methods (or literary-critical, as they are sometimes called) were the means to do so. In this chapter I shall rely upon this kind of exegesis in discussing the evidence for the historical relationship between ancient Judah and Israel, using archaeological data and a critical analysis of biblical texts. This kind of analysis also adopts certain methodological presuppositions, such as the indivisibility and interaction of all human activity, and the insistence that only human and natural causality can be taken into account. (These presuppositions are often attacked as subjective, but none of the attackers, as far as I know, ever questions their use outside the scope of the Bible.)

A very brief reminder of some of the major "cultural memories" from the preceding chapters may be helpful here. In the First History, the Pentateuch presents Israel as one part of a larger Abrahamic family that is promised land by the patriarchal god. The family of Jacob/Israel becomes a twelve-tribe nation that experiences formative events together before it enters the land it has been promised. In Joshua and Judges this twelve-tribe Israel begins to give way to more partial definitions; the conquest in Joshua does not cover the whole land, but focuses on a small area in Benjamin, though the land allocation covers all the tribes. In Judges the twelve-tribe Israel is restricted to a formal framework and a few later additions; most of the content presents the activity of individual tribes and their heroes, possibly exploring the possibilities of collaboration and even kingship. In 1 Samuel we encounter an Israel consisting of a small number of tribes led by Benjamin and excluding Judah (an exclusion we can already detect at points in Judges). In 2 Samuel–Kings, the story becomes one of a separate Israel and Judah, briefly united through David until Rehoboam, after which the separate kingdoms ("houses") once again go their own way. At the fall of Samaria, Israel ceases forever; it goes into exile and is replaced by foreign importees who adopt the trappings of Yahwism alongside their own idolatrous cults. Judah follows, though it is not lost in exile; it retains its king and its identity in Babylonia.

In the Second History, whose historical narrative begins properly with the death of Saul, the twelve-tribe Israel becomes the united Israel of which David is king and Jerusalem the eternal capital. The secession of some tribes creates a temporary political division that is finally brought to an end with the fall of Samaria, after which Israel has only one king, in Jerusalem. After the fall of Jerusalem, the books of Ezra and Nehemiah focus on what they regard as the only remnant of Israel, the descendants of those Judeans who went into exile. No other population of the territories of either Judah or Israel belongs to the people of Israel.

Judah's relationship to Israel in these narratives is variously described. The books of 2 Samuel and Kings do not join them into a single nation; the Pentateuch, Joshua and parts of Judges do, and so does Chronicles: for Ezra and Nehemiah, Judah (or rather, the exiles of Judah) *is* Israel. The Benjaminite memories, as they have been reconstructed, do not include Judah as part of the nation of Israel. But all sources agree that Benjamin became part of Judah after having been part of Israel.

To provide a modern critical history of ancient Israel and Judah one ought to include at least the Samaritan memories too. The fact that the biblical texts are our only major literary source does not justify equating ancient Israel or Judah with "biblical Israel." But this book *is* about biblical Israel, and in any case, the Samaritan memory includes the Pentateuch; that much cultural memory (with very slight differences)[3] is shared. Still, it is important to recognize that a modern history of ancient Israel should include post-722 Samaria on equal terms with Judah, both the kingdom and then the province.

What follows is by no means an account of ancient Israelite and Judean history, nor even of the history of the biblical Israels. The aim is to focus on some key episodes or features of the historical relationship between Israel and Judah, where the question of the relationship between

---

3.   The major difference of substance is the replacement in Deut 27:4 of Mt Ebal by Mt Gerizim, the site of the Samaritan's sanctuary.

Judah and Israel can be explored and tested. As much weight as possible (but no more!) will be attached to non-biblical evidence, our only direct source of confirmation of the textual memories in the Bible.

The Settlement of Israel and Judah in Palestine

By the overwhelming consent of informed archaeologists and historians, the Israel of the Pentateuch is not historical. In some cases, the story simply cannot be verified (by their very nature, we can never verify the stories of the ancestral family affairs in Genesis, for example); in others it can be denied (e.g. travel from Egypt, conquest). The origins of Israel have been identified, as a result of the West Bank surveys undertaken by Israeli archaeologists, collated with excavation results,[4] in small farming communities in the central Palestinian highlands that appeared at the beginning of the Iron age (ca. 1250 BCE), typically in clearings made from the heavily forested hills. Although there are numerous issues and disagreements about the chronology of these settlements and the place of origin of this population, the material culture points unambiguously to Canaan itself (including perhaps Transjordan). Nevertheless, the social, geographical and economic features of these settlements (intermarriage, economic cooperation, shared defence, economic self-sufficiency and lack of extensive contact with neighbouring areas) will have fostered, over generations, the growth of a distinctive ethnic identity different from the kinds of identity formed within the city-state systems of Late Bronze Age Canaan. From this population—and from similar ones that formed in Transjordan at around the same time—emerged a new kind of society, one that was based on relations between villages that were typically understood and expressed in terms of kinship and did not inherit the social and political structures of the city-state system.[5]

4. For a detailed presentation of the results of surveys and excavations region by region, see I. Finkelstein, *The Archaeology of the Israelite Settlement*; further, I. Finkelstein, Z. Lederman and S. Bunimowitz, eds., *Highlands of Many Cultures: The Southern Samaria Survey—The Sites*, vol. 1 (Tel Aviv: Institute of Archaeology, 1997); of the important Manasseh survey by Zertal, only vol. 1 is at present available in English: A. Zertal, *The Manasseh Hill Country Survey*. Vol. 1, *The Shechem Syncline* (Leiden: Brill, 2004); vols. 2–3 are at the time of writing still in Hebrew: *The Survey of the Hill Country of Manasseh*. Vol. 2, *The Eastern Valleys and the Fringes of the Desert* (Leiden: Brill, forthcoming) and *The Survey of the Hill Country of Manasseh*. Vol. 3, *From Nahal ʿIron to Nahal Shechem* (Haifa: University of Haifa, 1999).

5. An excellent description of this system is given in Liverani, *Israel's History*, 3–21.

This society did not extend to the territory mapped out in Joshua, which stretched out beyond the hill country as far as the Mediterranean coast; nor was it won by conquest: settlement and growth were in areas largely unpopulated and wooded. The villages existed together with larger cities (which also had their own "daughter" villages); contact between these and the farming settlements varied.[6] To what extent tribal identities developed (or possibly originated with the settlers) is unknown.

This whole process has been extensively discussed in the last twenty years. For the purposes of this study, however, the most important finding is that the areas later occupied by Judah and Israel appear to have been settled in separate processes, and the societies to have evolved at different rates, so that their emergence into statehood occurred at different times. The relevant archaeological data have been summarized as follows:

> Most striking of all is the paucity of occupation in Judah. This is no archaeological accident, but has been substantiated by considerable research. For example, comparing the number of sites in Judah to an equivalent area in Ephraim, we find ten times as many sites in Ephraim! The regions adjacent to the Judean hills reinforce this picture: The upper Shephelah experienced few, if any, attempts at settlement; no Israelite Settlement sites are known in the southern Hebron hills…and in the Beer-sheba Valley, Israelite Settlement did not begin until the 11th century BCE—and even then, only on a limited scale.[7]

Finkelstein comments that this lack of occupation is surprising, since the land was suitable for settlement and there were hardly any other occupants. But the terrain was relatively rockier and more densely wooded than further north.

The whole question of the settlement has been complicated further by the debate about chronology. There is no point in discussing this issue here: it can be followed elsewhere and is in any case ongoing: briefly, the traditional "high" chronology assigned Iron IIA, the period of Israelite and Judean state formation, to the tenth century, the period to which the figures of David and Solomon would be assigned; Finkelstein's "low chronology" dates this process rather to the ninth century and regards the founder of the Israelite kingdom as Omri. At the time of writing, the two positions have now converged somewhat and differ only by about half a century—though the crucial gap between them still leaves the reigns of

6. Finkelstein (*The Archaeology of the Israelite Settlement*) implies little or no contact; the evidence gathered by Zertal, however, suggests that there was such contact. The picture of a highland society isolated from the city-state system (and structures) that were still present in the Iron Age should not be overdrawn.

7. Ibid., 326.

David and Solomon in dispute.[8] Recently, Herzog and Singer-Avitz have proposed an extended Iron IIA, lasting 150–200 years. For Judah, they suggest a long and gradual process of development, beginning in the Shephelah (the lowlands to the west) and the Beersheba valley from the mid-tenth to late ninth or even mid-eighth century, divided into two sub-phases; for Israel, they divide Iron age II into three sub-phases. They argue that each society underwent quite different social processes in its transition towards statehood, partly as a result of different environmental factors.[9] There was, in other words, no single "Israel" and no common history, but just a parallel one. For the whole picture they have coined the term "variegated evolution."[10]

It is not even clear that the settlers in what were to become Israel and Judah actually arrived from the same direction. Finkelstein suggests that the Judean settlement either represents "a trickle from the principal areas of Israelite Settlement to the north" or "included sedentarizing pastoral groups who had already been active in the region."[11] On this view, the "Judeans" would have been of the same population stock as "Israelites" (the term "Israelite Settlement" seems to prejudge the issue, but this is almost certainly unintentional on Finkelstein's part), or they may not. He notes the absence of Judah from biblical accounts of any activity in the books of Judges and 1 Samuel ("during the 11th century,"[12]), but suggests that penetration from the north is suggested by Judg 1:4–9, and by the location of a place named [ה]אפרת) as an alternative name for Beth-lehem.[13] But, as Finkelstein also notes, there are indications in the biblical texts that Judah was settled from the south.[14] If Judah had been

---

8. The most recent presentation of the debate at the time of writing is A. Mazar, "The Debate over the Chronology of the Iron Age in the Southern Levant: Its History, the Current Situation, and a Suggested Resolution," in *The Bible and Radiocarbon Dating: Archaeology, Text and Science* (ed. T. E. Levy and T. Higham; London: Equinox, 2005), 15–30, with a reply by I. Finkelstein and E. Piasetzky, "The Iron I–IIA in the Highlands and Beyond," *Levant* 38 (2006): 45–61.

9. Z. Herzog and L. Singer-Avitz, "Redefining the Centre: The Emergence of State in Judah," *Tel Aviv* 31 (2004): 209–44, and "Sub-Dividing the Iron Age IIA: A Suggested Solution to the Chronological Debate," *Tel Aviv* 33 (2006): 163–95.

10. Herzog and Singer-Avitz, "Sub-Dividing the Iron Age IIA," 163, 181, 188.

11. Finkelstein, *The Archaeology of the Israelite Settlement*, 326.

12. Ibid., 327.

13. Gen 48:7; see N. Naʾaman, "Ephraim, Ephrath and the Settlement in the Judean Hill Country," *Zion* 49 (1984): 325–31 (Hebrew).

14. Many of the arguments have been assembled and reassessed recently by J. Blenkinsopp, "The Midianite–Kenite Hypothesis and Israelite Ethnic Origins" (unpublished).

colonized by "Israelites" from the north, we are faced with explaining how a "house of Judah" and then a kingdom of Judah ever came into being as distinct entities. Finkelstein's further argument that the "sacred centers" of Israel moved steadily south is based on a too literal reading of the biblical narrative. Yet in his more recent book with Silberman, he has apparently revised this opinion, and they now argue that

> in two earlier settlement waves—in the Early Bronze Age (c. 3500–2200 BCE) and in the Middle Bronze Age (c. 2000–1550 BCE) the indigenous highland population moved from pastoralism to seasonal agriculture, to permanent villages, to complex highland economies in a manner that was strikingly similar to the processes of Israelite settlement in the Iron Age I (1150–900 BCE). But even more surprising, the surveys (and the fragmentary historical information) indicated that in each wave of highland settlement, there always seemed to have been *two* distinct societies in the highlands—northern and southern—roughly occupying the areas of the later kingdoms of Judah and Israel.[15]

Liverani makes the same point from a different perspective; Shechem and Jerusalem were the main city states during the Amarna age. This reflected the topography of the highland region and the consequent boundaries of economic and political influence.[16] Why should Iron age I be different, especially when in Iron II that very pattern is reasserted?

We cannot demonstrate for certain that Israel and Judah were the result of different settlements from two different directions and at different times and evolved into statehood at different rates and by different processes. But as Finkelstein and Silberman put it, "there is no archaeological evidence whatsoever that this situation of north and south [sc. the two monarchies] grew out of an earlier political unity."[17] If we add to this that the biblical texts themselves contain strong clues to Israel and Judah as having achieved statehood separately (as was shown earlier), it is thus a reasonable conclusion that the populations of the future kingdoms of Israel and Judah should be treated, until we have any evidence to the

---

15. Finkelstein and Silberman, *The Bible Unearthed*, 153–55 (quote from 153). The whole question of agricultural expansion and its relationship to population density, which is sometimes invoked in Israelite settlement, is a thorny one: see, e.g., E. Boserup, *The Conditions of Agricultural Growth: The Economics of Agrarian Change under Population Pressure* (Chicago: Aldine, 1965; reissued New Brunswick: Aldine, 2005, with an Introduction by Nicholas Kaldor). If she is correct, there is no necessary correlation between an increasing population density in the Ephraimite highlands and an expansion of this population into the Judean highlands.

16. Liverani, *Israel's History*, 83–85

17. Finkelstein and Silberman, *The Bible Unearthed*, 158. For a detailed study of the tribe of Benjamin, see K. D. Schunck, *Benjamin* (Berlin: de Gruyter, 1963).

contrary, as having come into existence separately—and remained separate, whether or not any temporary unification of the two kingdoms was achieved.[18]

The issue is, then, how such a unity, or the belief in such a unity, came about: how the twelve-tribe biblical Israel (in its various forms) came into existence. We must first consider the possibility that this occurred through a period of single political leadership at an early stage. Currently, historians and archaeologists are divided on the question of whether this may have occurred in the tenth century (Iron IIA, David and Solomon): some believe in a unified Davidic rule (the notion of an "empire" has been largely dismissed even by those who accept a "United Monarchy"); others deny any kind of political unification at this time, at least centred on Jerusalem, on the grounds that Judah was insufficiently developed socially, politically and economically, and Jerusalem virtually uninhabited. Whether or not a "United Monarchy" *could* have existed (let alone whether it did), cannot be decided on the archaeological evidence at present. The Merneptah stela is of little help in answering this question: it relates to an earlier period (thirteenth century BCE) and there is no way of telling whether Judah was included in its "Israel." In recent years there has been a renewed debate about the status of Jerusalem at this time, with claims that structures and seals point to the city as an active centre and possibly the centre of David's kingdom. As with many such claims, only full publication and discussion will reveal their strength. But it is worth pointing out how much even these claims, far from establishing the biblical story, simply assume it. Can we, for example, conclude that any structures in Jerusalem during Iron IIA would have been built by David rather than, say, Saul, whose home base was close by? This conclusion would make sense of several biblical clues (the allotment of the city to Benjamin in some texts and the connection between Saul's family and Jerusalem in others). But all such argumentation of this kind is fruitless: we can set biblical and archaeological data side by side but that does not of itself produce any kind of confirmation. Archaeologically we know very little and nearly every interpretation assumes something about the textual evidence. So it is to this that we have to turn. Here the major problem is—narratively speaking—the unexplained separation of Judah in 1 Samuel from the twelve-tribe Israel and the appearance of a separate Judean kingdom. It is always possible that this separation is itself a fiction, but it

18. See further Avi Ofer, "The Monarchic Period in the Judaean Highland: A Spatial Overview," in *Studies in the Archaeology of the Iron Age in Israel and Jordan* (ed. A. Mazar; Sheffield: Sheffield Academic Press, 2001), 14–37

explains rather well the later, well-attested separation of the two areas. The question is, after all, not whether Israel and Judah may have been temporarily united in a single domain but whether Judah and Israel should be regarded as a single "nation," or, more specifically, whether Judeans would have at this time recognized themselves as "Israelite," in whatever terms they might have used to express their absolute identity with those to the north.

And the term that Judeans may have used raises a further problem. If the two kingdoms *had* been unified at this period, and even if that unified kingdom had been called "Israel," the subsequent relations between the two kingdoms are described as having relapsed into hostility. Had Judah once been part of an "Israel," would this have been remembered or forgotten? Would this memory persist to the point where Judeans would later, even after the end of the kingdom of Israel, call themselves "Israel"? The theory of a unified kingdom not only does not take fully into account the biblical narrative, but does not in fact solve the basic problem of Judah's adoption of the name centuries later.

If we take the full range of biblical and archaeological evidence together and weigh it carefully, we ought to conclude that the processes of original settlement and early political development, as archaeology reveals them, supply no basis for a consciousness of ethnic or social unity between the settlers of the central and the southern highlands. Archaeology cannot prove the existence of a "United Monarchy" nor, if such existed, that Jerusalem was its capital. Given that the biblical evidence, critically considered, also suggests separate state formation in both areas, there seems little reason to force the issue. It is rare enough that archaeological and biblical text agree so well.

The Joining of Benjamin and Judah

The next moment to consider is the union of Benjamin and Judah, already discussed in Chapter 4 as a literary or narrative problem. What can a historian say about this? Benjamin's subordination to Judah is conveyed very briefly indeed in the story of Israel's secession under Jeroboam I (1 Kgs 11–12). But it has also been suggested (see below) that the Joseph story reflects that union through a narrative about the sons of Jacob/Israel. The two accounts have been brought together by Yigal Levin in a consideration of what he calls the "Benjamin Conundrum."[19] Levin

19. Y. Levin, "Joseph, Judah and the 'Benjamin Conundrum,'" *ZAW* 116 (2004): 223–41, and "The Political Status of the Tribe of Benjamin and the Joseph Story," *Judea and Samaria Research Studies* 14 (2005): 35–52 (Hebrew with English

observes that—as noted in Chapter 3—the books of Samuel present Judah and Israel as uniting only under the rule of David, that this rule was strongly resisted by Benjamin and that the two "houses" were kept separate under David's immediate successors. Levin also notes the place of Benjamin among Israel, not Judah, in the "prefect list" attributed to Solomon (1 Kgs 4:18). In an earlier article, Levin argued that some Benjaminite clans remained "north of the border" after the secession[20] and commented that "had the Israelian version of events survived, it probably would have counted Benjamin among the northern tribes."[21] But in his view Rehoboam *did* hold on to Benjamin, yet only partly, with the border set at Mizpah, while the remainder of Benjaminite territory, in which he includes Bethel, remained in Israel.[22] After the destruction of Samaria, in his view, some of the "northern" Benjaminites went south— thus explaining the evidence of population movement that some interpretations of archaeological evidence have inferred for the late eighth century (see below).

This is a plausible reconstruction up to a point. However, it takes for granted the historicity of the "United Monarchy," and thus the political development and power of Judah, and so assumes that Rehoboam would have been able to retain—and continue to retain—part of the territory of Benjamin against the presumed wishes of the inhabitants and of the much more powerful kingdom of Israel. There is no hint in the biblical narratives that Benjamin was divided, and it would be expected that such a division would be challenged by Israel. A simpler explanation (without even making a decision about the general historicity of the "United Monarchy") is that Benjamin's association with Judah does not go back as far as this, but has been located during the reign of Rehoboam for other reasons—perhaps the simplest being that Judean memory had always regarded Benjamin as part of its own kingdom and as a free choice on the part of that tribe—in which case the choice logically would have been

abstract). The article provides a good account of scholarly discussion and bibliographical reference, to which the reader is directed.

20. Y. Levin and A. Faust, "The Ties Between the Tribes Asher and Benjamin," in *Judea and Samaria Research Studies: Proceedings of the Seventh Annual Meeting* (ed. Y. Eshel; Ariel: College of Judea and Samaria, 1998), 225–31 (Hebrew with English abstract).

21. Ibid., 227.

22. He also notes (in ibid., 229 n. 26) the double Benjamin list in Josh 18:21–24, 25–28 (that cover adjacent territories), which several commentators understand to reflect different administrative regions from the monarchic period (whether Solomon or Josiah).

made at the outset. If so, the "forgetting" of the process by which Benjamin came to be in Judah would be another example of the repressive activity of cultural memory. For it is significant that, as noted in Chapter 4, no decision of Benjamin to join Judah is actually recorded.

Levin's "Benjamin Conundrum" is offered as a challenge to those who doubt the historicity of the biblical account. He claims that, if the "Primary History" were "invented" in the reign of either Josiah or even the Persian era, the northern origin of the Benjaminites need not have been mentioned, nor need Benjamin have been given the "honour" of founding Israel. But here he uncharacteristically misreads the story, for, as we have seen, Saul is *not* given that honour. He never rules Judah, and as a king he fails. Levin's argument would have some point if the Saul story were regarded as a pure Judean invention, but not if we acknowledge the role of Benjamin and its own memories in the creation of the Judean account (as argued in Chapter 7 above). Having David the Judean fail where Saul the Benjaminite succeeds actually fits better a process of Judean succession to Benjamin, such as occurred in the political and religious transfer of power during the fifth century. It also better explains the memory of strong antagonism of Benjamin towards the house of David. For Levin maintains that over time that original antagonism ceased, and notes that in the "postexilic prophets," Haggai, Zechariah and Malachi, Benjamin is not mentioned separately and so has apparently been absorbed into Judah. But he ignores the evidence of Jeremiah and the entire Second History, which both must have reached their present form in the Persian period and yet carefully preserve the awareness of a separate Benjaminite identity—as do Ezra and Nehemiah. At least we can both agree that a memory of Saul *was* preserved and not invented by the creators of the books of Samuel, but it does not follow that the recollection itself is historical.

Levin then turns to the Joseph story and notes Redford's view that we have an Israelite version in which the patriarch is named "Jacob" and the leading "good brother" Reuben, and a Judean version in which he is named "Israel" and the leading good brother Judah, both versions dating to no earlier than the late seventh or sixth centuries.[23] Levin accepts the suggestion that the Joseph story is a fable about Judah persuading Jacob to relinquish Benjamin, and that it reflects the struggle between Judah and Joseph over Benjamin. But for Levin, the Joseph story as a whole has to be earlier if Benjamin belonged to Judah from the time of Rehoboam. If that were *not* the correct date, however, and the tussle for

23. D. B. Redford, *A Study of the Biblical Story of Joseph (Genesis 37–50)* (Leiden: Brill, 1970).

Benjaminite allegiance persisted into the Persian era, there is nothing to contradict Redford's other arguments for a later date for the Joseph story. Redford's view of the date of the story derives, of course, from his dating of the annexation of Benjamin to Judah. But if that is wrong, the Judean revision of the Joseph story can be still later and yet fulfil the same function. Indeed, any story in which Judah acts as an elder brother within the family of twelve brothers must postdate the acceptance of an "Israel-ite" identity by Judah, whether or not it postdates the union of Judah and Benjamin.

Levin then considers Ahijah's message to Jeroboam, where he is promised ten tribes, and Solomon one, which implies a unity of the two kingdoms. That implication in turn contradicts the impression elsewhere in Samuel–Kings that the unity between the two "houses" was only in the form of political unification under David. The problem in fact points to a solution: the notion of a ten-tribe Israel is not necessarily a Judean construct, but may reflect the structure (at some point) of the Israelite kingdom. The configuration of Judah itself is actually more of a problem: according to the biblical texts, it comprises variously one, two or two and a half tribes—or one, or two "houses" (Benjamin is described as a "house" in 2 Sam 3:19). The ambiguity suggests that the twelve-tribe system is itself the consequence of Judah's assuming membership of "Israel," extending the number of ten (Israelite) tribes to twelve. For, as Levin also agrees, the "ten tribes" of Jeroboam probably include Benja-min—leaving only one for Rehoboam. On his theory, Benjamin's two halves might have made possible a count of ten plus two, but the division of Benjamin is, as we have noted, nowhere mentioned in the narrative. Levin's solution is ingenious and attractive, but I do not, for the reasons given, find it persuasive, though I do agree with several of his observations.

Israel and Judah as Neighbouring Kingdoms

Until—or unless—the archaeological evidence relating to the period of David and Solomon becomes clearer (and this will entail more precise pottery dating, which may never be achieved), we can know nothing about the existence of these kings—or about Saul or Rehoboam. At best we can regard elements in the stories as historically plausible, which does not guarantee historicity. In any case, the kind of history that can be reconstructed critically is not represented by individual acts of persons so much as by social processes that leave material traces. Archaeology can reveal the process of state formation in both Israel and Judah with some chronological latitude, but the identification of any single monarch before

Omri or perhaps even before Ahab remains beyond its competence. Even here we can only confirm the names of Israelite and Judean kings from the contemporary or near-contemporary inscriptions of other nations. No Israelite or Judean royal inscriptions have yet come to light. The ease with which, in even current archaeological work, "time of David" automatically becomes "David" is unfortunate, if (usually) deliberate.

Finkelstein's "low chronology" mentioned earlier means that what on the "high chronology" was dated to the time of David and Solomon (tenth century BCE) is now to be dated to the ninth, and thus the true creator of the kingdom of Israel was Omri,[24] whose foundational role is probably reflected in the name *bit humriya* for the kingdom of Israel in Assyrian texts and "Omri" as in the Mesha stele. This reconstruction also appears to wipe out Rehoboam and Jeroboam (the two names are rather reminiscent of Tweedledum and Tweedledee). A further aspect of Finkelstein's reconstruction (also touched on earlier) is the emergence of the kingdom of Judah later than the kingdom of Israel. It calls into question the impression of an equal status between Judean and Israelite kingdoms given in the books of Kings. Insofar as Judah was a separate entity on Israel's southern border, and not a part of that kingdom, what was its status? Was it—as could be argued from a reading of the Tel Dan stela— a vassal chiefdom to its northern neighbour? Even so, there is no allusion to Judah as part of the kingdom of Israel and no pretext for taking over the name—though Judah is not mentioned in any contemporary inscription as a kingdom, including in the stela from Tel Dan, until after the fall of Samaria. But Judean memory might betray an awareness that Judah was for a short while involved in a "United Monarchy"—or something close—in which Israel was the dominant partner. The Judean king Jehoshaphat and an unnamed "king of Israel" apparently fight together against Aram, as equals, in 1 Kgs 22. Yet Jehoshapahat's son and successor is named as Jehoram/Joram, who married the daughter of Ahab (2 Kgs 8:16–18). Ahab's son and successor (after his brother Ahaziah) is also named Joram, however, and J. M. Miller has proposed that the two kings were one and the same, implying that a single king ruled both territories.[25] On this theory, a single king occupied both thrones, succeeding his brother-in-law Ahaziah of Israel before being killed. The text has Jehoram of Judah dying and being succeeded by Ahaziah, then both

---

24. Finkelstein and Silberman, *The Bible Unearthed*, 169–95.

25. Miller and Hayes, *A History of Ancient Israel and Judah*, 280–84. A further complication is that J(eh)oram of Judah's successor bore the same name as J(eh)oram of Israel's predecessor.

kings being killed by Jehu (2 Kgs 9).[26] According to Miller's theory the one king J(eh)oram was killed and the Israelite throne taken by Jehu, who also killed J(eh)orams's son Azariah, leaving Judah ruled by Azariah's queen Athaliah. According to the picture in 2 Kings, she would have been an enemy of Jehu, who was apparently then unable to regain control of Judah.

Such a course of events *might* have resulted in the creation of a single kingdom with the name of "Israel." But it is unlikely that this episode marks the birth of a "greater Israel." If a union of crowns did take place, it is recorded as having lasted only a few years, and the subsequent independence of Judah, together with the hostile relationship between Judah and Israel that the Judean sources remember, make it difficult to argue that Judeans subsequently took on the identity of Israelites. Israel was soon afterwards weakened by its wars with Aram and later engaged, in alliance with Aram, against Assyria. The story in 2 Kgs 14, according to which Amaziah of Judah challenged Jehoash of Israel to battle, might be understood in this context as disguising a bid for *independence*. It ends, however, in the capture and plunder of Jerusalem, more probably a genuine than an invented recollection. If so, the consequences of this for the status of the territory of Benjamin can only be guessed at. Shortly afterwards, 2 Kgs 16 relates that Ahaz, pressured by both Israel and Aram to join its coalition, appealed for protection to Assyria, which responded with an attack on Damascus (one that no doubt it intended anyway); but the outcome, inevitably, was Judah becoming an Assyrian client, freeing it from any threat from Israel. This sequence of events is consistent with what we can infer from other sources and from the subsequent relations between Assyria and Judah. If Israel and Judah thus found themselves on opposite sides over Assyria, following a period of difficult relations between them, it is hard to imagine that feelings of mutual belonging were generated, such as would lead to Judah retaining, let alone taking on, the name "Israel." Before the Assyrians, no doubt, the kings of Judah did their utmost to distance themselves from their northern neighbour; any hint of a common identity would be unwise.

Judah During and After the End of the Kingdom of Israel

The renewed Assyrian threat and the fall of Samaria mark a change in the regional power structure, which is most dramatically reflected in the

---

26. Jehu is the son of a certain Jehoshaphat (2 Kgs 9:14). Can we have great confidence in the reliability of the records of Judean or Israelite monarchs during this period? A number of names seem to be shared.

rapid growth of population in Judah during the remainder of the eighth century, up to tenfold on several estimates.[27] Jerusalem itself was enlarged by the incorporation of the western hill within the walls and was surrounded by new agricultural settlements—commensurate with the requirements of the enlarged city. The architecture and luxury goods begin to exhibit the social and economic indexes of a well-developed state.[28] In what must have become a more complex and therefore probably more centralized and bureaucratic state, the importance of Jerusalem increased considerably. Plausible reasons for this rapid development are the lack of external threat and the participation in the Arabian trade that ran through the main route across the Negev from Gaza to the Red Sea, and which the Assyrians controlled. The evidence of a large olive oil processing facility in Ekron (Tel Miqne), for example, points also to the involvement of Judean oil production in a wider trade network, again under Assyrian patronage.[29]

The dramatic rise in population throughout Judah and especially in Jerusalem has been attributed in particular to the destruction of Samaria by Sargon in 722, and the subsequent population transfers and the reorganization of the territory into Assyrian provinces, which occurred during Ahaz's reign (usually dated 735–715). M. Broshi, who first published in 1974 the results of Avigad's excavation on the "western hill" of Jerusalem between 1969 and 1976, attributed the expansion of the city to the influx of a refugee population from Samaria.[30] This interpretation has been widely followed, but a more detailed account of these developments has recently been offered by Finkelstein and Silberman,[31] which must be discussed here, because these authors propose a partial explanation for the adoption of Israelite identity by Judeans.

27. See the bibliography in Finkelstein and Silberman, "Temple and Dynasty."

28. See also D. W. Jamieson-Drake, *Scribes and Schools in Monarchic Judah* (Sheffield: Almond, 1991).

29. See D. Eitam and A. Shomroni, "Research of the Oil Industry During the Iron Age at Tel Miqne," in *Olive Oil in Antiquity: Israel and Neighbouring Countries from the Neolithic to the Early Arab Period* (ed. D. Eitam and M. Melzer; Padua: Sargon, 1996; originally published in English and Hebrew, University of Haifa, 1987).

30. M. Broshi, "The Expansion of Jerusalem in the Reigns of Hezekiah and Manasseh," *IEJ* 24 (1974): 21–26; see N. Avigad, *Discovering Jerusalem* (Oxford: Blackwell, 1980).

31. Finkelstein and Silberman, "Temple and Dynasty," with extensive bibliography; cf. Finkelstein and Silberman, *The Bible Unearthed*, 243–46, and *David and Solomon*, 136–38.

According to Finkelstein and Silberman, both the increase in Jerusalem's population and also the doubling of numbers in Judah over a few decades suggests large-scale immigration. This they attribute to the depredations by Sennacherib in 701—when the city was practically the only part of Judah left unscathed and would have brought many refugees to Jerusalem—but also to the earlier fall of Samaria. The most important element in their argument, from the point of view of this study, is their suggestion that many immigrants moved to Judah from the former kingdom of Israel with a resulting merger of Judean and Israelite identities.

The data from the Southern Samaria survey (1980–87) led by Finkelstein have been interpreted by him as indicating a severe decrease in population to the north of Jerusalem, between Shechem and Bethel.[32] His inference is that this movement occurred immediately after the fall of Samaria and was caused by "fear of deportation."[33] Foreign populations had been transferred by the Assyrians into this region, causing displacement. The simultaneous rise in population in Judah, then, is to be understood as follows:

> Not only did Judah develop from an isolated highland society into a fully developed state integrated into the Assyrian economy; its population dramatically changed from purely Judahite into a mix of Judahite and ex-Israelite. Perhaps as much as half of the Judahite population in the late eighth to early seventh century BCE was of north Israelite origin.[34]

As a result, runs the argument,

> These people must have come to Judah with their own local traditions. Most significantly, the Bethel sanctuary must have played an important role in their cult practices, and the memories and myths of the Saulide dynasty—which originated in this area—could have played an essential role in their understanding of their history and identity.[35]

This situation thus explains the reforms of Hezekiah, centralizing the cult in Jerusalem in response to the challenge of rival religious traditions and practices. The attachment of these new Israelite immigrants to their former cult-centre at Bethel—still easily accessible to them—would have underlined the need to strengthen the importance of Jerusalem as the proper place of worship. It also explains the creation of a tradition in which the founding kings of Judah, David and Solomon, became kings of

---

32. See Finkelstein, Lederman and Bunimowitz, eds., *Highlands of Many Cultures*, 898–906.
33. Finkelstein and Silberman, "Temple and Dynasty," 268.
34. Finkelstein and Silberman, *David and Solomon*, 137–38.
35. Finkelstein and Silberman, "Temple and Dynasty," 269.

"all Israel," and in which the "northern" memories about Saul were integrated with stories about David in such a way as to create a united memory of the past and a common identity.[36] A "United Monarchy" was, as it were, created *"within* the borders of Judah."[37]

Before considering this theory, it is worth drawing attention to the interesting study by Kratz of the problem that has a bearing on the reign of Hezekiah, but from a different perspective: the meaning of "Israel" in the book of Isaiah.[38] I drew attention in Chapter 1 to Kratz's distinction between the religious and political/ethnic definitions as an important clue to the solution of Judah's "Israelite" identity; here he looks for the origin of that identity in a particular text (and a particular time and place). Kratz is also aware of the problem of Judah's assumption of Israelite identity and he argues that the distinctive Isaianic title "holy one of Israel"[39] belongs in the earliest stratum of the book, and is not a product of a later revision associated with Second Isaiah. Hence the phenomenon also belongs to the late eighth century. But, as he acknowledges, the use of "Israel" to refer to Judah at this time is "unique and without any histori-cal analogy."[40] As he points out, it also has a *theological* and not a politi-cal meaning: the "Israel" in question is the "people of God" (as he puts it). Equally significant is the use of "Jacob" (42 times in the book as a whole), which, again, Kratz traces back to an early stratum of the book, confirming the existence of the tradition identifying Israel and Jacob.

Kratz notes[41] Rost's argument that Isaiah of Jerusalem spoke of Israel as a state from his early period until the Syro-Ephraimite war but there-after made a transition to including his own people under the name "Israel"; he also cites Høgenhaven's partial agreement: the innovation took place at the downfall of the nation of Israel in 722 BCE, when the name would have become available to be appropriated by Judah.[42] There is thus some pedigree to Finkelstein's and Silberman's theory that Judah "became" Israel from the late eighth century.

36. See also Finkelstein and Silberman, *David and Solomon*, 121–49.

37. Finkelstein and Silberman, "Temple and Dynasty," 279.

38. R. G. Kratz, "Israel in the Book of Isaiah," *JSOT* 31 (2006): 103–28.

39. Of the 31 occurrences of the term in the Bible, 25 are in Isaiah, plus an oracle of Isaiah quoted in 2 Kgs 19:22. Elsewhere it is found twice in Jeremiah and three times in Psalms.

40. Kratz, "Israel in the Book of Isaiah," 111.

41. Ibid., 122–23.

42. L. Rost, *Israel bei den Propheten* (Stuttgart: Kohlhammer, 1937), 48; J. Høgenhaven, *Gott und Volk bei Jesaja. Eine Untersuchung zur Biblischen Theologie* (Leiden: Brill, 1988), 17.

The only point at which I disagree with Kratz, as with Rost and Høgenhaven, is that this concept of "Israel" should be attributed to the eighth century. Kratz himself asks the crucial question: Why would this prophet adopt a term applying to a nation that he "regarded as an enemy"[43] to his own people? His answer proposes a theological development within the process of transmission of the book of Isaiah itself. The original prophetic *Denkschrift* in chs. 6–8, widely regarded as original to the prophet, does not use the term "Israel" of Judah, and additionally offers threats as well as promises to Judah. The immediately surrounding chapters (5 and 9), develop the threat that Judah will suffer the same fate as Ephraim and Samaria, and effectively merge the two "houses of Israel" into a single "Israel," united by an identical judgment from the same god, the god of Israel.

This process, the equation of the fates of Israel and of Judah, of the god of Israel with the god of Judah and the creation of the idea of a single nation out of that reflection, is one extrapolated from a theory of the growth of the text of Isaiah, and does not invoke any historical or social causation (other than a theological interpretation of the fact of Samaria's destruction). A purely *theological* explanation for the bringing together of "Israel" and Jacob, creating the notion of "Israel" in a religious sense, and even the idea of Judah as a "house" of Israel in a political sense also (if 8:14 is from the eighth century also[44]), might all be buttressed by pointing to the process reconstructed by Finkelstein and Silberman. Isaianic prophecies from the time of Ahaz about the coming destruction of Samaria (and Judah) could have been expanded after the fall of Samaria (following Høgenhaven), after their partial fulfilment, from a perspective in which the two nations were not just notionally and theologically linked, but socially and politically as well, with the god of Israel/Jacob who had punished Israel identified with the god of Judah who would punish them also. Some further discussion of Isaianic texts will be useful, but rather than obstruct the flow of the argument here, I will deal with this at the end of the chapter.

If we also consider (as Finkelstein and Silberman also note) that the books of Chronicles present the reign of Hezekiah as a time of

43. Kratz, "Israel in the Book of Isaiah," 114.

44. Kratz mentions the term "two houses of Israel" (ibid., 122) as an instance of the political use of Israel that distinguishes the two kingdoms: but if that were also assigned to the eighth century, it could make Kratz's theory redundant. Given that "two houses of Israel" is a unique expression in the entire Hebrew Bible (it recurs in 1 Esd 8:59) and does not represent the view of the books of Kings, its appearance in the eighth century would require some explanation.

reunification of "Israel" under the Davidic dynasty, then literary arguments can again be combined with archaeological reconstructions to
make a case for the late eighth century as the time in which Judah might
have adopted some Israelite traditions, including the cult of the "god of
Israel/Jacob." Indeed, the hypothesis of a migration of priests and levites
from Israel to Judah in the time of Hezekiah has long been offered as an
explanation for the absorption of "northern" traditions into Judah, in
particular the book of Deuteronomy.[45] This scenario is, I think, the most
powerful alternative to the theory I am arguing, that the development
occurred in the fifth century.

Yet there are difficulties in accepting this theory. Let me begin with
the archaeology. First, the presence of a significant Israelite population in
Judah in the late eighth century cannot be evidenced from the material
evidence, as Finkelstein and Silberman concede.[46] Second, the demographic data for "southern Ephraim" need to be used cautiously: comparison can only be made with maximal population densities between
Iron II and the Persian period, a span of at least two centuries. The period
of Judean demographic expansion might therefore have occurred
anywhere between the fall of Samaria and the fall of Jerusalem. Even if
certain measures that suggest preparation for war can be ascribed to
Hezekiah (and his "tunnel" cannot be certainly dated to him), it is not
necessary to date to his reign what may, in fact, be a symptom of a gradual (or even rapid) development of the Judean state arising from the
regional policies of the Assyrians. Judean memories of a golden Hezekian age should not influence the interpretation of archaeological data.
Nor should the verdict on a "wicked" king distract from the possibility
that the reign of Manasseh, long and prosperous, should be credited with
Judah's growth rather than Hezekiah's, as Knauf has, in fact, argued.[47]
This period also fits the archaeological data.

There are other uncertainties with a Hezekian dating. Some depopula-
tion of southern Ephraim may have occurred in the wake of the fall of
Samaria, but the reasons given for this are not entirely persuasive: that
the population feared deportation is possible, but whether such a threat
would have been powerful enough to displace farmers from the land on
which their livelihood depended is uncertain. Such a flight is also likely

45. A. C. Welch, *The Code of Deuteronomy: A New Theory of Its Origin*
(London: J. Clarke, 1924); Ginsberg, *The Israelian Heritage of Judaism*.

46. Finkelstein and Silberman, "Temple and Dynasty," 266.

47. E. A. Knauf, "The Glorious Days of Manasseh," in Grabbe, ed., *Good Kings
and Bad Kings*, 164–88. (Knauf also dates the first edition of the book of Isaiah to
the reign of Manasseh.)

to have been reversed once the threat of deportation had passed. Also, ultimately, if fears of this kind *had* prompted farmers to leave their own land, is it not likely that the arrival of Sennacherib in Judah, twenty years later, would have induced them to return to their original homelands, where they would be free of another threat of Assyrian reprisal?

Another problem is the status of Benjamin. Finkelstein and Silberman seem to accept that Benjamin was part of Judah at this time (following the First and Second Histories). If so, a theorized migration of Ephraimites to northern Judah could have strengthened longstanding kinship links between the two populations. But one would not expect Ephraimite farmers, if they did (improbably) migrate, to go to *Jerusalem*. Nor would there be any reason for Benjaminites themselves to move there at this time, if they were part of the kingdom of Judah and so not threatened by the Assyrians. The rise in *Jerusalem's* population therefore remains unexplained. The possibility that Benjamin may not have been part of Judah at this time might actually fit the data better. Part of the Assyrian reorganization of Samaria might have been to transfer administration of Benjamin to the vassal kingdom of Judah—a reasonable administrative decision. Unfortunately, we have no clear understanding of the southern border of the province of Samaria (i.e. the towns from which the Assyrians collected taxes directly rather than indirectly from vassal kings). Moreover, the territory of Benjamin does not seem to have suffered in Sennacherib's assault on Judah in 701, which might suggest it was not by then part of Judah. It could, of course, have been added to Judah under Manasseh in return for loyalty and as part of the economic reorganization and development of that region. In Knauf's view,[48]

> the shift of Benjamin from the sphere of Samaria into that of Jerusalem in the course of the seventh century was dictated by demographic and economic factors. When this shift was acknowledged, by changing the border between Judah and Samaria accordingly, is subject to speculation: it might have happened as early as 671, when Esarhaddon held court on the borders of Samaria and might have found it advisable to honor his loyal vassal.

If that were the case, a population move from Ephraim to Benjamin in Hezekiah's time makes even less sense, since both would have been within the province of Samaria.

Another complication is the effect of an influx of refugees from Judah during Sennacherib's campaign in 701. Finkelstein and Silberman

---

48. E. A. Knauf, "Bethel: The Israelite Impact on Judean Language and Literature," in *Judah and the Judeans in the Persian Period* (ed. O. Lipschits and M. Oeming; Winona Lake: Eisenbrauns, 2006), 291–350 (297).

recognize that this may have contributed to Jerusalem's growth—and indeed, this is a much better explanation for any expansion of Jerusalem under Hezekiah.

These considerations also affect, of course, Finkelstein's and Silberman's suggestion that the "memories and myths of the Saulide dynasty—which originated in the area"[49] may have played a role in the formation of the new "Israelite" identity. On their assumption that Benjamin had been part of Judah for a century or more, these traditions will already have been absorbed long before the reign of Hezekiah. Again, the possibility that Benjamin was part of Samaria at this time supports this part of their reconstruction better. But in any case, there is a more important objection to their suggestion: we must take into account not just the *content* of these memories from (mainly) Benjamin but also their often *highly polemical character* within the Judean narrative. How are the anti-Saulide and anti-Benjaminite elements in the First History to be explained? It makes no sense for these traditions to be absorbed at this time only so as to be attacked. The anti-Bethel polemics can also be accounted for only if Hezekiah's cult centralization is a fact and not just a theory.

But there are even doubts about Hezekiah's reform, where again the archaeologist may be relying too much on the biblical source. Cult reform was not an uncommon practice among ancient Near Eastern rulers, of course, and the role of a central, even dynastic, temple is likely to have been enhanced as the state itself grew more complex, bureaucratic and centralized. But the Judean First History devotes only six verses to this (2 Kgs 18:1–6), and while the Second History mightily expands the story (2 Chr 29–31), it is precarious to conclude that this expanded version account may contain a genuine memory rather than an imaginative embellishment of its hero's zeal. Indeed, the historicity of the reform itself has been challenged by several scholars.[50] In response to such objections, Finkelstein and Silberman argue that at Arad, Beersheba and Lachish evidence of the destruction of altars at cult centres points to a centralization policy, implemented in advance of the Assyrian destruction. But they also admit that "the stratigraphy is difficult";[51] and in each of the three cases the interpretation (as the authors note) has been

---

49. Finkelstein and Silberman, "Temple and Dynasty," 269.
50. L. Handy, "Hezekiah's Unlikely Reform," *ZAW* 100 (1988): 111–15; N. Naʾaman, "The Debated Historicity of Hezekiah's Reform in the Light of Historical and Archaeological Research," *ZAW* 107 (1995): 179–95; L. S. Fried, "The High Places (*Bamôth*) and the Reforms of Hezekiah and Josiah," *JAOS* 122 (2002): 1–29.
51. Finkelstein and Silberman, "Temple and Dynasty," 271.

challenged.[52] The removal, symbolically, of the presence of the protective deity from a city is in any case an unwise move in time of war, because it can reduce morale and signal the imminent defeat of the defenders.

Yet another problem is one that Kratz has noted, and that we have already encountered in our readings of the Judean histories: the clear distinction between the political and religious connotations of "Israel." From the moment that the twelve-tribe Israel gives way to the kingdom of Saul, the "Deuteronomic History" (Joshua–Kings), which, it is being claimed, originates in Hezekiah's Judah, ceases to refer to Judah as "Israel." It is the Second History that utilizes this concept, but in doing so also emphasizes the religious character of that Israel. As Kratz rightly observes, the key to the use of the name lies not in any political or social connections with its northern neighbour but in the shared worship of the "god of Israel." It is from this cultic merging that a common descent from Jacob/Israel is then derived. However, as demonstrated in Chapter 8, it is in Jeremiah and not Isaiah that we find the clearest evidence of *El Yisrael* being syncretized with *Yhwh Sebaoth*. This later context also suggests that the Isaianic texts considered by Kratz are in fact to be dated to the same period as Second Isaiah, where we also find the term "Jacob" applied to Judah (see below).

In conclusion, whatever the extent of population mix that occurred in the time of Hezekiah, or Manasseh, or both, such a process is not likely to have resulted in the adoption of the cult of the "god of Israel," involving that deity's identification with the god of Jerusalem. Hezekiah in particular is unlikely to have encouraged reverence for a deity who had already been defeated by Asshur, while Judeans would also be unlikely to regard themselves as part of a larger nation of "Israel" that had just lost it national independence.

But the fundamental flaw in the Finkelstein and Silberman thesis is that they simply do not consider any options outside the Iron age, and unless they do so, they cannot argue that their explanation is the best. This restricted panorama is endemic among archaeologists of ancient Israel, who specialize in the Iron age. What we really need is better archaeological data and analysis of the later periods, so that we can utilize the maximum resources of archaeology as well as text in determining the origin of "biblical Israel."

---

52. See the critique by D. Edelman, "Hezekiah's Alleged Cultic Centralization," *JSOT* (forthcoming).

The Reign of Josiah

The theory of a Josianic "golden age" is as well rooted in biblical scholarship as Hezekiah's and need not be reviewed in any detail.[53] It continues to be a widely favoured view that this king entertained a policy of uniting (or, in terms of the theory, re-uniting) the territories of Judah and Samaria under a single king and a single deity, but reservations are increasingly being voiced about the true history of his reign. Three issues need to be considered in particular here: first, the widespread scholarly view that Josiah had ambitions to extend his rule over the territory of the former kingdom of Israel and thus to recreate the "United Monarchy"; second, that he instituted a religious reform based on a lawbook that can be identified with some early form of Deuteronomy; and third, that he desecrated the altar at Bethel.

The identification of Deuteronomy with the lawbook found under Josiah marks a crucial point in the development of biblical criticism, and for many scholars remains a linchpin for the reconstructed history of Israelite and Judean religion. But the story does not automatically validate itself as history rather than an instance of the kind of legend that often accompanies the "discovery" of books and bestows upon them the endorsement of a long dead hero or saint.[54] The Deuteronomic lawcode itself (chs. 12–26) does not, in fact, define the extent of the "Israel" that it addresses: the twelve tribes are addressed only in the "Blessing of Moses" in ch. 33, and listed in ch. 27 at the ceremony on Gerizim and in 34:2, all of which are regarded as later additions to the book. Nor does it

53. On the historicity of Josiah's reforming activities, see M. Sweeney, *King Josiah of Judah: The Lost Messiah of Israel* (Oxford: Oxford University Press, 2001) and N. Naʾaman, "The King Leading Cult Reforms in His Kingdom: Josiah and Other Kings in the Ancient Near East," *ZABR* 12 (2006): 131–68. For further critique and discussion, see Grabbe, ed., *Good Kings and Bad Kings*, especially the articles by Uehlinger ("Was There a Cult Reform under King Josiah," 279–316), Davies ("Josiah and the Law Book," 65-77) and the response by R. Albertz ("Why a Reform Like Josiah's Must Have Happened," 27–46); see also E. Eynikel, *The Reform of King Josiah and the Composition of the Deuteronomistic History* (Leiden: Brill, 1996), who (following several other scholars) separates the lawbook discovery from the reform.

54. On the general issue of "historical" sources, see D. Henige, "In Good Company: Problematic Sources and Biblical Historicity," *JSOT* 30 (2005): 29–47; on the discovery of lost books, see, in particular, A. J. Droge, " 'The Lying Pen of the Scribes': Of Holy Books and Pious Frauds," *Method and Theory in the Study of Religion* 15 (2003): 117–47, and K. Stott, "Finding the Lost Book of the Law: Rereading the Story of the "Book of the Law" (Deuteronomy–2 Kings) in Light of Classical Literature," *JSOT* 30 (2005): 153–69.

mention Jerusalem or a single sanctuary, only "the place where Yhwh will let/make his name dwell." Whether or not this phrase designates a single exclusive place or only designated sites where the authentic worship of Yahweh is carried out cannot be determined from the text. The scholarly consensus that it does is influenced by the presumed historical context of the lawcode itself and is in no way grammatically superior. Clearly, the text *was* at some point read as an endorsement of Jerusalem and as a call to exclusivity—in Judah. But other sanctuaries are known from elsewhere, including Samaria and Egypt, where this statement may have been interpreted differently.

The dating of texts is determined in the first instance from a consideration of their implied social function, and there are several mismatches between Deuteronomy and the monarchic period. These include the proposal of a "constitutional monarch" with no real monarchic power (e.g. in matters of justice or warfare), the replacement of prophets by priests in the delivery of the war-oracle, the ban on divination and the identification of a population element called "Canaanite." Despite the impression of a consensus about the date of Deuteronomy, its Josianic origin has never been unchallenged.[55] But the dating of Deuteronomy is not relevant here; the question is whether Josiah's reign provides any clue to Judah's assumption of the identity of "Israel."

The account of Josiah's reform in the First History (2 Kgs 23) states that he (a) took idolatrous cult objects from the Jerusalem temple and burned them, carrying the ashes to Bethel, and also took other measures "from Geba to Beersheba" to purge the priesthood and cult; (b) pulled down and desecrated the altar at Bethel, including burning bones from the tombs; (c) removed the cult places from the "cities of Samaria," doing to them "as he had done to Bethel" and killing priests; he then celebrated a Passover in Jerusalem.

The account in the Second History (2 Chr 34) is slightly different: the reform occurs *before* the finding of the lawbook, but includes the same measures as reported in Kings: burning bones, destroying and desecrating altars, killing priests. Nothing is said of Bethel, however, and the subsequent finding of a lawbook precedes a covenant ceremony and Passover, at which "all Judah and Israel were present" (v. 18).

---

55. A discussion of the issues is clearly impossible here; a useful collection of essays representing numerous viewpoints is N. Lohfink, ed., *Das Deuteronomium: Entstehung, Gestalt und Botschaft* (Leuven: Peeters, 1985). An excellent account of early arguments for a post-exilic Deuteronomy is L. B. Paton, "The Case for the Post-Exilic Origin of Deuteronomy," *JBL* 47 (1928): 322–57, which nevertheless attempts to refute them all.

What do these accounts imply? According to Finkelstein and Silberman, they signify "a momentous chapter in the political and spiritual life of Judah," in which a written law code was read out to the people. The impulse detected behind this royal initiative was the transfer of power in the region, as Assyrian sovereignty gave way to Egyptian, probably on an agreed and orderly basis. Previous claims that there was a power vacuum beckoning Josiah to reconquer territory (on which a great deal of importance used to be laid) now seem erroneous in the light of Naʾaman's analysis of the relevant Assyrian texts.[56] Nevertheless, the notion that "a great, Pan-Israelite state" might have seemed ready for the making, inspired by the vision of a united Israel afforded in Deuteronomy, has not disappeared.[57] These were "messianic times," in which the "legendary kingdom of David" would become reality.

These enthusiastic assertions go a long way beyond the evidence: there is nothing in the memory of Josiah that suggests he intended to reconquer Samaria (and it is not an ambition that archaeology can confirm; there is no archaeological evidence of his presence beyond Judah). The scenario—this should be said bluntly—is a figment. Nor is Josiah's death any confirmation of such ambitions. Second Kings 23:29 says that "Pharaoh Necho slew him at Megiddo, when he saw him." The Second History records this as a battle, but almost certainly without the advantage of any independent evidence. Several historians implicitly prefer the Second History's account (or draw the same inference in the Kings version). But in a study of Judean foreign policy during Josiah's reign, Naʾaman has shown that Palestine was smoothly transferred from Assyrian to Egyptian control before Josiah reigned, leaving little scope for the proposed policy of Judean expansion. He has also suggested that the phrase "Pharaoh Necho slew him at Megiddo, when he saw him" suggests an interview rather than a battle: Josiah did not attempt any military opposition. Necho is reported as marching to the Euphrates "against (על) the king of Assyria": it is, however, agreed that he was marching to Assyria's defence, but in any case apparently unconcerned about any major invasion, or plans for invasion, on the part of a Judean monarch of the territory of Samaria that he had just acquired from Assyria.

If Josiah were executed, however, rather than killed in battle, he must have done something to offend the Pharaoh, and the possibility that he made some intervention that angered Necho is perfectly reasonable; some encroachment on or interference in neighbouring territory is

56. Naʾaman, *The Kingdom of Judah Under Josiah*.
57. The quotations are from Finkelstein and Silberman, *The Bible Unearthed*, 283–85.

possible, perhaps in Benjamin. Archaeology again cannot provide much assistance; but the cultural memories may. The most interesting feature of the story of Josiah's actions is the focus on Bethel in the First History and the absence of any mention of it in the Second. The extensive verbal parallels between the texts of Kings and Chronicles here imply that both come from a common source—generally regarded as an early version of what became 2 Samuel and Kings. But this conclusion permits two different inferences: that the Second History deliberately left out any mention of Bethel, or that the First History deliberately added it in. The choice between these alternatives is not made easier by the realization that the story with which Kings connects Josiah's desecration (in 2 Kgs 23:16–18) does not appear in Chronicles either—because all stories exclusively about the kingdom of Israel are absent. Again, we cannot know whether we are dealing with a case (or cases) of deliberate omission or of later expansion. A campaign against Bethel as part of an enlargement of Judean territory is not improbable, but equally not certain. It could have been added as a pretext for a later assault on the sanctuary, which according to the (not entirely reliable) archaeological evidence was destroyed not at this time, but in the Persian period.

The Kings narrative, at any rate, separates Josiah's visit to Bethel (which actually begins in v. 15) from his actions against the sanctuaries in Samaria where he is said to have done "just as he had done at Bethel" (v. 19). The note about activities in Samaria is not an afterthought: the Second History also describes such actions, though in different wording. The account of the earlier action, desecrating the altar at Bethel with the ashes of cult objects from the Jerusalem temple (2 Kgs 23:4), implies that Josiah was free to do this, and the later reference distinguishing Bethel from the sanctuaries of the "cities of Samaria" reinforces the impression that Bethel was not one of these sanctuaries, but lay *within* Josiah's own kingdom; the reference to Geba as a northern limit of his domain certainly implies that the land of Benjamin was under his jurisdiction.[58] Again we are faced with the question of whether Bethel was a city under Josiah's control (and thus "within Judah," and eligible to be regarded as "Benjamin") at the end of the seventh century. Alternatively, Josiah's desecration of a site outside his territory might have been what led to his execution, if Naʾaman's suggestion is correct. All this, of course, rests on the assumption that the story about the desecration of Bethel is not a piece of retrojected polemic!

58. See Josh 18:21; 1 Kgs 15:22; Neh 11:31. Its precise location is unclear: 1 Sam 13 suggests it is close to Gibeah. See the discussion in Lipschits, *The Fall and Rise of Jerusalem*, 138, who thinks Josiah pushed north to include Bethel.

The conclusion of Naʾaman's arguments is that "The picture of Josiah's reign, as reflected in this discussion, is far removed from the description of those years as reflected in the book of Kings, and no less distant from the sketch of his period presented in modern historiography."[59] There is, in fact, nothing here to detain us further in our investigation of how Judah became Israel. But the scholarly reconstruction of the Josianic era apparently has enough momentum to continue onwards even when the wheels are off.

The End of the Kingdom of Judah

Until quite recently, the period from 586 BCE until an indeterminate moment in the sixth century was treated by historians of ancient Israel and Judah as the "exilic period": the modern account of ancient Israel followed the scriptural one tracing the plot to Babylon and back. The Second History certainly leads the way along that track, with its Israelite genealogies converging on the exile, but the First History, too, ends with a snapshot of a Judean king in Babylonia: its brief reference to continuing events in Judah go no further than a year or two.

This perception has dramatically changed. The Babylonian exile is a minor aspect of the history of Judah, and the term "Neo-Babylonian period" is now replacing "exilic period," focusing on the events onstage rather than offstage. This focus has led to a revolution in the assessment of the biblical literature as well as the history of Judah. Yet the (sparse) data in the First History, and (fuller) data in the book of Jeremiah have always been available; they were simply not assessed from a perspective free of the ideology of the Judean histories themselves. It should also be fully appreciated that the political configuration of the Neo-Babylonian period in Judah did not end with the advent of Cyrus; precisely when or why Jerusalem was restored as the capital is unclear: the Second History does not say. But whatever its overall reliability, the book of Nehemiah suggests that at the middle of the fifth century the city was still in ruins. The reign of Mizpah as capital of Judah extends well into the Persian period and probably lasted around 150 years. This is perhaps not a great deal shorter than Jerusalem's own history as the capital city of the kingdom.

59. N. Naʾaman "The Kingdom of Judah Under Josiah," in *Ancient Israel and Its Neighbors: Interaction and Counteraction* (Winona Lake: Eisenbrauns, 2005), 329–98, quote from 384. But see also Naʾaman's defence of the historicity of Josiah's reform in his "The King Leading Cult Reforms."

The story of this period as recalled in Benjaminite memory has been covered in Chapter 8. This, too, does not go beyond the death of Gedaliah. Of the wider picture, several detailed studies have recently appeared, which need in due course to be supplemented by more reliable archaeological data (current political circumstances permitting).[60] I have already said enough in previous chapters about the likelihood of literary activity in Mizpah, and throughout this book the crucial role of Bethel has been indicated (discussed further in the following chapter). I have also suggested, following Kratz, that the title "Israel" adopted by Judah should be understood in a religious rather than a political sense. Hence it is not the transfer of the capital of Judah to Mizpah that directly caused Judah to adopt the title of Israel. That occurred because of one of the consequences of the political shift: the resurgence of Bethel, home of the cult of the god of Jacob/Israel, a cult probably practised throughout the territory of Benjamin.

To sum up the conclusions of this chapter, the possible alternative contexts that are proposed for the adoption of the identity of "Israel" by Judah fail fundamentally because they suppose a situation in which Judah is the stronger partner and thus unlikely to assume the name of the weaker. We are obliged, on the contrary, to look for a period when "Israel" was dominant and "Judah" subordinate, and a period of time in which an identity "Israel" could be absorbed by a population that also saw itself as "Judah" in such a way that the designation became fundamental and irreversible. (I considered but rejected such a context in a possible "united kingdom" under the Omrides.)

In discussing the alternative that is most fully argued, the reign of Hezekiah, I considered the suggestion made by Kratz that "Israel" is used in Isaiah as a religious term (he says "people of God"). I argued in Chapter 8 that Jeremiah offered direct evidence of a process of adopting the "god of Israel" into Judah, and I conclude this chapter with a review of other texts that indicate that process. First, Isa 2:3:

> And many people will go and say, "Come let us go up to the mountain of Yhwh, to the house of the God of Jacob, and he will teach us his ways, and we will walk in his paths: for out of Zion shall go forth the law, and the word of Yhwh from Jerusalem."

60.   Apart from the extremely valuable collection of papers in Lipschits and Blenkinsopp, eds., *Judah and the Judeans in the Neo-Babylonian Period* and Lipschits's monograph *The Fall and Rise of Jerusalem* (n. 42), a convenient summary of the topic can also be found in Middlemas, *The Troubles of Templeless Judah*, though it displays a traditional Jerusalem-based perspective on the period.

"Jacob" occurs at least 40 times in Isaiah, but is especially concentrated in chs. 40–55 (22 times). This is a totally unexpected phenomenon in a poet supposedly exiled among Zionists and addressing them. I use the term "deportation" precisely: the "exile" was a selective removal of leading Jerusalemites, whose descendants presumably were responsible for supporting the restoration of their beloved city:

> Hear this, O house of Jacob, who are called by the name of Israel, and have come out of the waters of Judah, who swear by the name of Yhwh, and make mention of the god of Israel, but not in truth, nor in righteousness (Isa 48:1).

I have argued elsewhere that the contents of Second Isaiah stem largely if not entirely from Judah in the fifth century, when the issue of Jerusalem's claims and the claims of its "children" were being advanced in a way that did not, as in Ezra and Nehemiah, seek to exclude the indigenous population.[61] For this poet, the returning Zionists (to whom he is sympathetic, if not even one himself) are part of "Israel"; they are "Jacob" and should be welcomed.

The usage recurs in Trito-Isaiah:

> And I will bring forth a seed out of Jacob, and out of Judah an inheritor of my mountains: and my elect shall inherit it, and my servants shall live there. (Isa 65:9)

A similar collocation in Lamentations fits the proposed period very well:

> Yhwh has swallowed up all the habitations of Jacob, and has not shown pity: he has thrown down in his wrath the strongholds of the daughter of Judah; he has brought them down to the ground: he has polluted the kingdom and its princes. He has cut off in his fierce anger all the horn of Israel: he has drawn back his right hand from before the enemy, and he burned against Jacob like a flaming fire, that devours round about. (Lam 2:2–3)

See also Lam 1:17 where Jacob is collocated with Jerusalem:

> Yhwh has commanded against Jacob
> that his neighbours should become his enemies;
> Jerusalem has become an impurity among them.

---

61. Davies, "God of Cyrus, God of Israel." Earlier arguments (apart from Duhm's own) are also well made by Barstad, *A Way in the Wilderness*, and *The Babylonian Captivity of the Book of Isaiah: "Exilic" Judah and the Provenance of Isaiah 40–55* (Oslo: Novus, 1997).

In the two collocations of Jacob and Judah in Hosea, on the other hand, the terms are not synonymous: "Judah" and "Jacob" apply to different entities:

> Ephraim is like a heifer that is trained, and loves to tread out the corn; and I put a yoke upon its fair neck: I will harness Ephraim; Judah shall plough, and Jacob break up the ground. (Hos 10:11)

> Yhwh has also a dispute with Judah, and will punish Jacob according to his ways; according to his doings will he recompense him. (Hos 12:2)

The same is true of the last collocation, in Mic 1:5:

> All this is because of Jacob's rebellion, and for the sins of the house of Israel. What is the transgression of Jacob? Is it not Samaria? And what are the high places of Judah? Are they not Jerusalem?

There is, then, a good deal of indirect evidence to associate the emergence of "Jacob" and "Israel" as terms that either embraced Judah or even denoted Judah exclusively, in literature that clusters around the Neo-Babylonian and Persian periods. There is no point in looking earlier for Judah's adoption of Israel (as a *religious* identity). The centre of the cult of the god of Israel/Jacob is Bethel, and it is now time to look more closely at this city and sanctuary as the cradle of "biblical Israel."

Chapter 10

BETHEL

Bethel and Jerusalem were sanctuaries that had, at least according to the cultural memories of Judah and Benjamin, enjoyed royal patronage, and while we must not assume that any policy of cult centralization was introduced into Judah before the Persian era, these had long been no doubt the sites of many official cultic celebrations as a result of their status. As a sanctuary that between 586 and the latter part of the fifth century BCE served Judah, Bethel is likely to have been the place where the cult of the "god of Jacob/Israel" was given Judean provincial patronage and thus officially established this cult among those who had previously worshipped Yhwh under other names, and especially in the Jerusalem cult. The unification of the cults of Jerusalem and Bethel is, under these circumstances, likely to have taken place. The cult of the god of Jacob/Israel is also likely to have been established at Mizpah, and if this, rather than Bethel, had become the dominant sanctuary, then the above comments will still apply; and the same also of other Benjaminite sanctuaries (such as Gibeon and Gilgal) that were functioning in the Neo-Babylonian period.

We have good evidence that Yhwh was a divine name already known in both Israel and Judah, and the amalgamation of Jerusalem and Benjaminite cults (and deities) was quite possibly already underway within a Judah that included the territory of Benjamin. But the opposite may equally be true, and the Benjaminite cults of the "god of Israel" were rejected in favour of the dynastic cult of Jerusalem. This is what the Judean memory suggests, though it may be unreliable. But undoubtedly much of the population of that part of Judah that comprised Benjamin will have participated in both cults and tended to regard "Yahweh the god of Israel" as a single deity. While we need not project monotheism on the Judean population at this time, the tendency to identify both Yahwehs (and their consorts) would be understandable.

My investigation of the origins of Judah's Israelite identity (leading to the presentation of a twelve-tribe nation) has been converging on Bethel, and it is now time to consider that city and its sanctuary and to close in on the birth of that "Israel." Several studies on Bethel have appeared in recent years,[1] and the latest of these, which appeared while this book was substantially completed, comes very close to my own thesis—but halts before the last, and crucial, step. The books referred to all contain accounts of the history of research and the reader can be referred to them for fuller information.

We begin with the fact that while Bethel is mentioned more times in the Hebrew Bible than any other sanctuary apart from Jerusalem, the identification of the site, while widely agreed to be the modern *Beitin*, only a few kilometres from Mizpah, is not certain, and an alternative identification with *el-Bireh* cannot completely be ruled out.[2] In any case, the site of *Beitin* has, by general consent, never been satisfactorily excavated[3] nor properly reported, and *el-Bireh* even less so.[4] Consequently, conclusions about the history of Bethel drawn from excavation are tenuous and generally unsatisfactory. Indeed, the location of the actual cult centre itself has not yet been determined; it may have been outside the city. Definitive statements about its occupation are therefore provisional, and we are left to rely largely on the biblical references. The following discussion should make clear just how provisional a lot of our knowledge of Bethel is.

Pfeiffer

Pfeiffer's work is concerned specifically with Bethel in the book of Hosea, whose contents he stratifies into three literary layers: the original Hoseanic oracles, a pre-Deuteronomistic redaction and a

---

1. H. Pfeiffer, *Das Heiligtum von Bethel im Spiegel des Hoseabuches* (Göttingen: Vandenhoeck & Ruprecht, 1999); K. Koenen, *Bethel: Geschichte, Kult und Theologie* (Freiburg: University of Freiburg; Göttingen: Vandenhoeck & Ruprecht, 2003); J. F. Gomes, *The Sanctuary of Bethel and the Configuration of Israelite Identity* (Berlin: de Gruyter, 2006); Knauf, "Bethel." The monograph by Melanie Kohlmoos, *Bet-El-Erinnerungen an eine Stadt: Perspektiven der alttestamentlichen Bet-El-Überlieferung* (Tübingen: Mohr Siebeck, 2006), was unfortunately not available to me.

2. The alternative was proposed by D. Livingston, "Location of Biblical Bethel and Ai Reconsidered," *WTJ* 33 (1970): 20–44.

3. See J. L. Kelso, "Excavations at Bethel," *BA* 19 (1956): 36–43, and *The Excavations at Bethel (1934–1960): Joint Expedition of the Pittsburgh Theological Seminary and ASOR* (Cambridge, Mass.: American Schools of Oriental Research, 1968).

4. Knauf ("Bethel," 306–8) states simply that "The archaeology of Bethel is non-existent: its archaeology is a mess," and demonstrates its shortcomings quite emphatically.

Deuteronomistic/post-Deuteronomistic redaction. Accepting that Bethel (like Dan) was instituted by Jeroboam as a state sanctuary, he proposes that its cult, where Yahweh was worshipped in the form of a calf, and the Exodus and conquest of the land were celebrated as a basis of divine protection, served to legitimate the new dynasty. Hence the original oracles of Hosea attacked Bethel as a symbol of the state itself, denying that its cult offered any security from impending disaster, as did the prophet Amos. The detail of these calf images in Exod 32 belongs to the pre-Deuteronomistic (post-722) redaction when the Exodus was separated from the now obsolete royal ideology but refurnished as a basis for future hope. Following the destruction of Jerusalem, Bethel continued to be popular among the Samarian population. The Deuteronomistic and post-Deuteronomistic redactors (post-586), on the other hand, undermined the status of Bethel, and reconfigured the figure of Jacob negatively (Hos 12), criticizing the calf images as idolatrous and removing the Exodus motif from Jacob and his sons to Moses. Bethel (Beth-aven) now became an idolatrous cult centre. This attitude reflected the claims of Jerusalem's cult to an exclusive status.

Pfeiffer's reconstruction is in its broad lines plausible enough, and matches what we may imagine to have been the attitudes towards Bethel adopted, first of all by an Israelite social critic (Hosea) and, later, by those for whom Bethel's usurpation of Jerusalem had to be reversed (the "Deuteronomists" and their successors). The intermediate stage of "pre-Deuteronomistic" redaction is more problematic, however: we might expect the period in which Bethel presumably flourished as a prestigious sanctuary *within Judah*—while simultaneously serving the population of Samaria also—to be reflected somewhere in Hosea, and indeed, as in the case of Jeremiah at Mizpah, we should probably reckon that the scroll-collection of Hosean oracles began at Bethel, and found its way, like the Amos collection, to Jerusalem during the fifth century.[5] But material reflecting this era is not, in fact, easy to find in Hosea. The minute literary dissection upon which Pfeiffer bases his analysis is also problematic: it is often hard to follow and even more often hard to validate since it involves a high degree of speculation. I have remarked on the drawbacks of this very detailed kind of literary analysis in Chapter 1 and again in Chapter 8.

But the study is nevertheless valuable in emphasizing that, like Amos and Jeremiah, Hosea also has not only an Israelite and a Judean stage of development, but reflects strong ideological shifts when these collections—which originally in the case of Hosea and Amos entirely addressed

5. On the history of the book of Amos, see my "Amos, Man and Book."

Israel, and in the case of Jeremiah both Judah and Israel—were transferred from Benjamin, where they must at some stage surely have resided, to Jerusalem. When this city and sanctuary regained their status, the contents of these collections were directed towards a "Zionist" population and a Jerusalem-centred ideology, though with relatively little textual expansion, since it was possible, or *made* possible, to re-read their old "Israel" as a new one.

Pfeiffer is right, I believe, to conclude, at least from an analysis of the Hosean material, that Bethel remained popular after the fall of Jerusalem and that the polemics against it stem from after this period and not from any attempt at centralizing the cult in Jerusalem after the fall of Samaria. But the role of Bethel as an active sanctuary for Judeans, rather than just a Deuteronomistic bogey, is somewhat overlooked in his study.

Koenen

Koenen gives a more comprehensive account of the city and sanctuary, but on religio-historical rather than literary-historical lines. As the seat of the royal Israelite state temple, Bethel contained a *maṣṣebah* and a calf statue (here Koenen invokes Exod 32), the latter an image of Yahweh as the god of the Exodus, identified with El. The temple was sacked by the Assyrians towards the end of the eighth century and the calf statue removed, but the cult remained active until the reign of Josiah. Its status thereafter is disputed: some scholars regard Bethel as having continued in the Neo-Babylonian period. If it did continue, however, no texts, he asserts, were written there.

During the monarchy Bethel functioned in the same way as other ancient Near Eastern cities, including Jerusalem. Its theology is inferred from aetiological narratives and from the attacks on it by Amos and Hosea. The sanctuary was represented (following Gen 28) as standing at the centre of the earth, at the foot of a "ladder" connecting earthly and heavenly temples. Thus it guaranteed welfare and prosperity for the city and the kingdom. Amos attacked Bethel as part of his social critique and Hosea as part of his political and cultic critique. After the fall of the Israelite kingdom, Bethel lost prominence and this theology lapsed. Along with its sanctuary it came to be regarded as a place of wickedness and idolatry. But the worship of Yahweh survived without the calf images (a move, Koenen suggests, towards aniconism). The old Bethel traditions either became patriarchal ones, attached to the figure of Jacob or were transferred to Jerusalem, which came to be regarded in Judah as the sole legitimate place of divine presence.

Unlike Pfeiffer, Koenen does not rely on a detailed analysis of the biblical texts, but unfortunately tends to assume many of them to be historical, and thus diverges at crucial points from Pfeiffer. He accepts that the sanctuary was attacked by Josiah and is therefore uncertain whether its cult continued to function afterwards. Also, unlike Pfeiffer, he regards the patriarchal connection as secondary, despite the fact that this raises problems for the meaning of the term "god of Israel," which, as we have seen, means primarily "god of Jacob" and only secondarily "god of the kingdom (of Israel)." His reservations about the role of Bethel during the Neo-Babylonian period could be justified on a purely archaeological assessment, but since the archaeology is so uncertain, we need to rely on logic, inference and the archaeology of the texts. On balance, it is surely likely that such a prestigious sanctuary would continue to play an important role—or have its role revived—when Jerusalem's sanctuary was stripped of all political support and probably derelict.

Koenen's suggestions about the theology of the cult of Bethel are especially intriguing, and although the suggestion that Bethel hosted an aniconic cult is perhaps precarious, the suggestion that some of its traditions were moved to Jerusalem is probable. The question remains, however, whether this removal would have taken place after the fall of Samaria or after the reinstatement of Jerusalem in the fifth century. If Bethel lay in the territory of Judah (within Benjamin) then the earlier date is possible. The key consideration is, however, whether the anti-Bethel polemic is part of a Hezekian policy of addressing the interests of recent immigrants from Samaria (on the hypothesis advanced most recently by Finkelstein and Silberman and discussed in the previous chapter) or belongs with the anti-Benjaminite polemic in the books of Judges and Samuel, which, I have argued, makes less sense under Hezekiah than in the early Persian period.

Gomes

Gomes's monograph is the most relevant of all those being considered, since it also advocates the thesis of this book: Bethel as a shaper of Israelite identity. Unfortunately, his discussion of nearly every aspect of Bethel's history and cult, often without any significant resolution, tends to obscure his central argument. By way of compensation, however, he is particularly attentive to the pro- and anti-Bethel propaganda in the biblical texts and recognizes that much of the negative portrayal of the sanctuary reflects its rivalry with Jerusalem. He also provides a very clear and quite full summary of his case,[6] which is often clearer than the corresponding arguments.

Like both Pfeiffer and Koenen, Gomes suggests that Bethel was a legitimate Yahwistic shrine even after the fall of Samaria. The concession of 2 Kgs 17 about the Yahwistic religion of the inhabitants originating from there provides strong support for this conclusion. But his major contribution is in defending the claim that "the sanctuary of Bethel was at the heart of the configuration of Israelite identity."[7]

Gomes analyzes the profile of Bethel in the books of Kings, in Genesis then in Joshua–1 Samuel—three blocks of material that were identified earlier in this book as presenting different "Israels"—then in Amos and Hosea and certain Psalms, and finally in "Post-Exilic Writings" (Zechariah, Ezra–Nehemiah, Chronicles). These representations of Bethel are finally ordered into a historical sequence. Gomes regards the earliest "sounding" (as he puts it[8]) as the report of Bethel's conquest by the "house of Joseph" in the "period of the Judges," which he links to its reported destruction "in 1240–1235." Here he succumbs to that marvellous over-precision beloved of some biblical archaeologists, and especially characteristic of Kelso's interpretation of the archaeology of the site. Such an exact dating is impossible on archaeological grounds and is clearly reached by bringing in an interpretation of the biblical data. On the basis of Judg 1:22, Gomes also concludes that Yahweh was the tribal deity of this "house," and that the story of Jacob's encounter with the deity at Bethel stems from the sanctuary's role in forming the identity of "northern tribes," since it was also the sanctuary at which Samuel performed annual rites. He also notes its connection with Benjamin. Jeroboam's reform at Bethel is seen to reflect his concern with the figure of Jacob as Israelite ancestor and in particular to exploit Bethel's association with the traditions of exodus and conquest.[9]

The report in 2 Chr 13 (but absent from Kings) that Bethel was annexed by Abijah and temporarily became part of Benjamin is identified as the basis of Josh 18:21–28, but the site was quickly recaptured and became prosperous in the eighth century, where both Israelite (Hosea) and Judean (Amos) prophets gave their oracles. As Hosea in particular indicates, during this time the cult became syncretistic. The Assyrians probably did not destroy Bethel (as Hosea predicted) but rather looted it

6. Gomes, *The Sanctuary of Bethel*, 213–23.
7. Ibid., 34.
8. Ibid., 212.
9. Following the majority opinion, Gomes disagrees with Pfeiffer and Koenen in regarding the calves as pedestals and not divine images.

(following Koenen), and Sargon II recognized it as a centralizing force for his importees (2 Kgs 17). Its cult there accommodated both Israelites and the newly transplanted populations, and it thus served to fashion yet another new Israelite identity. In one of his very few disagreements with the biblical narrative, Gomes finds Josiah's alleged destruction of Bethel "enigmatic," and doubts whether this story can be historically correct. During Jerusalem's demise under the Babylonians, Bethel continued to function, but hosted an annual memorial of the destruction of Jerusalem, and on the eve of the Persian takeover of the empire, sought an accommodation over Jerusalem. The book of Ezra suggests that no compromise occurred, but during the late fifth century Bethel *was* incorporated in the Judean *qahal*, since its population was included in the move of one tenth of the population to Jerusalem. Yet after 350 the city is unmentioned in Chronicles. Only in the Hellenistic period is Bethel finally established as part of Judah.

Into this framework (as noted, largely following the biblical narrative) Gomes fits the various attitudes towards Bethel found in the biblical texts. He begins with the Elohist (dated to the reign of Jeroboam I), the author of the major part of the Jacob story, including the Bethel cult foundation story that highlights Israel's ancestor. The near-contemporary Yahwist (Gen 12–13) tries to claim Bethel-Ai for Judah by linking it with Hebron in the Abraham cycle. Next, Amos and Hosea, "recognising that Bethel was at the heart of Israelite identity,"[10] and in the case of Amos associated with Jeroboam II, focus their critique on it. For Hosea, the calf image was the origin of Israelite idolatry, though Gomes argues that Hosea had no problem with the image itself, only with its abuse, since he views Bethel as for the most part a genuine Yahwistic sanctuary, linked to Jacob and to the Exodus. Even in ch. 12, where Hosea's prophecies were adapted for exilic use, this view of Bethel is maintained, but Hosea's attacks on the abuses practised there enable the Deuteronomistic redactor to deliver a severe critique of the sanctuary. Following the Cross version of the Deuteronomistic History theory, Gomes finds the core of the attack on Bethel in 1 Kgs 12, where Dtr1 (Josianic) denounces Bethel, but Dtr2 (exilic) extends this to other high places in Samaria. The post-exilic redactor then intensifies the polemic (1 Kgs 13), warning southern prophets against it. In his view, Bethel was seen especially as a threat during the rebuilding of the Jerusalem temple, when groups of Samarians tried to integrate with the Judeans.

Gomes also notes other traces of anti-Bethel polemic in Judges and 1 Samuel. The conquest of Bethel in Judg 1:22–23 is unfavourably

10. Gomes, *The Sanctuary of Bethel*, 219.

contrasted with the exploits of Judah; Bethel is renamed as "Bochim" (= "place of weeping") in Judg 2:1, 5; Deborah is set up as an alternative to the Bethel priesthood, while during the reigns of David and Solomon the place is not even mentioned. The "exilic Yahwist" seems to be reclaiming Bethel for Judah in Gen 28, while the Priestly writer's support for Bethel can be seen in Genesis and in editorial touches in Judges. P also offers a "sanitised picture of Jacob."[11] Indeed, P makes the Bethel theophany and the naming of the sanctuary the climax of the patriarchal promise theme. Gomes argues that in the absence of Jerusalem, the exilic writer is ready to embrace Bethel as the alternative. This claim is explained by identifying the Bethel priesthood as Aaronide, despite the fragile evidence. In Zechariah, Gomes finds Bethel included in the "people of the land" (7:2), as also in the lists in Ezra and Nehemiah, where Bethel is now assigned to Benjamin.

Finally, the Chronicler (ca. 350) omits the sanctuary of Bethel altogether (the city itself is mentioned twice, in 1 Chr 7:28 and 2 Chr 13:19), while emphasizing the importance of Jacob (see also the discussion above in Chapter 5). Gomes therefore concludes that "the exilic and post-exilic writers all recognize the central role of Bethel in configuring the identity of Israel. Unless Bethel is brought under the submission of Judah, there is no hope for complete unity."[12]

The major drawback of Gomes's study, in my opinion, is that he is too tied to conventional literary-critical methods, to the prevailing consensus and to the reliability of the biblical texts—with the important exception of the Josianic attack on Bethel, when he follows Niehr[13] in dismissing it as a likely "postexilic fiction."[14] He is also absolutely right in seeing that Bethel, far from simply falling into disuse and abuse, remained a strong cultic centre in the Neo-Babylonian and Persian periods and contributed a good deal to the memories enacted in the cult of "biblical Israel." Gomes has managed to see a good deal of the wood, despite his detailed attention to the trees; his focus on the role of Bethel as the key to the identity of "Israel" is crucial and important. Indeed, this book absolves me of the need to labour the reader further with argument in favour of Bethel's importance.

---

11. Ibid., 221.

12. Ibid., 222.

13. H. Niehr, "Die Reform des Joschija: Methodische, historische und religions-geschichtliche Aspekte," in *Jeremia und die "deuteronomistische Bewegung"* (ed. W. Gross; Weinheim: Athenäum, 1995), 33–54.

14. Ibid., 46–49.

Gomes has, however, missed the implications of the destruction of Jerusalem for Bethel's influence on Judean identity and its role in promoting the new "biblical Israel" through the union of Judean and Israelite religious traditions under Benjaminite patronage. The one "Israel" for which Bethel is *most* responsible is the one in which Judeans finally enter as children of Jacob, and Judah as one of Jacob's twelve sons.

Knauf

Knauf's essay on Bethel as a literary centre exhibits its author's command of linguistic, archaeological, anthropological and literary-critical expertise combined with a typically fresh interpretation of the issues. It is also important to the argument of this book about literary activity in Benjamin during the sixth–fifth centuries BCE. Knauf's thesis is

> that Bethel played a part of equal importance to Babylon in the literary history of the Neo-Babylonian period, and was only superseded by Jerusalem in the Persian period; and notably, that it was the northern traditions which came to Judah via Bethel, a process which started when Judah incorporated Bethel and its local temple, school and library.[15]

The evidence for the functioning of the Bethel sanctuary throughout the sixth century[16] is, he claims, provided by the story of the pilgrims in Jer 41:4 and 48:13, which seems to use "Bethel" as a divine name, echoed in various divine names in the Elephantine archive, and Zech 7:2–3 (internally dated to 518). Knauf also proposes a more "refined" analysis of linguistic development within Israel and Judah that includes Archaic, Classical, Transitional Classical, Late Biblical and Mishnaic Hebrew (the latter dating back to the Persian period), and also distinguishes Judean from Israelite Hebrew.[17] The watershed between the various kinds of Classical Hebrew and Late Biblical Hebrew is not (as widely claimed) the Babylonian exile but ca. 400 BCE, with Transitional Classical Hebrew dating between the seventh and fifth centuries.

It is Israelite Hebrew that especially concerns Knauf, and he recognizes it as comprising several dialects. It has also strongly influenced Mishnaic Hebrew, a fact that he explains as follows: "[b]etween 630 and 620, the Israelite south—Benjamin—was joined to Judah and remained Judean throughout the Babylonian and Persian periods. In the 6th century, more than 50% of the inhabitants of Yehud were descendants of speakers

---

15. Knauf, "Bethel," 295.
16. See also Gomes, *The Sanctuary of Bethel*, 51–54.
17. Knauf, "Bethel," 309–16.

of (southern) Israelite Hebrew."[18] He adds that in the sixth century the scribes of Bethel edited and wrote literature in Judean Hebrew, and as a consequence Biblical Hebrew has some Israelite Hebrew loanwords.[19] In fact, he regards these as having already entered Judean Hebrew by the end of the seventh century. The fall of Jerusalem can only have increased this impact.

Knauf's reconstruction of relations between Bethel and Jerusalem[20] contains four stages. First, ca. 650–586, Bethel and its traditions are incorporated into Judah. Second, ca. 586–ca. 520, Bethel and its traditions are supreme in Judah. Third, ca. 520–445, Jerusalem is re-established as a cultural but not political centre; Jerusalem traditions are reintroduced from Babylonia and cause conflict with those of Bethel. Finally, Bethel and its school and sanctuary are destroyed; ca. 450–ca. 300 Bethel traditions are integrated into the "constitution of Yehud" (the Torah) but can still be distinguished. The traces that each stage has left are then elaborated. In the first stage (650–586), the Jacob cycle, the exodus tradition, Hosea and the "Book of Saviours" are produced in Bethel, and 1 Sam 8–2 Kgs 2 and Isa 6–32 in Jerusalem. In the second stage (586–520), at Bethel the Abraham cycle is added to the Jacob cycle, while Hosea, Amos, Micah and Zephaniah are developed into a "Book of Four Prophets." Jeremiah is also begun, the existing Jerusalem literature is edited and Pss 75–52 (belonging to the Asaphite collection) are written. During this time, in Babylonia, Ezek 1–39 is written and other literature taken from Jerusalem (Exod 1–Josh 11; 1 Sam 8–2 Kgs 10 and perhaps Isa 5–32) is developed. The third stage (520–445) sees the editing of the exilic and Benjamin literature in Jerusalem, and thereafter the remainder of the scriptural canon, completed by ca. 150 BCE.

A good deal of this quite elaborate (often argued but sometimes also asserted!) reconstruction fits with the observations and arguments made earlier in this book. My own agnostic stance towards detailed literary critical argumentation discourages me from commenting on some of the proposals. Knauf does not, moreover, comment on the main issue of this book, which is the Judean identity of Israel: however, his comments suggest that he might endorse this suggestion.

Knauf takes for granted what had been earlier argued by Blenkinsopp: that Bethel was the major sanctuary of Judah during the Neo-Babylonian and early Persian periods. (He has further argued that the priesthood of

18. Ibid., 316.
19. He gives as examples תשוקה, רעש and אל שדי.
20. Knauf, "Bethel," 319.

Aaron was originally located there also.)[21] As Blenkinsopp points out, Jerusalem had been, according the biblical record, so thoroughly destroyed that an alternative site have would become necessary. There were, of course, other cult centres within the province of some antiquity: Gibeon, Mizpah and Gilgal,[22] which probably also recognized the "god of Jacob/Israel," and which, during the neo-Babylonian period, but perhaps also earlier, served Samaria as well as Judah, as Blenkinsopp notes with respect to Mizpah.[23] He discusses Jer 41:4–8 (considered in Chapter 8) but also Zech 7:1–7, dated to the "fourth year of Darius." This verse displays some awkward syntax, leaving it open to ambiguous interpretation: ...וישלח בית־אל צר־אצר (7:2). The modern translations generally render "the people of Bethel sent Sar-Eser…" The objective of the envoy is to enquire about continued fasting and lamenting over the sanctuary of Jerusalem in the early Persian period, and the passage refers to priests stationed there, to the deity *Yahweh Sebaoth* and to a lament observed (for a period of seventy years) for the destruction of Jerusalem. According to Hag 1:1 and Zech 1:1, the initiative for rebuilding this temple had recommenced in Darius's second year (see also Ezra 3:8), while Ezra 6:15 states that the temple was not finished until Darius's sixth year. On Zech 7:2, Gomes[24] follows the standard interpretation and thus concludes that "A relationship clearly existed between Bethelites and the Jerusalem Temple."[25] Blenkinsopp reads differently: "Sar-Ezer…had sent to Bethel," but argues that the reference to Bethel interrupts the introduction to the oracle and the oracle itself and is secondary, as betrayed by the resumptive use of "the word of Yhwh came" in v. 4.[26]

21. J. Blenkinsopp, "Bethel in the Neo-Babylonian Period," in Lipschits and Blenkinsopp, eds., *Judah and the Judeans*, 93–107. See also his "The Judean Priesthood During the Neo-Babylonian and Achaemenid Periods: A Hypothetical Reconstruction," *CBQ* 60 (1998): 25–43. He notes that Bethel's succession to Jerusalem had been proposed earlier by T. Meek, "Aaronites and Zadokites," *AJSL* 45 (1929): 149–66; R. North, "Aaron's Rise in Prestige," *ZAW* 66 (1954): 191–99; H. G. Judge, "Aaron, Zadok and Abiathar," *JTS* 7 (1956): 70–74.

22. The continued use of (the comparatively well-excavated) Beersheba is unlikely; though there is evidence of destruction in the early sixth century followed by population decline, it apparently lay within the limits of Judah as portrayed in Nehemiah (11:27, 30) and was (sparsely) resettled.

23. Blenkinsopp, "Bethel in the Neo-Babylonian Period," 99.

24. Cf. also Middlemas, *Templeless Judah*, 134–36.

25. Gomes, *The Sanctuary of Bethel*, 187.

26. Edelman, *The Origins of the "Second" Temple*, 147 n. 3, proposes that the text be translated "Bethel-Sharezer sent."

Given the problems with dating the rebuilding of Jerusalem and its temple during the time of Darius,[27] it may be better to avoid deriving any historical implications from this verse, though on either interpretation (but not Edelman's) Bethel is conceded by the writer of the phrase to have been Jerusalem's replacement. This is the place to remember that for cultural memory forgetting is as important as remembering, and that what Judean memory has forgotten about Bethel is as important as what it has remembered. Fortunately, the antagonism that Bethel engendered among the "Zionist" Judeans has prevented them from entirely forgetting, as the First History shows—though the Second History seems to have managed to overlook it.

Judean antagonism against Bethel is also investigated by Yairah Amit in the same volume as the Blenkinsopp essay.[28] Although she attributes this to the rivalry between Bethel and Jerusalem in the sixth century, she believes that the Judean cult had been centralized in Jerusalem under Josiah, which would have provided a further pretext for open polemics against Bethel. Yet while it is reasonable to conclude that indirect polemics might reflect a period of tension when both sanctuaries were active, direct polemic against Bethel could also be attributed to the time when Jerusalem sought to impose an exclusive status against not only Bethel, but other sanctuaries in Samaria. The dating of this exclusivist claim remains problematic, and the most important of the scriptural books in this connection, Deuteronomy, is less unambiguous than it is generally taken to be. The formula "the place where Yhwh will cause his name to reside" does not require a single sanctuary but might mean any sanctuary designated as a residence of the "name" of the god. The commonly accepted connection of Deuteronomy with Josiah has influenced the translation here, and a different historical context might favour the alternative. (There were, after all, other Yahwistic temples besides Jerusalem in the Persian period.) At all events, the polemic against Bethel in 1 Kgs 12–13, 2 Kgs 23 and Amos (passim) points to it having been regarded as the chief rival to Jerusalem, as its geographical location would suggest—though this rivalry need not have existed during the Judean monarchy, but when these texts were written (in the case of Amos, when it was taken over and edited as a Judean memory). The stories associated with the transfer of the ark, and the golden calf episode (connected with the legend of Josiah's destruction of Bethel) show that Bethel–Jerusalem

27. See ibid., 80–149 (Haggai–Zechariah) and 150–208 (Ezra).

28. Y. Amit, "Epoch and Genre: The Sixth Century and the Growth of Hidden Polemics," in Lipschits and Blenkinsopp, eds., *Judah and the Judeans*, 135–51, especially 139–43.

rivalry constituted a major issue within Judean cultural memory. Amit has argued that this antagonism may have its roots in the sixth century but must have achieved its literary expression in the period when Jerusalem reasserted its supremacy over Bethel (religiously) as well as over Mizpah (politically).[29]

It is thus highly probable, if not virtually certain, that between the destruction of the Jerusalem sanctuary and its restoration as the central Yahwistic temple of Judah, Bethel played a dominant role. The worship of Yahweh obviously continued in Judah during this time, and while Bethel need not have claimed an exclusive status, its history as a royal sanctuary and the antagonistic echoes in Judean memory strongly imply that it functioned as the focus of Judean religious life for a period that extended over more than a century, while simultaneously continuing to serve in some capacity the population of Samaria as well (perhaps even as its most venerable sanctuary). I have argued that it succeeded in uniting the royal cults of the both defunct kingdoms with the result that the god of the patriarch Israel, also in the guise of Yhwh Sebaoth, Jerusalem's deity, was worshipped in both territories, bringing the people of Judah for the first time, and forever afterwards, into the family of Jacob.

29. Ibid.

Chapter 11

REFLECTIONS AND IMPLICATIONS

Many peoples shall come and say,
"Come, let us go up to the mountain of Yhwh,
to the house of the God of Jacob;
that he may teach us his ways
and that we may walk in his paths."
For out of Zion shall go forth instruction,
and the word of Yhwh from Jerusalem (Isa 2:3)

The history of scholarship is littered with many firm conclusions and even more agreed ones. But the history also shows that most conclusions have a limited shelf-life. Some are disproved; others go out of fashion; some become irrelevant. But this fact does not diminish the value of scholarship. Biblical scholarship is a conversation and a quest as well as a science. If we can rarely decide definitively what is right, we can often declare emphatically what is *not* right. We also learn to ask new and better questions; and, most importantly, perhaps, we realize that scholarship, like history-writing, answers the questions of its own time and can therefore never reach any definitive goal. In other words, understanding better does not necessarily mean knowing more answers: it can mean knowing better questions.

This book, like its predecessor, *In Search of "Ancient Israel"*, is certainly not intended as a definitive "solution" but as a contribution to a set of related problems and an invitation to explore them further. Every single question touched upon deserves and demands more detailed treatment. But what seems to me most important is the way in a mixture of approaches and a range of varied bits of evidence here come together to point towards the same conclusion—perhaps one that many readers will already regard as obvious: *"Israel" in the Hebrew Bible is not a historical community but an identity claimed by several communities.* Indeed, there are other "Israels" outside the Bible, but those within it represent the ancient Judean cultural memories. I have suggested that Judeans adopted the cult of the "god of Israel" in the sixth century, identifying this deity with the god of Jerusalem's cult, and sharing worship with others from Samaria (another "Israel") and of course with the people of Benjamin who had belonged both to Israel and more lately also to Judah (and were thus already members of an "Israel" that included Judah). Over a period of a century and a half, Judeans came to recognize ("remember") themselves as descendants of the Jacob whose ancestral god they worshipped and who had founded the sanctuary of Bethel. Those who took over authority in Judah under the Persians, at some time in the middle to late fifth century, and re-established Jerusalem and its cult (I think "Zionists" is precisely the right term) did not reject this identity, but defined their "Israelite" identity in various ways: extending their claims over the territory of Samaria as well as Judah or, on the contrary, excluding these and claiming themselves to be exclusively "Israel"—the two polarized positions perhaps reflecting the tensions between Judah and Samaria that eventually developed into a rift. On the other hand, we know that this cult was shared not only widely in "Beyond the River" (outside the territory of the "Samaritans"), but in numerous communities throughout the empires of Persia and its successors, Parthia, the Hellenistic monarchies and Rome.

There remains, then, huge uncertainty about how the various Israels reflected in the Judean canon functioned within Judean society and among its neighbours. But the presence of different definitions is reflected in the codifying of Judean cultural memories that eventually became canonized. In ancient times that canonization played a major role in defining and stabilizing "Judaism," the dominant expression of Israel. This canon became also part of the canon of a new religion, Christianity (producing in turn another "Israel"). In modern times the double canonization has led to these cultural memories being completely misunderstood and abused as "history" by Christian fundamentalism and Jewish Zionism. This false "history" has therefore become part of the cultural memory of these modern constituencies.

Biblical Israels and their Historical Contexts

How far can we translate the ancient cultural memories into our modern critical version of history, rather than just co-opting them into our own cultural memories (which is their legitimate function within Jewish and Christian worship and the respective identities that these religions entail)? What follows is merely my own suggestion; not much more than a guess. The chronologically earliest historical Israel may well be the small group of tribes centred on Benjamin who are remembered as forming a kingdom under Saul. This is a Benjaminite memory, probably dominant within the later kingdom of Israel and later adopted by Judeans, who reconfigured the story of this Israel as a kingdom saved from Philistine defeat by the Judean hero David. In addition, apparently having few memories of their own about their origins, Judeans adopted and adapted the memories of conquest of their land and early struggles against local enemies that originated with Benjaminites and may have also been "remembered" by other Israelites. I have argued that such a Benjaminite/Israelite history was written in Mizpah in the sixth century BCE, and the Jerusalemite–Judean version that now constituted the later part of the First History (the "Former Prophets") was created after Jerusalem once again became the centre of Judah in the second half of the fifth century. In each case specific reasons for the production of these memories have been suggested.

The books of Kings, Chronicles and Ezra reflect different attitudes towards what was now Samaria, implying a disagreement within Judah about the status of the former territory of the kingdom of Israel. It is difficult to map the political and social history that these positions presumably reflect.[1] But the First and Second Histories are complex and composite literary products, and their component scrolls have also their own independent textual histories. While their broad ideological positions can be discerned and to some extent correlated with historical contexts, the growth of this literature itself is complex and should not be simplified. However, there seems to me little doubt that the formation of the Judean cultural memories written in the scriptural canon took place entirely within the so-called Second Temple Period (a term we really ought to abandon; it reflects Zionist theology and is not an accurate historical description).[2]

It is the current consensus that the so-called Samaritan schism did not occur in the Persian period, but perhaps late in the third century or even early in the second (Ben Sira 50:26, describing those who live in Shechem as "foolish," may reflect a late stage in the process of disaffection). The books of Ezra and Nehemiah seem to reflect that schism and should therefore be dated well after the period they claim to relate. But their ideology of internal separation, which is also present in Deuteronomy, and which renames the "peoples of the land" as "Canaanites" (and which Ezra–Nehemiah invokes) may reflect a two stage-process in which first a ruling clique claiming to be the true "Israel" established its

---

1. For one such attempt, see Jon L. Berquist, "Constructions of Identity in Post-colonial Yehud," in Lipschits and Oeming, eds., *Judah and the Judeans*, 53–66, which shows a keen awareness of the multilayered aspects of identity.

2. This conclusion follows largely the historical context offered by Liverani's for his "invented history" (*Israel's History*, 250–360).

authority over the religious and political life of Judah and in the process sought to make Jerusalem the exclusive cult centre, at least in Judah; then, in a second stage, the ideology takes a sectarian form as exclusive Judean groups seek to claim this exclusive Israelite identity for themselves, even redefining "exile" in the process as an ongoing experience. This second stage can be seen in the Qumran literature, but the books of Ezra and Nehemiah themselves may belong to a second sectarian stage themselves: the original separation of the two main characters (which is perfectly obvious) points to two distinct groups making similar kinds of claims.

The books of Chronicles represent a view that insists on the supremacy of Jerusalem over Judah and Samaria. This seems to reflect a dispute between the two territories over religious leadership and thus to mark the beginnings of the rift between them, which would lead to two "Israels" centred in Jerusalem and Shechem. The political reunification of both territories that probably took place in the Ptolemaic period may have led to a competition over religious hegemony for the whole region. The Pentateuch, with its single twelve-tribe nation, reflects the cultural memories of both Judah and Samaria and so appears to predate that rift. Even within that twelve-tribe Israel, there are differences in how identity is configured, illustrated by the books of Leviticus, Numbers and Deuteronomy; these presumably reflect claims on behalf of priestly, scribal and military (nationalistic?) interests. It would be useful to see how far these interests can be correlated with those that we can identify within early Judaism (such as Pharisee, Sadducees, Hasmoneans).

The fully fledged portrait of the Pentateuch demonstrates the ultimate incorporation of Judah into an Israelite nation. But we should avoid the temptation to arrange the biblical Israels into too neat a chronological sequence. Just as they exist synchronically on the pages of the Bible, they can also have existed simultaneously in Judah during the Persian and Hellenistic periods, before the memories were all canonized.

In relation to the Pentateuchal Israel, I am aware that I have said little about the tribal system. This is widely suspected as being an artificial scheme. Such a conclusion does not deny that "Benjamin," "Judah," "Ephraim," "Manasseh" and others correspond to real geographical, social or political entities. Indeed, memory of descent from the eponymous Jacob/Israel may have been embedded within the kingdom of Israel. If so (and this is only a surmise), the number of tribes may have grown to ten, as the precise wording of 1 Kgs 11:35 (עשרת השבטים) might betray. The extension to twelve would then be the mechanism by which Judah is included in Israel. Presumably eleven was not thought a suitable number, not because neither soccer nor cricket had then been invented, but for cultural reasons: certain numbers are unlucky or evil. The problem of increasing ten to twelve while having a total of only eleven was apparently solved in more than one manner, as several of the inconsistencies between various versions of the scheme show. There was no agreed mechanism among the guardians of the Judean memory as to how the system should be constructed. Once only three tribal identities were left within Judah, the complement of the full twelve hardly mattered—only the actual number. But Genesis also goes further, and incorporates this Israelite genealogy into a wider one, anticipating (or reflecting) the spread of the cult of Yhwh (and of "Judaism") widely throughout the area once known as "Across the River" (*eber ha-nahar*) —and so perhaps creating the "Hebrews" as a generic name for this Aramaic-speaking and largely Yahweh-worshipping population.[3]

But these suggestions lie beyond what I have tried to argue in this book. My main concern has been to show how "biblical Israel" is not a historical datum but a construction of cultural memory that defines not the community of the past but that of the present. It is not at all a common denominator of literature and archaeology: it exists only as a literary phenomenon. Attempts to write a history of correlating biblical and archaeological data are misguided until and unless the character of the literary Israels is understood

A few further implications may be noted. Much has been written (some of it intelligent; most of it not) about so-called minimalism, as if it were a clearly defined and ideologically driven programme or "school." There are in fact many scholars who argue for later dates and less historical reliability than the (dwindling) majority, and while most employ exactly the same methods as have been traditional used in biblical scholarship, they do not all share any single ideological viewpoint. I hope that the ridiculous polarization of "minimalism" and "maximalism" can be forgotten, and those who favour earlier dates and a higher degree of historical reliability for the biblical texts will propose arguments against the view that I have in effect argued here: that *no text or passage in which Judah belongs to Israel should be dated before the Neo-Babylonian period at the earliest, and perhaps not before the Persian period.*

Finally: these issues are not antiquarian. The problems inherent in the definitions of "Jew/Judean" and "Israelite" persist today and remain

---

3. This suggestion takes further a conclusion reached by N. P. Lemche, " 'Hebrew' as a National Name for Israel," *Studia Theologica* 33 (1979): 1–23, and D. R. G. Beattie, "What does Hebrew Mean?" (paper presented at the Queen's University Institute of Byzantine Studies, Belfast, May 23, 2007).

problematic. The Bible still rules as a modern cultural memory among Jews and Christians (and in certain ways among Muslims too). Terms such as "secular Jew" and "Arab Israeli" point dramatically to the difficulties, even today, of simplifying the essence of "Israel"—or "Jew" or "Judaism"—in the modern world. The term "Israel" has acquired again a national and political identity after two millennia of religious identity, and the tensions between the political, cultural and religious identities denoted by the term are highly visible. But these tensions can be seen already in the Bible itself and its various Israels. While biblical historians cannot resolve these modern tensions, they should be aware that their roots lie in the ancient concepts of "Israel," and that while religion (or in secular contexts, culture—though it is a religious culture) and genealogy still serve as major codes for Jewish identity, the identity of "Israel" remains something that is *produced* rather than *given*. In that respect, those who assert Jewishness are no different from the rest of us with our own equally constructed nationalities, cultures and identities—among which a closely related identity, "Palestinian," is even now in the making.

BIBLIOGRAPHY

Aaron, David. *Etched in Stone: The Emergence of the Decalogue.* London: T&T Clark, 2006.

Abu El-Haj, Nadia. *Facts on the Ground: Archaeological Practice and Territorial Self-Fashioning in Israeli Society.* Chicago: University of Chicago Press, 2001.

Ahlström, Gösta W. *The History of Ancient Palestine from the Palaeolithic Period to Alexander's Conquest.* Sheffield: Sheffield Academic Press, 1993.

Albertz, Rainer. *History of Israelite Religion in the Old Testament Period.* 2 vols. London: SCM Press. Louisville: Westminster John Knox, 1994. German edition, *Religionsgeschichte Israels in alttestamentlicher Zeit.* Göttingen: Vandenhoeck & Ruprecht, 1992.

—"Why a Reform Like Josiah's Must Have Happened." Pages 27–46 in Grabbe, ed., *Good Kings and Bad Kings.*

—*Die Exilzeit. 6 Jahrhundert v. Chr.* Berlin: Kohlhammer, 2001.

Alt, Albrecht. "The Settlement of the Israelites in Palestine." Pages 133–69 in *Essays on Old Testament History and Religion.* Garden City, N.Y.: Doubleday, 1966. Originally published as *Die Landnahme der Israeliten in Palästina.* Leipzig: Reformationsprogramm der Universität, 1925.

Amit, Y. "Epoch and Genre: The Sixth Century and the Growth of Hidden Polemics." Pages 135–51 in Lipschits and Blenkinsopp, eds., *Judah and the Judeans.*

Assmann, Jan. *Das kulturelle Gedächtnis. Schrift, Erinnerung und politische Identität in frühen Hochkulturen.* 2d ed. Munich: Beck, 1999.

—*Moses the Egyptian: The Memory of Egypt in Western Monotheism.* Cambridge, Mass.: Harvard University Press, 1997.

—*Religion and Cultural Memory: Ten Studies.* Translated by Rodney Livingstone. Stanford: Stanford University Press, 2006. Trans. of *Religion und kulturelles Gedächtnis.* Munich: Beck, 2000.

Auld, A. Graeme. *Kings Without Privilege: David and Moses in the Story of the Bible's Kings.* Edinburgh: T. & T. Clark, 1994.

—*Joshua, Moses and the Land: Tetrateuch–Pentateuch–Hexateuch in a Generation Since 1938.* Edinburgh: T. & T. Clark, 1980.

Avigad, Nahman. *Discovering Jerusalem.* Oxford: Blackwell, 1980.

Babha, Homi K. *The Location of Culture.* London: Routledge, 1994.

Barr, James. "Story and History in Biblical Theology." *Journal of Religion* 56 (1976): 1–17.

Barstad, Hans. *The Babylonian Captivity of the Book of Isaiah: "Exilic" Judah and the Provenance of Isaiah 40–55.* Oslo: Novus, 1997.

—"Lebte Deuterojesaja in Judäa?" *Norsk Teologisk Tidsskrift* 83 (1982): 77–87.

—*A Way in the Wilderness: The "Second Exodus" in the Message of Second Isaiah.* Manchester: Manchester University Press, 1989.

Barth, Fredrik. *Ethnic Groups and Boundaries*. Boston: Little, Brown & Co., 1969.

Beattie, D. R. G. "What does Hebrew Mean?" Paper presented at the Queen's University Institute of Byzantine Studies, Belfast, May 23, 2007.

Ben Zvi, Ehud. *Signs of Jonah: Reading and Rereading in Ancient Yehud*. London: Sheffield Academic Press, 2003.

Berquist, Jon L. "Constructions of Identity in Postcolonial Yehud." Pages 53–66 in Lipschits and Oeming, eds., *Judah and the Judeans*.

Blenkinsopp, Joseph. "Bethel in the Neo-Babylonian Period." Pages 93–107 in Lipschits and Blenkinsopp, eds., *Judah and the Judeans*.

—"The Judean Priesthood During the Neo-Babylonian and Achaemenid Periods: A Hypothetical Reconstruction." *Catholic Biblical Quarterly* 60 (1998): 25–43.

—"Memory, Tradition and the Construction of the Past in Ancient Israel." *Biblical Theology Bulletin* 27 (1997): 76–82. Repr. on pages 1–17 in Joseph Blenkinsopp, *Treasures Old and New*. Grand Rapids: Eerdmans, 2004.

—"The Midianite–Kenite Hypothesis and Israelite Ethnic Origins." Unpublished.

Boserup, Ester. *The Conditions of Agricultural Growth: The Economics of Agrarian Change Under Population Pressure*. Chicago: Aldine, 1965. Reissued with an Introduction by Nicholas Kaldor, New Brunswick: Aldine, 2005.

Brannigan, J. *New Historicism and Cultural Materialism*. Basingstoke: Macmillan, 1998.

Braun, Roddy L. "Reconstruction of the History of Israel." Pages 92–105 in *The Chronicler as Historian*. Edited by M. Patrick Graham, Kenneth G. Hoglund and Steven L. McKenzie. Sheffield: Sheffield Academic Press, 1997.

Brett, Mark, ed. *Ethnicity and the Bible*. *Leiden:* Brill. 1996.

—"Interpreting Ethnicity: Method, Hermeneutics, Ethics." Pages 3–23 in Brett, ed., *Ethnicity and the Bible*.

Bright, John. *A History of Israel*. Philadelphia: Westminster, 1959. 4th ed, Louisville: Westminster John Knox, 2000.

Broshi, Magen. "The Expansion of Jerusalem in the Reigns of Hezekiah and Manasseh." *Israel Exploration Journal* 24 (1974): 21–26.

Brueggemann, Walter. *David's Truth in Israel's Imagination and Memory*. Philadelphia: Fortress, 1985.

Carroll, Robert. *Jeremiah: A Commentary*. OTL. Philadelphia: Westminster, 1986.

Chapman, Stephen. *The Law and the Prophets: A Study in Old Testament Canon Formation*. Tübingen: Mohr, 2000.

Clines, David J. A. "The Old Testament Histories." Pages 85–105 in *What Does Eve Do To Help? And Other Readerly Questions to the Old Testament*. Sheffield: JSOT Press, 1990.

Clines, David J. A., and J. Cheryl Exum. *The New Literary Criticism and the Hebrew Bible*. Sheffield: JSOT Press, 1993.

Cohen, Ronald. "Ethnicity: Problem and Focus in Anthropology." *Annual Review of Anthropology* 7 (1978): 379–403.

Cross, Frank M., Jr. "The Structure of Deuteronomic History." Pages 9–24 in *Perspectives in Jewish Learning*. Chicago: College of Jewish Studies. Repr. as "The Themes of the Book of Kings and the Structure of the Deuteronomistic History." Pages 274–89 in *Canaanite Myth and Hebrew Epic: Essays in the History of the Religion of Israel*. Cambridge, Mass.: Harvard University Press, 1973, and pages 79–94 in Knoppers and McConville, eds., *Reconsidering Israel and Judah*.

Davies, Philip R. "Amos, Man and Book." Pages 113–31 in *Israel's Prophets and Israel's Past: Essays on the Relationship of Prophetic Texts and Israelite History in Honor of John H. Hayes*. Edited by Brad E. Kelle and Megan Bishop Moore. London: T&T Clark, 2006.

—"Biblical Foundations of Judaism." Pages 113–20 in vol. 1 of *The Encyclopaedia of Judaism*. Edited by J. Neusner, A. Avery-Peck and W. S. Green. 3 vols. Leiden: Brill, 2000.

—"God of Cyrus, God of Israel: Some Religio-Historical Reflections on Isaiah 40–55." Pages 207–25 in *Words Remembered, Texts Renewed: Essays in Honour of John F. A. Sawyer*. Edited by Graham Harvey, Wilfred Watson and Jon Davies. Sheffield: Sheffield Academic Press, 1995.

—*In Search of "Ancient Israel"*. Sheffield: Sheffield Academic Press, 1992.

—"Josiah and the Law Book." Pages 65–77 in Grabbe, ed., *Good Kings and Bad Kings*.

—"'Pen of Iron, Point of Diamond' (Jer 17:1): Prophecy as Writing." Pages 65–81 in *Writings and Speech in Israelite and Ancient Near Eastern Prophecy*. Edited by M. Floyd and E. Ben Zvi. Atlanta: Scholars Press, 2000.

—"Scenes from the Early History of Judaism." Pages 145–82 in *The Triumph of Elohim*. Edited by D. V. Edelman. Kampen: Kok Pharos, 1995.

—"What *Is* Minimalism, and Why Do So Many People Dislike It?" Pages 76–86 in *Historie og konstruktion. Festskrift til Niels Peter Lemche I anledning af 60 års fødselsdagen den 6. September 2005*. Edited by Mogens Müller and Thomas L. Thompson. Copenhagen: Museum Tusculanums, 2005.

—"Whose History? Whose Israel? Whose Bible? Biblical Histories, Ancient and Modern." Pages 104–22 in *Can a History of Israel Be Written?* Edited by L. L. Grabbe. Sheffield: Sheffield Academic Press, 1997.

Davis, Thomas W. *Shifting Sands: The Rise and Fall of Biblical Archaeology*. Oxford: Oxford University Press, 2004.

Dearman, J. Andrew. "Composition and Context in Jeremiah 36." *Journal of Biblical Literature* 109 (1990): 403–21.

Dever, William G. "The Patriarchal Traditions." Pages 102–20 in Hayes and Miller, eds., *Israelite and Judaean History*.

Dietrich, Walther. *Prophetie und Geschichte*. Göttingen: Vandenhoeck & Ruprecht, 1972.

Droge, A. J. "'The Lying Pen of the Scribes': Of Holy Books and Pious Frauds." *Method and Theory in the Study of Religion* 15 (2003): 117–47.

Duhm, Bernhard. *Das Buch Jesaia*. HAT. Göttingen: Vandenhoeck & Ruprecht, 1892.

—*Das Buch Jeremia*. KHAT. Tübingen: Mohr, 1901.

Edelman, Diana. "Did Saulide-Davidic Rivalry Resurface in Early Persian Yehud?" Pages in 70–92 in *The Land That I Will Show You: Essays in the History and Archaeology of the Ancient Near East in Honor of. J. Maxwell Miller*. Edited by M. P. Graham and A. Dearman. Sheffield: Sheffield Academic Press, 2001.

—"Ethnicity and Early Israel," Pages 25–55 in Brett, ed., *Ethnicity and the Bible*.

—"Hezekiah's Alleged Cultic Centralization." *Journal for the Study of the Old Testament* (forthcoming).

—*The Origins of the "Second Temple": Persian Imperial Policy and the Rebuilding of Jerusalem*. London: Equinox, 2005.

Eissfeldt, O. "Der Geschichtliche Hintergrund der Erzählung von Gibeas Schandtat (Richter 19–21)." Pages 54–80 in *Kleine Schriften*, vol. 2. Edited by R. Sellheim and F. Maass. Tübingen: Mohr, 1963.

Eitam , David, and Amir Shomroni. "Research of the Oil Industry During the Iron Age at Tel Miqne." Pages 37–56 in *Olive Oil in Antiquity: Israel and Neighbouring Countries from the Neolithic to the Early Arab Period.* Edited by D. Eitam and M. Melzer. Padua: Sargon, 1996.

Esler, Philip F., ed. *Ancient Israel: The Old Testament in Its Social Context.* Minneapolis: Fortress, 2006.

Eynikel, Erik. *The Reform of King Josiah and the Composition of the Deuteronomistic History.* Leiden: Brill, 1996.

Finkelstein, Israel. *The Archaeology of the Israelite Settlement.* Jerusalem: Israel Exploration Society, 1988.

Finkelstein, Israel, Zvi Lederman and Shlomo Bunimowitz, eds. *Highlands of Many Cultures: The Southern Samaria Survey—The Sites,* vol. 1. Tel Aviv: Institute of Archaeology, 1997.

Finkelstein, Israel, and Eli Piasetzky. "The Iron I–IIA in the Highlands and Beyond." *Levant* 38 (2006): 45–61.

Finkelstein, Israel, and Neil Asher Silberman. *The Bible Unearthed: Archaeology's New Vision of Ancient Israel and the Origin of Its Sacred Texts.* New York: Free Press, 2001.

—*David and Solomon: In Search of the Bible's Sacred Kings and the Roots of the Western Tradition.* New York: Free Press, 2006.

—"Temple and Dynasty: Hezekiah: The Remaking of Judah and the Rise of the Pan-Israelite Ideology." *Journal for the Study of the Old Testament* 30 (2006): 259–85.

Freedman, David Noel. "Deuteronomistic History, The." Pages 226–28 in *The Interpreter's Dictionary of the Bible: Supplementary Volume.* Edited by K. Crim. Nashville: Abingdon, 1976.

Fried, Lisbet. "The High Places (*Bamôth*) and the Reforms of Hezekiah and Josiah." *Journal of the American Oriental Society* 122 (2002): 1–29.

Geus, Cornelius H. J. de. *The Tribes of Israel: An Investigation into Some of the Presuppositions of Martin Noth's Amphictyony Hypothesis.* Assen: Van Gorcum, 1976.

Ginsberg, H. L. *The Israelian Heritage of Judaism.* Texts and Studies of the Jewish Theological Seminary of America. New York: Jewish Theological Seminary of America, 1982.

Gomes, J. F. *The Sanctuary of Bethel and the Configuration of Israelite Identity.* Berlin: de Gruyter, 2006.

Gottwald, Norman. *The Tribes of Yahweh: A Sociology of the Religion of Liberated Israel, 1250–1050 B.C.E.* Maryknoll, N.Y.: Orbis, 1979.

Grabbe, Lester L., ed. *Good Kings and Bad Kings.* London: T&T Clark International . 2005.

Greifenhagen, Folker V. *Egypt on the Pentateuch's Ideological Map: Constructing Biblical Israel's Identity.* London: Sheffield Academic Press, 2002.

—"Ethnicity In, With, or Under the Pentateuch." *Journal of Roman Studies* 3 (2001): 1–17.

Guillaume, Philippe. *Waiting for Joshua: The Judges.* London: T&T Clark International, 2004.

Gunkel, Hermann. *The Folktale in the Old Testament.* Sheffield: Almond, 1987. German original, *Das Märchen im Alten Testamen.* Tübingen: Mohr, 1917, 1921.

—*The Legends of Genesis*. New York: Schocken, 1964. German original, *Genesis*, Göttingen: Vandenhoeck & Ruprecht, 1901 (Introduction).

Gunn, David M. *The Fate of King Saul: The Interpretation of a Biblical Story*. Sheffield: JSOT Press, 1980.

Halbwachs, Maurice. *On Collective Memory*. Edited and translated by Lewis A. Coser. Chicago: University of Chicago Press, 1992.

Halpern, Baruch. *David's Secret Demons: Messiah, Murderer, Traitor, King*. Grand Rapids: Eerdmans, 2001.

—"Sybil, or the Two Nations." Pages 291–338 in *The Study of the Ancient Near East in the Twentieth Century*. Edited by J. S. Cooper and G. M. Schwarz. Winona Lake: Eisenbrauns, 1996.

—"Text and Artifact: Two Monologues." Pages 311–40 in Silberman and Small, eds., *The Archaeology of Israel*.

Handy, Lowell K. "Hezekiah's Unlikely Reform." *Zeitschrift für die alttestamentliche Wissenschaft* 100 (1988): 111–15.

Hasel, Michael G. "*Israel* in the Merneptah Stela." *Bulletin of the American Schools of Oriental Research* 296 (1994): 45–61.

Hayes John H., and J. Maxwell Miller. *Israelite and Judean History*. London: SCM Press. Philadelphia: Westminster, 1977.

Heard, R. Christopher. *Dynamics of Diselection: Ambiguity in Genesis 12–36 and Ethnic Boundaries in Post-Exilic Judah*. Atlanta: Scholars Press, 2001.

Henige, David. "In Good Company: Problematic Sources and Biblical Historicity." *Journal for the Study of the Old Testament* 30 (2005): 29–47.

Hens-Piazza, G. *The New Historicism*. Minneapolis: Fortress, 2002.

Herzog, Zeev, and L. Singer-Avitz. "Redefining the Centre: The Emergence of State in Judah. *Tel Aviv* 31 (2004): 209–44.

—"Sub-Dividing the Iron Age IIA: A Suggested Solution to the Chronological Debate, *Tel Aviv* 33 (2006): 163–95.

Heym, Stefan. *The King David Report*. New York: Puttnam, 1973.

Hjelm, Ingrid. *The Samaritans and Early Judaism: A Literary Analysis*. Sheffield: Sheffield Academic Press, 2000.

Høgenhaven, Jesper. *Gott und Volk bei Jesaja. Eine Untersuchung zur Biblischen Theologie*. Leiden: Brill, 1988.

Holladay, William. *A Commentary on the Book of the Prophet Jeremiah*. 2 vols. Minneapolis: Fortress, 1986–89.

Jameson, Fredric. *The Political Unconscious: Narrative as a Socially Symbolic Act*. Ithaca, N.Y.: Cornell University Press, 1981.

Jamieson-Drake, David W. *Scribes and Schools in Monarchic Judah*. Sheffield: Almond, 1991.

Japhet, Sara. *I & II Chronicles*. London: SCM Press, 1993.

—*The Ideology of the Book of Chronicles and Its Place in Biblical Thought*. Frankfurt: Peter Lang, 1989.

Jepsen, Alfred. *Die Quellen des Königsbuches*. 2d ed. Halle: Niemeyer, 1956.

Johnstone, William. *1 & 2 Chronicles*. 2 vols. Sheffield. Sheffield Academic Press, 1997.

Jones, G. H. *1 and 2 Kings*, vol. 1. New Century Bible. London: Marshall, Morgan & Scott, 1984.

Jones, Sian. *The Archaeology of Ethnicity: Constructing Identities in the Past and Present*. London: Routledge, 1997.

Judge, H. G. "Aaron. Zadok and Abiathar." *Journal of Theological Studies* 7 (1956): 70–74.

Kelso, James L. "Excavations at Bethel." *Biblical Archaeologist* 19 (1956): 36–43.

—*The Excavations at Bethel (1934–1960): Joint Expedition of the Pittsburgh Theological Seminary and ASOR*. Cambridge, Mass.: American Schools of Oriental Research, 1968.

Killebrew, Anne. *Biblical Peoples and Ethnicity: An Archaeological Study of Egyptians, Canaanites, Philistines, and Early Israel 1300–1100 B.C.E*. Atlanta: Society of Biblical Literature, 2005.

King, P. J., and L. E. Stager. *Life in Biblical Israel*. Louisville: Westminster John Knox, 2001.

Klein, Ralph W. "Chronicles, Book of 1–2." Pages 92–1002 in vol. 1 of *The Anchor Bible Dictionary*. Edited by D. N. Freedman. New York: Doubleday, 1992.

Knauf, E. Axel. "Bethel: The Israelite Impact on Judean Language and Literature." Pages 291–350 in Lipschits and Oeming, eds., *Judah and the Judeans*.

—"Does Deuteronomistic Historiography Exist?" Pages 388–98 in *Israel Constructs Its History*. Edited by A. de Pury and T. Römer. Sheffield: Sheffield Academic Press, 2000.

—"The Glorious Days of Manasseh." Pages in 164–88 in Grabbe, ed., *Good Kings and Bad Kings*.

—"Towards an Archaeology of the Hexateuch." Pages 275–94 in *Abschied vom Jahwisten: Die Komposition des Hexateuch in der jüngsten Diskussion*. Edited by J. C. Gertz, K. Schmid and M. Witte. Berlin: de Gruyter, 2002.

Knoppers, Gary N., and J. G. McConville, eds. *Reconsidering Israel and Judah: Recent Studies in the Deuteronomistic History*. Winona Lake: Eisenbrauns, 2000.

Knowles, Melody D. *Centrality Practiced: Jerusalem in the Religious Practices of Yehus and the Diaspora in the Persian Period*. Atlanta: Society of Biblical Literature, 2006.

Koenen, K. *Bethel: Geschichte, Kult und Theologie*. Freiburg: University of Freiburg. Göttingen: Vandenhoeck & Ruprecht, 2003.

Kohlmoos, Melanie. *Bet-El-Erinnerungen an eine Stadt: Perspektiven der alttestamentlichen Bet-El-Überlieferung*. Tübingen: Mohr Siebeck, 2006.

Kratz, Reinhard G. *The Composition of the Narrative Books of the Old Testament*. London: T&T Clark International, 2005. German original, *Die Komposition der erzählenden Bücher des Alten Testaments*. Göttingen: Vandenhoeck & Ruprecht, 2000.

—"Israel als Staat und Volk." *Zeitschrift für Theologie und Kirche* 97 (2000): 1–7.

—"Israel in the Book of Isaiah." *Journal for the Study of the Old Testament* 31 (2006): 103–28.

Lemche, Niels Peter. *The Canaanites and Their Land: The Tradition of the Canaanites*. Sheffield: JSOT Press, 1991.

—"The Greek 'Amphictyony': Could It Be a Prototype for the Israelite Society in the Period of the Judges?" *Journal for the Study of the Old Testament* 4 (1977): 48–59.

—" 'Hebrew' as a National Name for Israel." *Studia Theologica* 33 (1979): 1–23.

—*The Israelites in History and Tradition*. Louisville: Westminster John Knox, 1998.

Levin, Yigal. "Joseph, Judah and the 'Benjamin Conundrum.' " *Zeitschrift für die alttestamentliche Wissenschaft* 116 (2004): 223–41.

—"The Political Status of the Tribe of Benjamin and the Joseph Story." *Judea and Samaria Research Studies* 14 (2005): 35–52 (Hebrew with English abstract).

Levin, Yigal, and Avram Faust. "The Ties Between the Tribes Asher and Benjamin."
    Pages 225–31 in *Judea and Samaria Research Studies: Proceedings of the Seventh
    Annual Meeting*. Edited by Y. Eshel. Ariel: College of Judea and Samaria, 1998
    (Hebrew with English abstract).
Linville, James R. *Israel in the Book of Kings: The Past as a Project of Social Identity*.
    Sheffield: Sheffield Academic Press, 1998.
Lipschits, Oded. *The Fall and Rise of Jerusalem*. Winona Lake: Eisenbrauns, 2005.
Lipschits Oded, and Joseph Blenkinsopp, eds. *Judah and the Judeans in the Neo-
    Babylonian Period*. Winona Lake: Eisenbrauns, 2003.
Lipschits, Oded, and Manfred Oeming, eds. *Judah and the Judeans in the Persian Period*.
    Winona Lake: Eisenbrauns, 2006.
Liverani, Mario. *Israel's History and the History of Israel*. London: Equinox, 2005.
—*Myth and Politics in Ancient Near Eastern Historiography*. Edited and With an
    Introduction by Zainab Bahrani and Marc Van De Mieroop; London: Equinox,
    2002.
Livingston, David. "Location of Biblical Bethel and Ai Reconsidered." *Westminster
    Theological Journal* 33 (1970): 20–44.
Lohfink, N., ed. *Das Deuteronomium: Entstehung, Gestalt und Botschaft*. Leuven:
    Peeters, 1985
Lundbom, Jack R. *Jeremiah: A New Translation With Introduction and Commentary*. 3
    vols. New York: Doubleday, 1999–2004.
McKane, William. *Jeremiah*. 2 vols. ICC. Edinburgh: T. & T. Clark, 1986–96.
McKenzie, Steven L., Thomas Römer and H. H. Schmid, eds. *King David: A Biography*.
    Oxford: Oxford University Press, 2000.
—*Rethinking the Foundations: Historiography in the Ancient World and in the Bible—
    Essays in Honor of John Van Seters*. Berlin: de Gruyter, 2000.
Mazar, Amihai. "The Debate Over the Chronology of the Iron Age in the Southern
    Levant: Its History, the Current Situation, and a Suggested Resolution." Pages 15–
    30 in *The Bible and Radiocarbon Dating: Archaeology, Text and Science*. Edited by
    Thomas E. Levy and Thomas Higham. London: Equinox, 2005.
—"Remarks on Biblical Traditions and Archaeological Evidence Concerning Early
    Israel." Pages 85–98 in *Symbiosis, Symbolism and the Power of the Past: Canaan*.
    Edited by W. G. Dever and S. Gitin. Winona Lake: Eisenbrauns, 2002.
Mazar, B. *Biblical Israel: State and People*. Jerusalem: Magnes, 1992.
Meek, T. "Aaronites and Zadokites." *American Journal of Semitic Languages and
    Literatures* 45 (1929): 149–66.
Mendels, Doron. *Memory in Jewish, Pagan and Christian Societies*. London: T&T Clark,
    2004.
Mendenhall, George E. "The Hebrew Conquest of Palestine." *Biblical Archaeologist* 25
    (1962): 66–87.
Middlemas, Jill. *The Troubles of Templeless Judah*. Oxford: Oxford University Press,
    2005.
Miller, J. Maxwell. "The Israelite Occupation of the Canaan." Pages 213–84 in Hayes and
    Miller, eds., *Israelite and Judaean History*.
Miller, J. Maxwell, and John H. Hayes. *A History of Ancient Israel and Judah*.
    Philadelphia: Westminster. London: SCM Press, 1986.
Moore, Megan Bishop. *Philosophy and Practice in Writing a History of Ancient Israel*.
    London: T&T Clark International, 2006.

Mowinckel, Sigmund. *Zur Komposition des Buches Jeremia*. Kristiania: J. Dybwad, 1913.

Mullen, Theodore, Jr. *Ethnic Myths and Pentateuchal Foundations: A New Approach to the Formation of the Pentateuch*. Atlanta: Scholars Press, 1997.

—*Narrative History and Ethnic Boundaries: The Deuteronomistic Historian and the Creation of Israelite National Identity*. Atlanta: Scholars Press, 1993.

Na'aman, Nadav. "The Debated Historicity of Hezekiah's Reform in the Light of Historical and Archaeological Research." *Zeitschrift für die alttestamentliche Wissenschaft* 107 (1995): 179–95.

—"Ephraim, Ephrath and the Settlement in the Judean Hill Country." *Zion* 49 (1984): 325–31 (Hebrew).

—"The King Leading Cult Reforms in His Kingdom: Josiah and Other Kings in the Ancient Near East." *Zeitschrift für Orientalische und Biblische Rechtsgeschichte* 2 (2006): 131–68.

—*The Kingdom of Judah Under Josiah*. Tel Aviv: Institute of Archaeology, 1992. = "The Kingdom of Judah under Josiah." *Tel Aviv* 18 (1991): 3–71. Reprinted in pages 329–98 of *Ancient Israel and Its Neighbors: Interaction and Counteraction*. Winona Lake: Eisenbrauns, 2005.

Nelson, Richard D. *The Double Redaction of the Deuteronomistic History*. Sheffield: JSOT Press, 1981.

Nicholson, E. W. *Preaching to the Exiles: A Study of the Prose Tradition in the Book of Jeremiah*. Oxford: Blackwell, 1970.

Niehr, H. "Die Reform des Joschija: Methodische, historische und religionsgeschichtliche Aspekte." Pages 33–54 in *Jeremia und die "deuteronomistische Bewegung"*. Edited by W. Gross. Weinheim: Athenäum, 1995.

North, R. "Aaron's Rise in Prestige." *Zeitschrift für die alttestamentliche Wissenschaft* 66 (1954): 191–99.

Noth, Martin. *Das Buch Josua*. Tübingen: Mohr, 1940. 2d ed. 1953.

—*The History of Israel*. London: A. & C. Black, 1958. German original, *Geschichte Israels*. Göttingen: Vandehoeck & Ruprecht, 1950, 4th ed. 1959.

—*A History of Pentateuchal Traditions*. Englewood Cliffs: Prentice–Hall, 1972. German original, *Überlieferungsgeschichte des Pentateuch*. Stuttgart: Kohlhammer, 1948.

—*The Old Testament World*. Philadelphia: Fortress, 1966. German original, *Die Welt des Alten Testaments*. Berlin: Töpelmann, 1940, 4th ed. 1960.

—*Das System der zwölf Stämme Israels*. Stuttgart: Kohlhammer, 1930.

—*Überlieferungsgeschichtliche Studien I; Die sammelnden und bearbeitenden Geschichtswerke im Alten Testament*. Halle: Niemeyer, 1943. English translation, *The Deuteronomistic History*. Sheffield: JSOT Press, 1981.

Ofer, Avi. "The Monarchic Period in the Judaean Highland: A Spatial Overview." Pages 14–37 in *Studies in the Archaeology of the Iron Age in Israel and Jordan*. Edited by A. Mazar. Sheffield: Sheffield Academic Press, 2001.

Paton, L. B. "The Case for the Post-Exilic Origin of Deuteronomy." *Journal of Biblical Literature* 47 (1928): 322–57

Perdue, Leo G. "Jeremiah in Modern Research." Pages 1–32 in *A Prophet to the Nations: Essays in Jeremiah Studies*. Edited by Leo G. Perdue and Brian W. Kovacs. Winona Lake: Eisenbrauns, 1984.

Person, Raymond F., Jr. *The Deuteronomic School: History, Social Setting, and Literature*. Atlanta: Scholars Press, 2002.

Pfeiffer, H. *Das Heiligtum von Bethel im Spiegel des Hoseabuches*. Göttingen: Vandenhoeck & Ruprecht, 1999.

Provan, I., V. Phillips Long and Tremper Longman. *A Biblical History of Israel*. Louisville: Westminster John Knox, 2003.

Rad, Gerhard von. "The Form-Critical Problem of the Hexateuch." Pages 1–78 in *The Problem of the Hexateuch and Other Essays*. Edinburgh: Oliver & Boyd, 1966. Original 1938.

—"The History of the Patriarchs." *ET* 72 (1960–61): 213–16.

—*Old Testament Theology*. 2 vols. Edinburgh: Oliver & Boyd, 1962–65. Repr. London: SCM Press, 1975. German original, *Theologie des alten Testaments*. 2 vols. Munich: Kaiser, 1967, 7th ed. 1978.

Redford, Donald B. *A Study of the Biblical Story of Joseph (Genesis 37–50)*. Leiden: Brill, 1970.

Rezetko, Robert. *Source and Revision in the Narratives of David's Transfer of the Ark*. London: T&T Clark International, 2007.

Richter, Wolfgang. *Die Bearbeitung des "Retterbuches" in der deuteronomischen Epoche*. Bonn: Hanstein, 1964.

—*Traditonsgeschichtliche Untersuchungen zum Richterbuch*. Bonn: Hanstein, 1966.

Ricoeur, Paul. *Memory, History, Forgetting*. Chicago: University of Chicago Press, 2004.

Rofé, A. "Ephraimite versus Deuteronomistic History." Pages 462–74 in Knoppers and McConville, eds., *Reconsidering Israel and Judah*.

Rogerson, John W. "Frontiers and Borders in the Old Testament." Pages 116–26 in *In Search of True Wisdom: Essays in Old Testament Interpretation in Honour of Ronald E. Clements*. Edited by Edward Ball. Sheffield: Sheffield Academic Press, 1999.

—*Old Testament Criticism in the Nineteenth Century: England and Germany*. London: SPCK, 1984.

Rogerson, John W., and Philip R. Davies. *The Old Testament World*. 2d ed. London: T&T Clark International, 2005.

Römer, Thomas C. *The So-Called Deuteronomistic History*. London: T&T Clark International, 2005.

Rost, Leonhard. *Israel bei den Propheten*. Stuttgart: Kohlhammer, 1937.

Rowley, Harold H. *From Joseph to Joshua*. London: British Academy, 1950.

Schearing, Linda S., and Steven L. McKenzie, eds. *Those Elusive Deuteronomists*. Sheffield: Sheffield Academic Press, 1999.

Schorn, Ulrike. *Ruben und das System der zwölf Stämme Israels*. Berlin: de Gruyter, 1997.

Schunck, K. D. *Benjamin*. Berlin: de Gruyter, 1963.

Shavit, Yaacov. "Archaeology, Political Culture, and Culture in Israel." Pages 48–61 in Silberman and Small, eds., *The Archaeology of Israel*.

Silberman, Neil Asher. *Digging for God and Country: Exploration, Archeology, and the Secret Struggle for the Holy Land, 1799–1917*. New York: Knopf, 1982.

Silberman, N. A., and D. B. Small, eds. *The Archaeology of Israel: Constructing the Past, Interpreting the Present*. Sheffield: Sheffield Academic Press, 1997.

Smend, Rudolf. "Das Gesetz und die Völker." Pages 494–509 in *Probleme biblischer Theologie*. Edited by H. W. Wolff. Munich: Kaiser, 1971.

Smith, George Adam. *The Historical Geography of the Holy Land*. 25th ed. London: Collins, 1983. Originally published 1897.

Soggin, J. Alberto. *An Introduction to the History of Israel and Judah*. 2d ed. London: SCM Press, 1993.

—*Joshua*. London: SCM Press, 1972.

Sommer, Benjamin D. "New Light on the Composition of Jeremiah." *Catholic Biblical Quarterly* (1999): 646–66.

Sparks, Kenton L. *Ethnicity and Identity: Prolegomena to the Study of Ethnic Sentiments and Their Expression in the Hebrew Bible*. Winona Lake: Eisenbrauns, 1998.

Stott, Katherine. "Finding the Lost Book of the Law: Re-reading the Story of the 'Book of the Law' (Deuteronomy–2 Kings) in Light of Classical Literature." *Journal for the Study of the Old Testament* 30 (2005): 153–69.

Sweeney, Marvin. *King Josiah of Judah: The Lost Messiah of Israel*. Oxford: Oxford University Press, 2001.

Thiel, W. *Die deuteronomistische Redaktion von Jeremia*. 2 vols. Neukirchen–Vluyn: Neukirchener, 1973–81.

Thompson, Thomas L. *The Historicity of the Patriarchal Narratives*. Berlin: de Gruyter, 1974.

—*The Origin Tradition of Ancient Israel*. Sheffield: JSOT Press, 1987.

Uehlinger, Christophe. "Was There a Cult Reform Under King Josiah." Pages 279–316 in Grabbe, ed., *Good Kings and Bad Kings*.

Van Seters, John. *Abraham in History and Tradition*. New Haven: Yale University Press, 1975.

—"The So-Called Deuteronomistic Redaction of the Pentateuch." Pages 58–77 in *Congress Volume: Leuven, 1989*. Edited by J. A. Emerton. Leiden: Brill, 1991.

de Vaux, Roland. *The Early History of Israel*. 2 vols. London: Darton, Longman & Todd, 1978. French original, *Histoire ancienne d'Israel*. Paris: Lecoffre, 1971.

Veeser, H. A., ed. *The New Historicism*. London: Routledge, 1989.

Veijola, Timo. *Die ewige Dynastie: David und die Entstehung seiner Dynastie nach der deuteronomistischen Darstellung*. Helsinki, Suomalainen Tiedeakatemia, 1975.

—*Das Königtum in der Beurteilung der deuteronomistischen Historiographie*. Helsinki, Suomalainen Tiedeakatemia, 1977.

Watts, James W. *Persia and Torah: The Theory of Imperial Authorization of the Pentateuch*. Atlanta: Society of Biblical Literature, 2001.

Welch, Adam C. *The Code of Deuteronomy: A New Theory of Its Origin*. London: J. Clarke, 1924.

—*Post-Exilic Judaism*. Edinburgh: William Blackwood & Sons, 1935.

Wellhausen, Julius. *Prolegomena to the History of Israel: With a Reprint of the Article Israel from the "Encyclopaedia Britannica"*. Preface by W. Robertson Smith. Edinburgh: A. & C. Black, 1985. Repr. with Foreword by Douglas Knight. Atlanta: Scholars Press, 1994. Trans. of *Prolegomena zur Geschichte Israels*. 2d ed. Berlin: G. Reimer, 1883

Wesselius, Jan-Wim. *The Origin of the History of Israel: Herodotus' Histories as the Blueprint for the First Books of the Bible*. London: Sheffield Academic Press, 2002.

Whybray, R. N. *The Making of the Pentateuch: A Methodological Study*. Sheffield. Sheffield Academic Press, 1987.

Westermann, Claus. *Genesis 12–36: A Commentary*. London: SPCK, 1985. German original, *Biblische Kommentar:altes Testament. Band 1, 2. Teilband, Genesis. Genesis, 12–36*. Neukirchen–Vluyn: Neukirchener, 1981.

Williamson, H. G. M. "Confirmation or Contradiction? Archaeology and Biblical History." The St George's Cathedral Lecture 12. Perth, Australia, 2004.

—*Israel in the Books of Chronicles*. Cambridge: Cambridge University Press, 1977.

Wright, G. Ernest. *God Who Acts: Biblical Theology as Recital*. London: SCM Press, 1952.

—"History and the Patriarchs." *Expository Times* 71 (1959–60): 292.

Younger, K. Lawson, Jr. *Ancient Conquest Accounts: A Study in Ancient Near Eastern and Biblical History Writing*. Sheffield: JSOT Press, 1990.

Zertal, Adam. *The Manasseh Hill Country Survey*. Vol. 1, *The Shechem Syncline*. Leiden: Brill, 2004.

—*The Survey of the Hill Country of Manasseh*. Vol. 2, *The Eastern Valleys and the Fringes of the Desert*. Leiden: Brill, forthcoming.

—*The Survey of the Hill Country of Manasseh*. Vol. 3, *From Nahal ʿIron to Nahal Shechem*. Haifa: University of Haifa, 1999.

Zevit, Ziony. *The Religions of Ancient Israel: A Synthesis of Parallactic Approaches*. London: Continuum, 2000.

INDEXES

INDEX OF REFERENCES

INDEX OF AUTHORS